THE ❋ FOOD ❋ OF
PORTUGAL

BOOKS BY JEAN ANDERSON

The Art of American Indian Cooking (with Yeffe Kimball)

Henry the Navigator, Prince of Portugal

The Family Circle Cookbook (with the Food Editors of *Family Circle*)

*The Doubleday Cookbook (with Elaine Hanna)

Recipes from America's Restored Villages

The Green Thumb Preserving Guide

The Grass Roots Cookbook

Jean Anderson's Processor Cooking

**Half a Can of Tomato Paste & Other Culinary Dilemmas (with Ruth Buchan)

Jean Anderson Cooks

Jean Anderson's *NEW* Processor Cooking

Jean Anderson's Green Thumb Preserving Guide

The *NEW* Doubleday Cookbook (with Elaine Hanna)

Micro Ways (with Elaine Hanna)

Jean Anderson's Sin-Free Desserts

The New German Cookbook (with Hedy Würz)

Winner of the R.T. French Tastemaster Award, Best Cookbook of the Year (1975)
**Winner of the R.T. French Tastemaster Award, Best Specialty Cookbook of the Year (1980)*

THE ✳ FOOD ✳ OF
PORTUGAL

Jean Anderson

COLOR PHOTOGRAPHY BY
THE AUTHOR

Hearst Books
New York

It is the policy of William Morrow and Company, Inc., and its imprints and affiliates, recognizing the importance of preserving what has been written, to print the books we publish on acid-free paper, and we exert our best efforts to that end.

Library of Congress Cataloging-in-Publication Data

Anderson, Jean, 1929-
    The food of Portugal / Jean Anderson; color photography by the
author.
      p. cm.
    Includes bibliographical references and index.
    ISBN 0-688-13415-7 (pbk.)
    1. Cookery, Portuguese.   2. Portugal—Social life and customs.
    I. Title.
    TX723.5.P7A53   1994
    641.59469—dc20
                                                 94-8377
                                                      CIP

Printed in the United States of America

      7 8 9 10

BOOK DESIGN BY BETH TONDREAU

For Narcisse Chamberlain,
amiga e redatora (friend and editor),
who proofed both the cooking and the copy

A GENERAL ACKNOWLEDGMENT

So many people, over the past thirty years, have had a hand in shaping this book, so many people in all corners of Portugal who took time from their busy lives to share with me their knowledge of the local harvests of land and sea, their mastery of the regional food and drink. Therefore at the outset I say to one and all, *"Obrigada!"* For the names of those, in both the United States and Portugal, who have been particularly helpful and for the resources that I continue to find indispensable, please see the fuller Acknowledgments and the Bibliography at the end of the book.

Contents

Introduction

You might think that a country no bigger than Alabama would produce few gastronomic surprises, a cuisine of limited scope. Certainly I never expected to find such bounty or culinary virtuosity when I first visited Portugal thirty years ago. And never, ever did I dream that this lusty cooking would absorb me the better part of the next thirty years.

When friends and colleagues heard that I was writing a Portuguese cookbook, the question they invariably put to me was "But isn't it just like Spanish cooking?"

No, it isn't, although Portuguese and Spanish cooks both rely heavily upon many of the same ingredients—tomatoes, garlic and olive oil, to name three. It's difficult to sum up the differences in broad strokes because they're often quite subtle. Take gazpacho, for example: The Portuguese versions are much thicker, brimming with crumbles of yeasty homemade bread, so that they more nearly resemble those extraordinary "dry soups" called *açordas*. Then there's flan. The Portuguese renditions are smoother and spicier than the Spanish because they are often thickened with egg yolks (as opposed to whole eggs) and flavored only with cinnamon—except sometimes for the merest suggestion of orange, lemon or Port. But rarely do they contain vanilla, the beloved seasoning of the Spaniards directly next door.

I've often wondered how the two neighboring countries can be so different, right down to what goes on the dinner table, despite shared terrain and roots. But dissimilar they are, mostly because Portugal, stuck down there on the southwesternmost corner of Iberia, was not only isolated for centuries from the rest of Europe, but was also lured overseas by the ocean that lapped its southern and western shores.

It was the Portuguese, remember, who launched Europe's Age of Discovery in the early fifteenth century; the Portuguese who designed a ship that could sail both with and against the wind (the caravel); who charted the west coast of Africa; who rounded the Cape of Good Hope; who plucked Madeira and the Azores from the "Green Sea of Gloom," as the Atlantic was then known; who discovered Brazil; and who, not least, found the water route to the East's treasury of spices. Vasco da

Gama was Portuguese and today lies buried in the impressive Jerónomos Monastery at Belém, a Lisbon suburb. Within full view of its intricate Manueline portal stand both the Tower of Belém—marking the spot on the Tagus River from whence Da Gama sailed—and the soaring Monument to the Discoveries, with Prince Henry-the-Navigator at its helm gazing seaward.

Vasco da Gama's ships brought precious spices—curry, cinnamon, cloves, nutmeg, pepper—directly to Portugal at the turn of the sixteenth century. And as Portugal's overseas empire expanded, the other exotics of the East (among them rice and tea), of Africa (coffee, broad beans and peanuts), not to mention New World pineapples, peppers sweet and incendiary, tomatoes and potatoes found their way into local kettles, too.

It is the ingenious use of Old World foods and New, the intrepid teaming of ingredients that most distinguishes Portuguese cooking from the Spanish. Who but a Portuguese with an eye on her escudos, for example, would have dared such stunning juxtapositions as trout and ham . . . salt cod and eggs and olives . . . clams and sausage . . . and come out a winner? And who would have thought to recycle the shrimp cooking water with yesterday's bread, creating a masterpiece known as *açorda de mariscos*?

I first tasted this classic "dry soup" at Guincho, a seaside resort near Lisbon. The *açorda* was brought to table in a square earthen dish for me to admire. And a picture it was, trimmed with pink, plump shrimp, scatterings of freshly chopped coriander and strategically placed raw whole eggs. These the waiter promptly stirred down into the steaming mixture, thereby cooking the eggs and thickening and coloring the *açorda* all in a few deft strokes.

To be honest, I didn't think I'd like *açorda de mariscos* and had ordered it as an educational experience. To my surprise, I scraped my plate. Now I order it whenever I am within sound of the Portuguese surf.

For more than thirty years now I have been poking about Portugal, lifting the lids of pots bubbling on country stoves, getting my hands in the dough—quite literally. And in the earth. I have dug potatoes in the Minho, joined the women gathering grapes along the Douro River during the Port wine harvest—for this *is* women's work; the men's job is to run the grapes downhill in wicker shoulder baskets, then dump them into the *lagars* (concrete vats) where they will later be trampled. I have also separated windfalls of olives from acorns in the Alentejo and, miserable sailor that I am, I have even put to sea on the fishing boats of Madeira.

I have dined both simply and sumptuously in Portuguese homes and shall never forget the *caldo verde* (the green cabbage soup that is considered the national dish of Portugal) served me by a complete stranger in a one-room fieldstone hut at the end of a squiggly mountain road. I had lost my way in the northerly Minho Province in the fog that so often frequents its mountains in early spring, and had stopped to ask directions. An old woman swathed in black answered my knock and, seeing how cold and tired I was, insisted that I rest a bit and revive myself before moving on. I sat at a scrubbed pine table beside the mound of intensely emerald collards she had been shredding, watched as she tossed handfuls of them into a pot bubbling over an open fire. She stirred the pot once, twice, let it mellow several minutes, then produced a brown pottery bowl and ladled the steaming jade liquid into it. She then cut for me a thick wedge of *broa* (the rough, yeast-raised corn bread of the north) and poured a glass of *vinho verde*, the region's crackling green wine, so called because it comes from green mountains and valleys, and also because it is drunk young. I don' know that I have ever enjoyed a meal more. Certainly I have seldom felt more revitalized. And try as I would to press a few escudos upon my savior, she staunchly refused.

By sundown I had wound my way down from savage purple peaks to the mouth of the Minho and beaches the color and consistency of confectioners' sugar. That night I feasted upon fresh-caught river eel (*lampreia*), as red and rich as beef, lightly curried in the manner of the Minho Province (the Portuguese often use curry powder, but in amounts so small that only its musky flavor, not its bite, comes through).

I have returned to Portugal every year since that original trip thirty years ago, sometimes two or three times a year, and know of no nation where the countryside, climate, produce and cooking all shift so abruptly in a few short miles.

There is the hardscrabble Trás-os-Montes, or land "behind the mountains," in the northeasternmost corner or Portugal where farmers grow cabbage of uncommon succulence, dry-cure fine-fleshed hams to the hue of mahogany and harvest awesome crops of the nuttiest, sweetest potatoes on earth. There are the tart tiny oranges of the sandy Setúbal Province directly south of Lisbon, the giant red tomatoes of the Alentejo, the almonds and figs of the surf-creamed Algarve, the honey-sweet pineapples of the Azores, the cherimoyas and bananas of Madeira.

I have worked my way from the mainland to Madeira and the Azores time and again, from seashore to mountaintop and back, from the Minho and Trás-os-Montes on the northern frontier with Spain through the rice paddies of Aveiro, the orchards of espaliered fruit of Estremadura, to the russet plains of the Alentejo, where miles of corks and olives, misshapen as scarecrows, dance over the horizon. I have visited the Algarve's famous almond orchards in winter when warm winds off Morocco fatten the trees' buds and loose a blizzard of snowy blossoms. I have walked in the fig groves in summer when the fruit hangs heavy from every branch. The Moor has left his mark on this southernmost Portuguese province, both architectural and culinary. (The excruciatingly rich egg, almond, and fig sweets of the Algarve are believed to be Moorish in origin, as indeed are Portugal's egg sweets in general.)

I have broken bread in castles, convents, sophisticated Lisbon restaurants and salty *tascas* (bistros). I have interviewed cooks trained and untrained, haute and humble; I have prowled markets in towns large and small, and returned to the fish auctions of Cascais, Portimão, and Albufeira more often than I can remember. And I came away from Portugal this last trip convinced that we Americans know more about the cooking of the People's Republic of China than we do about that of this "most foreign" of Western European countries despite the fact that there are many Portuguese communities scattered across the face of America.

To my mind, Portuguese cooking is one of the most imaginative and exuberant of the Western world. Yet it is economical, *approachable,* because it calls for few ingredients beyond the inventory of our own markets. What distinguishes Portuguese recipes is their innovative teaming—of meats with fish, fish with fruits, fruits with eggs, eggs with fish, eggs with beans and so on. Typical, too, is the fact that nothing is wasted, ever.

Does anyone make better soup than the Portuguese? I doubt it. Certainly no one makes better bread. And no one, I suspect, knows more ways to prepare salt cod.

In the culinary tour of Portugal set down in the pages that follow, my purpose is to share my great love of Portugal, my unbounded admiration for Portuguese cooks who can transform four simple ingredients—flour, salt, yeast and water—into such a memorable loaf of bread, who can then create a classic (and a meal) from that bread by combining it with water, garlic, coriander and eggs. Or who can take that same bread, cut it into croutons, brown them in butter, strew them through a cinnamony egg-yolk custard and emerge with yet another classic, this one the beloved *sopa dourada* (soup of gold).

I have learned much over the years from Portuguese cooks who not only gave generously of their time and talent, but also happily handed over cherished family recipes. Now I am eager to share the wealth—a repertoire of some 165 favorite recipes obtained from several dozen visits to Portugal. This is not, I hasten to add, a definitive book on Portuguese cooking, merely an introduction to it. I have eliminated a number of beloved dishes—among them certain egg sweets and salt cod recipes—because of our own growing awareness of the dangers of too much sodium, too much sugar, and too much cholesterol. And of necessity I have also excluded a few recipes based upon items unavailable here. (There is just no substitute for the lampreys of the Minho, for example.)

I have aimed, rather, for regional variety, and concentrated upon what I consider to be the very best of Portuguese cooking.

À vossa saúde!

New York, New York, 1994   JEAN ANDERSON

PART ONE

THE
FOOD AND WINE
❋ OF ❋
PORTUGAL

The Land of Portugal

❋

For thirty years now, I've been in love with Portugal. And no matter how often I return or how long I stay, my passion shows no sign of cooling. It's not just the Portuguese people I warm to, or Lisbon (to my mind one of Europe's loveliest capitals). It's the look of the land. Nowhere will you find greater diversity packed into such a small area. Savage purple crags (tipped with snow in winter) plummet onto rumpled uplands of green . . . rivers, on their rush to the sea, course through vineyards as intricately terraced as Himalayan tea plantations . . . and land's end promontories, matted with heather and gorse, plunge sheer to some of the sugariest beaches on earth.

All of these I love. But no more so than the rolling brown plains of the Alentejo Province, the "cork and olive country" where sheep peacefully graze among scarlet windflowers and *montes* (cubistic clusters of farm buildings) gleam so whitely under the downpouring sun they look to be icebergs off course. And no more so, certainly, than the merry country markets where great ropes of sausages, garlic and onions swing alongside bunches of fresh coriander as big as bridal bouquets, where slatted baskets, still streaming sea water, shimmer and glint with sardines, salmonetes and shrimp, where broad beans are bedded on leaves of cabbage and cabbages are piled up beside tomatoes, the better to catch and please the eye.

What follows is a brief photographic tour of the sunny little country I've adopted as my second home. It's quaint, it's colorful, and even though I've logged thousands of miles there and reached into its remotest corners, Portugal never fails to surprise and delight me.

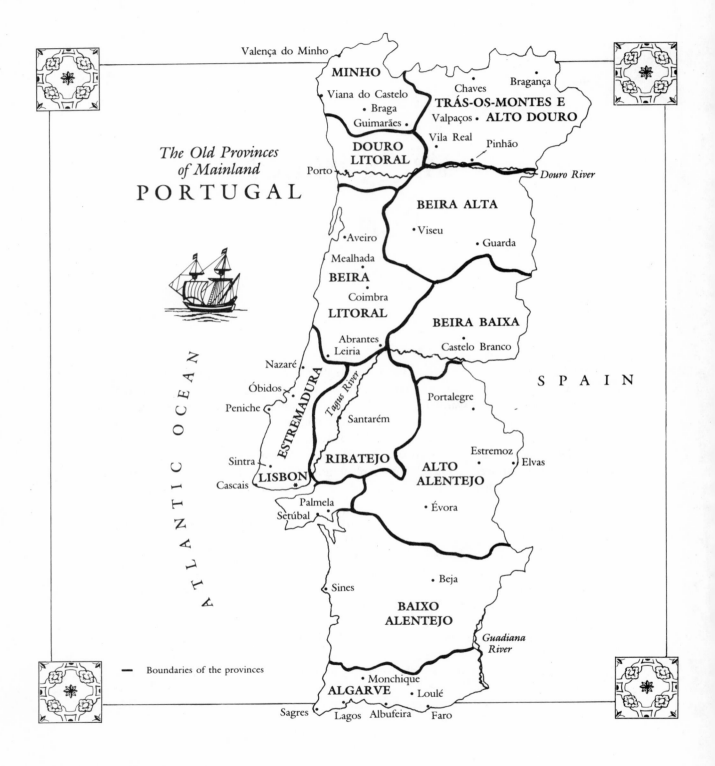

The Old Provinces
of Mainland
PORTUGAL

ATLANTIC OCEAN

SPAIN

Valença do Minho

MINHO
• Viana do Castelo
• Braga
Guimarães

TRÁS-OS-MONTES E
ALTO DOURO
Chaves   • Bragança
Valpaços
• Vila Real   Pinhão

DOURO
LITORAL
Porto •   Douro River

BEIRA ALTA
• Viseu
• Guarda

•Aveiro

Mealhada
•

BEIRA
•
Coimbra

LITORAL

BEIRA BAIXA
• Castelo Branco

Abrantes
Leiria •

Nazaré •

Óbidos •

Peniche •

Portalegre
•

ESTREMADURA

Tagus River

Santarém
•

Sintra •

Cascais

LISBON
*

RIBATEJO

ALTO
ALENTEJO

Estremoz
•   • Elvas

• Évora

Palmela
•
Setúbal •

• Sines

• Beja

BAIXO
ALENTEJO

Guadiana
River

— Boundaries of the provinces

• Monchique
ALGARVE   • Loulé

Sagres   Lagos Albufeira   Faro

Pousada de Palmela, near Lisbon; foreground, *sopa de pedra* ("stone soup") and *broa* (yeast-raised corn bread)

LEFT, Mercado da Ribeira, Lisbon; TOP, shredding collards for *caldo verde,* the famous Portuguese "green soup." The herb above is fresh coriander.

ABOVE, Casa do Leão Restaurant, Lisbon, and antique-shop sign made of Portuguese tiles.

RIGHT, the Alfama, old Moorish quarter of Lisbon.

On an Atlantic sea cliff at Guincho Beach near Lisbon, *açorda de mariscos* ("dry" shellfish soup) and *pão* (country bread).

TOP TO BOTTOM: Sardines grilling on a Lisbon street; Azeitão goat cheeses; Redondo pottery; Algarve egg and almond sweets.

Nazaré, fishing village north of Lisbon, and flour mill near Óbidos.

TOP, Sines, Alentejo; LEFT, Fisherman's Beach at
Albufeira, Algarve; ABOVE, clamming in the Aveiro
Lagoon, Beira Litoral.

LEFT, Porto on the Douro River. The *rabelo* (boat) once carried fermenting grape juice downriver from vineyard to Port wine lodge.

BELOW, Port wine vineyards, Douro River valley.

Monte (village) and grazing sheep in Alentejo province (Portugal's cork and olive country). BELOW, farmer plowing with oxen in the Trás-os-Montes (land "behind the mountains").

TOP, farmland high in the interior of Madeira; straw huts (*palheiros*) keep cattle safely off the steep slopes at night. ABOVE, blending wine in a Madeira wine lodge; RIGHT, Funchal market.

LEFT, Prince Henry-the-Navigator, Funchal, Madeira.

ABOVE, fish market in Angra do Heroísmo, Terceira Island, Azores. BELOW, São Miguel Island, Azores; black lava drywalls crisscross fields of wheat, cane, and corn.

Surf-casting near Sagres, Algarve. BELOW, clams *cataplana* on the beach at Praia do Carvoeiro, Algarve.

Tiled house in the Alfama,
Lisbon.

Cape St. Vincent lighthouse, near Sagres, Algarve.

The Language of
Portuguese Food, Drink
and Dining

Anyone who visits Portugal will be confronted by completely alien food words and phrases. Menus are full of them, as are guidebooks and, needless to say, cookbooks. This chapter is arranged alphabetically, like a glossary, to introduce the American to rudimentary kitchen and restaurant Portuguese, to attune the ear and focus the eye.

À ALENTEJANA: In the style of the Alentejo Province, meaning plenty of garlic, olive oil and paprika.

ABÓBORA: Pumpkin; the Portuguese grow several kinds of pumpkins unknown to us—small orange ones, which are boiled, puréed and blended into tarts and puddings (acorn or butternut squash substitute nicely); and *chila* (or *gila*), a gourd with long, pale strands of flesh that are candied and added to a variety of sweets for texture and flavor. Spaghetti squash, I've discovered, works almost as well (see page 286 for *Doce de Chila*).

AÇAFRÃO: SAFFRON; the Portuguese, unlike the Spaniards, use saffron sparingly.

ACEPIPES VARIADOS: Assorted hors d'oeuvre.

AÇORDA: A dry soup; see box.

AÇUCAR: Sugar; when Portugal began colonizing Madeira Island early in the fifteenth century, Prince Henry-the-Navigator had his settlers plant cuttings of sugarcane from Sicily, which thrived in the island's volcanic soil. Cane is still an important crop on Madeira, as indeed it is in the former Portuguese colony of Brazil. With sugar readily available, it's scarcely surprising that the Portuguese developed an appetite for desserts so sweet they set your teeth on edge. *Note: In the desserts included in this book, I have reduced the quantity of sugar to levels more tolerable to American palates.*

ADEGA: A wine cellar or cave.

AGRIÕES: Watercress; you've never seen more luxuriant watercress than that which grows beside the *levadas* (irrigation ditches) and streams of Madeira. It flourishes along riverbanks in mainland Portugal, too; and cooks, in addition to using lavish quantities of it to trim plates and platters, often use it in green soups or sauté it with milder greens to add a touch of tartness.

ÁGUA: Water; it's perfectly safe to drink tap water in Lisbon and Porto, but elsewhere about the country, better stick with *água mineral* (bottled mineral water) either *com gás* (bubbly) or *sem gás* (without gas, i.e., "still"). See THE BEER AND BOTTLED WATERS OF PORTUGAL, page 64.

AGUARDENTE: The "firewater" of Portugal, distilled from grape pips (*Bagaceira*), or from the arbutus or "strawberry tree" berries of the Algarve (*Medronho*), or from the morello cherry (*Ginjinha;* this *eau de vie* is particularly popular on the island of Madeira), or even from figs (*Aguardente de Figo,* an old Algarve favorite).

AIPO: Celery; it's used surprisingly little in Portugal, either for cooking or for eating out of hand.

 Açordas and Migas— Dry Soups and Stews

These porridgy bread-thickened mixtures, invented years ago by frugal country cooks, are beloved all over Portugal. They are based upon stale bread, broth from boiling vegetables, shellfish stock, even boiling water, and when skillfully made can be very good indeed. An *açorda* is soupier than a *migas,* and in fact is considered a soup. Portugal's two most popular *açordas*—the first from the coastal Estremadura Province, where Lisbon is located; the second from the inland Alentejo—are *Açorda de Mariscos* (shellfish-bread-egg soup laced with fresh coriander) and *Açorda à Alentejana* (a garlic-bread-egg soup, also intensely aromatic of fresh coriander); see Recipe Index.

Migas are drier, thicker, meatier than *açordas,* and when preparing them, Alentejo cooks don't stint on meat drippings. Mounded as they are in huge terra-cotta bowls and wreathed with chunks of fried pork or beef and pork combined, *migas* are sturdy country fare; see Recipe Index.

Another type of dry soup, *sopa seca,* is much eaten in the mountainous midriff and North of Portugal. The technique for making it is altogether different: Shreds of boiled chicken, veal, pork, ham, sausage (and whatever else might be at hand) are layered into a huge earthen bowl with sliced boiled carrots and potatoes, slabs of husky bread and sprinkles of chopped mint. The lot is then doused with boiling stock and shoved into a quick oven to dry for fifteen to twenty minutes. *Sopa seca* is an odds-and-ends dish, an ingenious way to recycle leftovers into a substantial main dish. In some areas of the country *sopa seca* is seasoned with fresh coriander, but in the northerly Minho Province, according to António Guedes of Quinta da Aveleda in Penafiel, mint is the essential herb.

ALECRIM: Rosemary; although rosemary grows as big as bushes in most parts of Portugal, it is not widely used as a kitchen herb. Occasionally an imaginative home cook will tuck a few sprigs of rosemary into the pan in which she's roasting kid; sometimes she will add it to stew. But those who rely most upon rosemary are classically trained restaurant and hotel chefs.

ALETRIA: Vermicelli; also a dessert made of vermicelli; see THE EGG SWEETS OF PORTUGAL.

ALFACE: Lettuce; despite the fact that the people of Lisbon have been nicknamed "lettuce eaters," I've never found lettuce of good variety or great quality in Portugal. Iceberg's the thing—except in top-notch hotels and restaurants for which farmers now raise more colorful varieties. The Portuguese themselves eat few salads, other than sliced tomatoes, roasted peppers, or iceberg lettuce drizzled with oil and vinegar. But I do find a bowl of crisp mixed greens the perfect partner for Portugal's robust soups, stews, grills and roasts, and because we Americans are blessed with such a bounty of greens, I do urge you to round out your Portuguese dinners with salads.

ALHEIRA: See THE SAUSAGES AND HAMS OF PORTUGAL.

ALHO: Garlic; no Portuguese could cook without it.

ALHO FRANCÊS or **ALHO-PORRO:** Leek; a popular addition to soups and stews.

ALMOÇO: Lunch; the Portuguese usually lunch between 1:30 and 3:00 P.M. and few of the better big-city restaurants open before 12:30 or 1:00 P.M.

ALMÔNDEGA: Meatball; the Portuguese aren't as fond of meatballs as the Spaniards.

ALMONDS: AMÊNDOAS; almond trees grow not only in the Algarve but also in the remote Trás-os-Montes in the northeastern corner of Portugal. The nuts, after having been blanched and ground to powder, are stirred into an awesome number of sweets.

In addition, whole blanched almonds are browned in olive oil and served with glasses of white or tawny Port.

ALPERCE: Apricot; you'll see loads of apricot trees in the Algarve and, in midsummer, huge straw mats of apricots and figs drying in the sun. Although the fresh apricots are superbly sweet and juicy, the Portuguese prefer the more concentrated flavor of dried apricots and mix them into an assortment of sweets.

À MADEIRENSE: In the style of Madeira, which usually means with tomatoes, onions and garlic, and possibly a shot or two of Madeira wine.

À MANEIRA: In the manner of.

AMÊIJOAS: Clams; Portugal's clams are very small, thin-shelled and sweet, scarcely bigger than cockles (*conquilhas*). The best of them come from the Santa Maria Lagoon around Faro, fed both by rivers tumbling out of the mountains and by the Atlantic Ocean. Because of recent problems with polluted waters, the government now tests each batch of lagoon clams scrupulously before allowing them to be sold. *Amêijoas* are so fragile, it takes very little heat to force them open, spilling their savory juices. The best American substitutes would be the Pacific butter clams or, failing those, the tiniest littlenecks you can find. Even these, you'll discover, may require thirty minutes or more of *gentle* simmering in such Portuguese classics as *Caldeirada* and *Cataplana* to open fully.

AMEIXA: Plum; with their fondness for sweets, the Portuguese have turned their fine, small green plums into "sugarplums." You'll find them in shops everywhere in the old fortified town of Elvas on the Spanish border, some hundred miles east of Lisbon. Called simply *frutas doces* (sweet fruits), they are both plumped and preserved in sugar syrup, drained well, then packed in little wooden boxes. They are one of the specialties for which Elvas—indeed, Portugal—is famous. And they are delicious. I like to keep a box of them beside me in the car as a sort of elegant K-ration when I poke about the remoter reaches of Portugal where restaurants and cafés are scarce.

AMÊNDOAS: See Almonds.

AMENDOIMS: Peanuts; these do grow in Portugal, but are used primarily for oil, not for nibbling.

À MINHOTA: In the manner of the northern Minho Province, usually meaning that the recipe contains bits of ham and sometimes *vinho verde,* the sprightly green wine of the region.

À MODA: In the style of.

ANANÁS: Pineapple; Portugal's pineapples are without peer, especially those of the Azores, which are grown in hothouses and ripened under waftings of woodsmoke. They are crisp, honey-sweet, and tender to the core. The Portuguese eat them cores and all. So do I.

ANCHOVAS: Anchovies.

ANHO: Lamb; it's less popular among the country people than *cabrito* (kid) because sheep are more highly prized for their wool and milk than their meat. The majority of Portugal's fine cheeses are made of ewe's milk.

À PADEIRA: Baked in an earthenware casserole at quick heat. A *padeiro* is a baker, and in the old days, farm women would carry their one-dish dinners to the village baker's brick or stone oven to be baked in retained heat as soon as the loaves of bread were done.

APERITIVO: Apéritif.

APPLE: **MAÇA;** a baked apple is *maça assada.*

APRICOT: See **ALPERCE.**

ARROZ: Rice; few people realize how important rice is to Portugal. You see it growing in lagoons and paddies up and down the West Coast. This is, for the most part, short-grain rice, which cooks down to creaminess and makes ambrosial rice pudding. But longer-grained rice is also grown; cooks stir it into a variety of soups and fricassees. It also shows up on nearly every lunch and dinner plate in tandem with

potatoes (even at some of Lisbon's sophisticated restaurants).

ARROZ-DOCE: Translated literally, this means "sweet rice." Actually it's rice pudding—and does anyone make it better than the Portuguese? I doubt it. See Recipe Index.

ASPARAGUS: ESPARGO; not a vegetable popular among the country people (except for *espargo bravo,* or wild asparagus, which is foraged in the fields). The cultivated variety is too expensive for many Portuguese. But you will find asparagus listed on many restaurant menus, and if you're lucky enough to be invited to a *quinta* (estate) or *solar* (manor house) in the spring asparagus season, you are likely to be served it—steaming hot and dripping with hollandaise or drawn butter. Like most other Europeans, the Portuguese prefer the chunky, ivory-hued stalks to the green.

ASSADEIRA: A large shallow roasting pan; just the thing for turkeys and large joints of lamb, mutton or pork.

ASSADO NO FORNO: Baked or roasted in the oven; the term is now often written more simply *assado,* as in *lombo de porco assado* (roast loin of pork).

À TRANSMONTANA: Prepared in the hearty style of the Trás-os-Montes Province. Such dishes will probably be studded with bits of sausage, may contain dried beans and have no shortage of garlic and onions.

ATUM: Tuna; See *THE FISH AND SHELLFISH OF PORTUGAL.*

À VAPOR: Steamed.

AVES: Poultry; the most popular farm-raised fowl in Portugal are chicken, duck and turkey—in more or less that order.

AZEDA: Sorrel; it grows wild in much of Portugal, and the Portuguese, great gleaners and gatherers, pick the tart tongue-shaped leaves to add tang to soups. They also toss small quantities of sorrel into a skillet with turnip or other greens and sauté all lightly together in olive oil. *Note: In Portugal, greens are more likely to be sautéed or braised than boiled or steamed.*

AZEDADO: Sour.

AZEDO: See *THE SAUSAGES AND HAMS OF PORTUGAL.*

AZEITÃO: See *THE CHEESES OF PORTUGAL.*

AZEITE: Olive oil, or, to give its full and proper name, *azeite de azeitonas.* Olive oil is the preferred frying medium of the Alentejo and Algarve provinces, but it is sometimes too expensive for the poorer people to use. No problem. They simply substitute the cheaper *azeite de amendoins* (peanut oil) or *óleo alimentar* (vegetable oil), then add a tablespoon or two of olive oil just before serving to inject rich olive flavor. It works. See *THE ROBUST OLIVE OIL OF PORTUGAL* on page 56.

AZEITONAS: Olives; these grow all over Portugal, but nowhere plumper or tastier than on the red-brown plains of the Alentejo in the vicinity of Elvas and Beja. Black olives (*azeitonas pretas*) are more popular in Portugal than the green (*azeitonas verdes*).

BACALHAU: Dried salt cod; see box.

BACON: **TOUCINHO;** see *THE SAUSAGES AND HAMS OF PORTUGAL.*

BANANA: You'll find banana plantations all along the lower slopes of Madeira's south shore, where giant hands of these fat little fruits, sweet as sugar, are harvested. They land at Funchal's bouncy market, also at Lisbon's vast Mercado da Ribeira.

Both markets welcome tourists and are the fastest way to get a fix on what's cooking.

BANHA: See *THE SAUSAGES AND HAMS OF PORTUGAL.*

BARBO: Barbel; see *THE FISH AND SHELLFISH OF PORTUGAL.*

BARLEY: See **CENTEIO.**

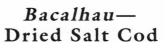

Bacalhau—
Dried Salt Cod

Not long after Columbus discovered America, the Portuguese were fishing Newfoundland's Grand Banks for cod, the first Europeans to do so. By 1506, António Bello writes in his *Culinária Portuguesa* (Lisbon, 1936), one-tenth of the fish sold in the ports of the Douro and Minho was *bacalhau.* It was the Portuguese, he continues, who learned to salt cod at sea, to bring it home and sun-dry it into board-stiff slabs that could be kept many months, then reconstituted in water. Escoffier, in a paper entitled *La Morue,* credited the Portuguese with introducing "the gastronomic values of this precious fish to Europe." The Portuguese, it's said, know 365 ways to cook *bacalhau,* one for each day of the year.

Today, supplies of cod are so severely depleted that few Portuguese sail, as in years past, for the Grand Banks each April (to return only in October). Portugal now buys much of its salt cod from Norway, and the price, for many, is beyond reach. "To think," said Manuel Paulino Revéz, assistant director of the Escola de Hotelaria e Turismo do Algarve, "that *bacalhau* is now a V.I.P. fish!"

BARRIGAS DE FREIRA: One of the devastating convent sweets for which Portugal is so famous. See *THE EGG SWEETS OF PORTUGAL*.

BASIL: MANJERICÃO; basil is not commonly used in cooking in Portugal. You see it most during the merry Feast of Saint Anthony on June 12 and 13 in Lisbon when boys and girls give little pots of frilly "bush basil" to their sweethearts. In Portugal, *Santo António* is the patron saint of lovers. He was born, in fact, in a little house in the Alfama—old Moorish quarter—and it's in the Alfama's careening cobbled streets that celebrations are liveliest.

BATATA: Potato; the potatoes of Portugal are nut-sweet, full of deep earthy flavor, and firm enough not to disintegrate in the pot. Small wonder they are served twice a day (often in the company of rice). In this book's recipes, you'll notice that I am quite specific about which potatoes to use—new potatoes, for example, or Maine or Eastern potatoes. There's a good reason for this: I am attempting to duplicate the particular taste and texture of the different varieties of potatoes grown in Portugal.

BATATA FRITA: Potato chip; the most popular snack food in Portugal. Whenever you visit a *pousada* (government inn) and order a drink, a little plate of chips freshly fried in olive oil will arrive along with your cocktail.

BAUNILHA: Vanilla; for some unexplained reason, the Portuguese use very little vanilla. It was, of course, the Spaniards who discovered it in Mexico (and they do use plenty of it). The Portuguese prefer to flavor their sweets with cinnamon, which *they* found in the East Indies, and also with oranges and lemons, which the Moors introduced to Iberia.

BAY LEAF: LOURO; one of the most popular culinary herbs of Portugal.

BEAN: FEIJÃO. Beans are almost as much a staple in Portugal as potatoes and rice, especially dried beans, which you see by the gunnysackful at every country market. Among the most popular varieties:

feijão branco (white bean), *feijão encarnado* (red), *feijão prêto* (black), *feijão manteiga* (butter bean), *feijão de frade* (black-eyed pea), *feijão de vaca* (cow pea). Among fresh beans, *vagens* or *feijão verde* are runners or green beans, and *favas,* of course, are favas (which see).

BEBIDAS: Drinks or beverages; the Portuguese serve few mixed drinks, far preferring to sip their own fine wines. They're right.

BEEF: See **BIFE.**

BEER: CERVEJA; see *THE BEER AND BOTTLED WATERS OF PORTUGAL* on page 64.

BEJA: See *THE CHEESES OF PORTUGAL.*

BEM PASSADO: "Well done," as in a well-done piece of meat.

BERINGELA: Eggplant; a fairly popular restaurant vegetable, but not in the provincial homes of Portugal.

BESUGO: Sunfish.

BICA: See *THE COFFEES OF PORTUGAL.*

BIFE: Beef; quite honestly, Portuguese beef isn't very good. Except for the choice cuts served in luxury hotels and restaurants, it's shoe-leather tough. The country people, quite understandably, favor pork, chicken and *cabrito* (kid), all of which are outstanding.

BIFES: Steaks—of beef, pork, lamb, even tuna (*bifes de atum*).

BISCOITO: Cookie; the Portuguese aren't great cookie bakers, except for religious feasts or festivals. Half a dozen different kinds of cookies are made for Easter (*Páscoa*), but I frankly find them uninteresting. The Portuguese do excel, however, at making cakes, puddings and pastries.

BOILED: COZIDO; this also happens to be the name of the Portuguese Boiled Dinner; see Recipe Index.

BOLINHOS: Little balls, as in *Bolinhos de Bacalhau,* Codfish Balls; see Recipe Index.

BOLO: Ball; also cake, which see.

BORREGO: Lamb; but also sometimes yearling mutton.

BOUQUET GARNI: RAMO DE CHEIROS; as with the more traditional *bouquet garni,* the composition of *ramo de cheiros* varies according to what is being cooked. Essential to it, however, are garlic (*alho*), parsley (*salsa*), and bay leaf (*louro*). Optional additions include leek (*alho francês*), fennel (*funcho*) and celery (*aipo*).

BRAISED: GUISADO. *Note: Guisado has often been translated as meaning "stewed," but in fact the method for it approximates our technique of braising because comparatively little liquid is used.*

BRASA: Ember or live coal; you will frequently see entries on Portuguese menus followed by the phrase *nas brasas,* meaning charcoal grilled. It's a favorite way to cook fresh sardines and such sausages as *chouriço* and *linguiça.*

Bread: See **PÃO.**

BREADED: PANADO; what makes Portuguese breaded foods singularly good is the quality of the bread crumbs. They are, of course, nothing more than crumbled stale bread but, oh, the Portuguese bread! It is to my mind the world's best. Because the Portuguese like their breading "to stick," they air-dry breaded cutlets or chops briefly before browning them.

BREAKFAST: See **PEQUENO ALMOÇO.**

BROA: The sturdy yeast-raised corn bread of the Minho Province. Often it contains whole wheat or barley flour as well as white flour and cornmeal. At the every-Thursday market in Barcelos about an hour's drive north of Porto, hundreds of large flat loaves of *broa,* still floury from the bakers' ovens and many of them scored across the top with a tick-tack-toe design, are bought straight off the backs of vans before they can be properly unloaded and displayed.

BUTTER: MANTEIGA; Portuguese butter, although heavily salted, is more often used than olive oil in the North of the country for frying and browning food. It is, however, frequently combined with lard, bacon drippings or olive oil.

CABBAGE: COUVE; nearly every Portuguese house has its cabbage patch, even those in the heart of Lisbon's Alfama, or old Moorish quarter, for no vegetable is more appreciated in Portugal. By most accounts, the choicest is *couve gallego* or Galician cabbage, an intensely emerald, non-heading, tender-leafed variety much like collards that is integral to *Caldo Verde* (which see). But the crinkly jade Savoy is much used, too, as are kale and tight, pale-green heads much like American cabbages.

CABREIRO: See *THE CHEESES OF PORTUGAL.*

CABRITO: Kid or young goat; one of the most esteemed meats in Portugal.

CAÇA: Game; venison still shows up on menus during the autumn hunting season, and occasionally wild boar. Game birds are far more prevalent.

CACAU: Cocoa; only recently has chocolate become popular in Portugal; most people still prefer their sugar diluted by nothing more than egg yolks and perhaps a pinch of cinnamon.

CAFÉ: See *THE COFFEES OF PORTUGAL.*

CAKE: BOLO; the Portuguese make excellent sponge cakes and dark, dense loaves loaded with spices and/or dried fruits.

CALDEIRADA: A fish and/or shellfish "muddle" prepared throughout mainland Portugal, the Azores and Madeira. Recipes vary from place to place, but mixtures of fish, lean and oily, are common to most *caldeiradas,* as are onions, garlic and intensely red ripe tomatoes.

CALDO: A for-the-most-part clear soup or broth—as opposed to *sopa,* which is invariably strewn with bits of vegetable and/or meat and routinely thickened with potatoes.

CALDO VERDE: Green Soup; the unofficial national dish of Portugal. See Cabbage and Recipe Index.

CAMARÃO: Shrimp; Portugal is blessed with an abundance of shrimp, both large and small, which are brinier than our Gulf Coast shrimp. Portuguese cooks scoff at the notion of deveining shrimp and, as often as not, cook them in their shells.

CANELA: Cinnamon; no spice is more essential to Portuguese cooking than cinnamon because it's used in savories as well as sweets. Vasco da Gama gets credit for importing shiploads of cinnamon to Portugal. (One boatload, it's said, fetched more than enough to pay for the entire East Indies expedition. It may be so.) As for its use today, powdered cinnamon (*canela em pó*) is not only stirred into a vast repertoire of cakes and puddings, but also frequently sprinkled or stenciled on the tops of them in stylized hearts-and-flowers designs. Stick cinnamon (*canela em pau*) is widely used, too, some cooks even going to the trouble to pulverize it themselves for a powder of intensely cinnamony flavor.

CANJA: A clear chicken soup containing either rice or, more recently, little pasta seeds, which the Portuguese call "pearls." The best *canjas* (and every cook has one in her inventory), begin with aromatic chicken broth; they contain shreds of breast meat, sprinklings of mint and healthy squirts of lemon juice. See Recipe Index.

CAPÃO: Capon; these plump castrated cocks are becoming popular in Portugal, but they aren't yet a match for *galinha* (stewing hen) or *peru* (turkey).

CARACÓIS: *Escargots* or snails; see *THE FISH AND SHELLFISH OF PORTUGAL).*

CARAPAU: Horse mackerel; see *THE FISH AND SHELLFISH OF PORTUGAL.*

CARIL: Curry powder; it is frequently added to soups and stews for zip, but in amounts so small it's flavor is unidentifiable. Thanks to Vasco da Gama's discovery of a water route to the East's treasury of spices, curry has been known to Portuguese cooks for centuries. Today you can find it in the remotest country kitchen.

CARIOCA: See *THE COFFEES OF PORTUGAL.*

CARNE: Meat, in general; *carne de porco* is pork; *carne de vaca,* beef.

CARNEIRO: Mutton; it's more popular in Portugal than lamb because it comes from sheep that have outlived their profitability.

CARROTS: CENOURAS; Portuguese carrots are so orange and sweet they're candied or boiled into marmalade. Their worth as a vegetable isn't overlooked, either. In fact they are the favorite accompaniment to most meats. The Portuguese method of preparing carrots couldn't be simpler: They are peeled, chunked or sliced, boiled until tender, then sometimes—but not always—turned in a little butter or meat drippings.

CASA DE CHÁ: Tearoom or, as it is alternatively known, *Salão de chá* (tea salon). Tearooms are a favorite rendezvous for stylish Portuguese ladies and dispense not only tea but also coffee and diet-busting arrays of sweets.

CASEIRO: Homemade (which Portugal's best breads and cakes are).

CASTELO BRANCO: See *THE CHEESES OF PORTUGAL.*

CATAPLANA: A hinged, hermetically sealed metal cooker popular in the Algarve and Alentejo that looks like a giant clamshell. Introduced by the Moors, it's used today to cook anything from fish to fowl but is most famous for a single recipe—*Amêijoas na Cataplana*—baby clams cooked in a *cataplana* with rounds of sausages and dots of ham in a ruddy tomato sauce; see Recipe Index.

CAULIFLOWER: See **COUVE-FLOR.**

CAYENNE: **PIMENTA-DE-CAIENA;** the Portuguese use it less frequently than *colorau*, the powder of a hot paprika or red pepper not as explosive as cayenne. Still, cayenne is employed in small quantities to add bite to soups, stews, fricassees and sauces.

CEBOLA: Onion; Portuguese onions are big and yellow and more forthright than the fawn-skinned Spanish onions. There are little white onions, too, no doubt cousins of our silverskins, which are plunked whole into stews or used to garnish platters.

CEBOLADA: A soft golden paste made by sautéing onions briefly in olive oil, often with garlic, then steaming them slowly twenty minutes or more until very sweet and moist. The technique of making *cebolada* is known as *refogado* (which see).

CEBOLINHO: Chives; indispensable to classical chefs but not to country cooks.

CELERY: **AIPO.**

CENOURAS: See Carrots.

CENTEIO: Barley; *farinha de centeio* (barley flour) is kneaded into many rough country breads along with a high-gluten flour to compensate for its own lack of gluten. Such breads are dark and chewy—and piled high at every village market.

CEREJA: Cherry; the bulk of the harvest is boiled into jams and jellies.

CERVEJA: Beer; see *THE BEER AND BOTTLED WATERS OF PORTUGAL* on page 64.

CERVEJARIA: A beer parlor; some of these are surprisingly sedate and good places for a quick snack or buying the makings of a picnic.

CHÁ: Tea; because of its historic links with the East, Portugal has no shortage of fine aromatic teas.

CHÁVENNA: Teacup; many Portuguese recipes still call for teacups of this or that in preference to metric measures.

CHEESE: **QUEIJO;** see *THE CHEESES OF PORTUGAL.*

CHEFE DE MESA: The headwaiter.

CHERNE: Stone bass; a lean white fish with wide appeal.

CHERRY: **CEREJA.**

CHICKEN: In what world capital other than Lisbon can you be awakened by the crow of a rooster? I can't think of any, certainly not any Euro-

---

The Cheeses of Portugal

Sheep and goats graze the mountains of northern Portugal, the vast plains of the Alentejo, the suburbs of Lisbon, even until a few years ago, postage-stamp plots smack-dab in the middle of Lisbon's old Moorish Quarter. They provide meat and, more importantly, milk, from which assorted *queijos* (cheeses) are made, some to rival the finest of France. Unfortunately (or maybe *not* so unfortunately) you'll have to go to Portugal to taste most of them.

AZEITÃO: Little golden rounds of sheep cheese made on quintas (estates) around the affluent town of Azeitão, which lies on the mountainous Setúbal peninsula directly across the Tagus River from Lisbon. Averaging about half a pound apiece, *Azeitão* cheeses are tangy, creamy, fine-textured. When perfectly ripe, they are not cut but dipped into with a spoon. One favorite combination: Azeitão and *marmelada*, a stiff amber paste made from quince.

continued on next page

The Cheeses of Portugal

BEJA: One of the outstanding sheep cheeses of the Alentejo, this one comes from farms near the town of Beja. It is moderately salty, weighs four to five pounds and is made from February to June. Connoisseurs prefer *Bejas* when fresh and buttery. Most, however, are aged one to two years into semihardness and piquancy.

CABREIRO: When young and soft, these lightly salted little goat cheeses from the vicinity of Castelo Branco are as fine as any cheese Portugal produces. The fresh ones, alas, are both highly perishable and highly popular and thus rarely make it as far away as Lisbon. What *cabreiro* cheeses aren't eaten fresh are briefly aged, developing a wrinkled crust, pale-gray cast, and a flavor reminiscent of Roquefort (although no blue veining of mold).

CASTELO BRANCO: This velvety white sheep cheese from farms around Castelo Branco looks and tastes so much like Portugal's celebrated *Queijo da Serra* (which see) that only experts can tell the two apart; any subtle differences of flavor are determined by what herbs and grasses the sheep eat. *Castelo Branco* is made from late fall right through the spring, and when the cheese "runs," it is pronounced perfect. It is also aged into rounds as hard and sharp as Parmesan. (Like Parmesan, it is used more often for cooking than for eating.)

ÉVORA: Maybe the best cheese of the entire Alentejo. Like the *Beja* and *Serpa* cheeses (which see), this one is made of sheep's milk, and mostly between February and June. It is somewhat smaller than the *Beja*, slightly saltier than *Queijo da Serra*, and is eaten both fresh (when it is deliciously creamy and piquant) and fully ripe (firm and pleasantly biting).

MERENDEIRAS: You see these fresh sheep cheeses at country markets and fairs all over the Alentejo Province. They weigh just a few ounces each and usually are sold completely submerged in olive oil in little terra-cotta crocks. Smaller cheeses of this type, the famous *Queijinhos de Évora*, are the local lunch-pail staple.

QUEIJO ARREGANHADO: A rough, lean cheese from Castelo Branco made of the thin "first milk" of the ewe. Mild and mellow, but difficult to find except in season in the region where it's made.

QUEIJO DA ILHA: An outstanding Cheddar-like cow's-milk cheese from the Azorean island of São Jorge. Known locally as *Queijo da Terra* (cheese of the earth or land), it ages well to a firmness and flavor suggestive of Parmesan. Many Lisbon shops sell grated *Queijo da Ilha* much as American shops sell grated Parmesan, and like Parmesan, it is used primarily for cooking. Because of the success of *Queijo da Ilha*, other Azorean islands have begun making cheese. Pico produces two fine ones: a low-butterfat white cow's-milk cheese known as "Cheese of the North" and a far richer, creamier goat-and-cow's-milk blend called "Cheese of the South" (the better of the two).

QUEIJO DA SERRA: This queen of Portuguese cheeses, when runnily ripe, is as buttery and well-balanced of flavor as the choicest Brie. *"Serra,"* as it is familiarly known, is a rich (35 to 40 percent butterfat) cheese made of the milk of long-horned sheep, which graze the lofty heaths of the

The Cheeses of Portugal

Serra da Estrêla (Mountains of the Star) in northeastern Portugal. Indeed, so integral to the cheese's flavor is this diet of wild herbs that the *Serra*-producing region has been demarcated much like the regions of Portugal's fine wines. All phases of the making of *Queijo da Serra* are now scrupulously controlled to ensure cheeses of uniformly high quality. Depending upon the weather, *Queijo da Serra* is made from October to April or May, the first cheeses coming from the loftier towns and farms, the later ones from lower down the mountain, where frosts arrive later. Those knowledgeable about such things consider the very finest *Serra* to be the *Cabeça da Velha* from the town of Seia. Although the Portuguese prefer a *Serra* that is runny (*amanteigado*) and ammoniac (available only in winter and spring), many of them are also ripened until firm and pungent. These *curado Serras* are compact, smooth, ivory-hued, and weigh two to four pounds each.

QUEIJOS FRESCOS: Fresh sheep and goat cheeses are made on farms all over Portugal. Most are produced (and should be eaten) in winter, and most are no more than two to three inches across. Two of the best come from towns near Lisbon—Sintra and Mafra. The *queijos frescos* of Sintra are made into delicately cinnamony tarts called *queijadas;* see Recipe Index. Although their name implies that *queijos frescos* are only eaten fresh, they are also aged to some extent, their flavors intensifying, textures firming, and colors assuming the richness of old ivory.

RABAÇAL: A semi-soft sheep-and-goat's-milk cheese from the Portuguese heartland

that is eaten both fresh and sun-cured (in which case the flavor is plenty strong).

REQUEIJÃO: This white farmer's cheese, sold in little straw baskets and served on fig or cabbage leaves, is made of boiled sheep's milk, sometimes in combination with a little goat's milk. It is somewhat firmer and drier than the conventional *queijo fresco,* which it resembles in flavor. The Portuguese like to sprinkle *requeijão* with cinnamon and sugar and serve it as dessert.

SERPA: The third of the Alentejo's "sacred trinity of cheeses" and, in the opinion of many, the best. Like *Beja* and *Évora* cheeses (which see), *Serpa* is made of sheep's milk during the winter and spring and eaten both fresh (when it's soft and buttery) and aged (when it's sharp and semi-hard). The aging process is unique: *Serpas* are ripened one to two years in cool caves, cleaned regularly, and brushed with a paste of olive oil and paprika, which accounts for their distinctive orange rinds. Some people liken *Serpa* (named for the town from which it comes) to the more famous *Queijo da Serra,* but its flavor is nuttier and its texture drier.

TOMAR: Snowy little sheep cheeses, each scarcely more than a bite, from the old Knights Templar stronghold of Tomar some seventy-five miles north of Lisbon. They are lightly salted, fairly dry, and taste of both woodsmoke and nuts.

Note: A surprisingly good round, red-skinned "Dutch" cheese is made in Portugal and also, quite recently, a dead-ringer for Camembert in the northern lagoon town of Aveiro.

pean capital. Chickens are kept everywhere in Portugal, both for eggs and for eating. Young birds (*frangos*) are broiled or grilled; old hens (*galinhas*) are stewed or fricasseed.

CHICK-PEA: **GRÃO-DE-BICO** or, more popularly, just *grão*. Dried chick-peas are one of the economical, nutritious foods upon which creative Portuguese country cooks have built a soups-to-sweets repertoire of recipes.

CHILA (GILA): A pumpkinlike gourd; see **ABÓBORA**.

CHIVES: **CEBOLINHO**.

CHOCO: Cuttlefish; an everyday item in fishing villages, where it's unloaded from gaily painted fishing boats.

CHOPS: **COSTELETAS;** pork chops are the most popular, veal chops second.

CHOURIÇO. See *THE SAUSAGES AND HAMS OF PORTUGAL*.

CHURRASCO: Charcoal-grilled meats or chicken, usually on a spit or skewer. In the north of Portugal you see crudely lettered, enchantingly decorated *Churrasqueiria* signs, meaning *churrasco* is the house specialty. Most of these little restaurants are owned by *retornados,* men who worked overseas in such places as Brazil ("The Capital of Churrasco"), pocketed a little change, then came home to Portugal to make a better life for their families who had waited patiently behind.

CINNAMON: See **CANELA**.

CLAMS: See **AMÊIJOAS**.

CLARA: Egg white; the Portuguese addiction to egg yolks is so acute that cooks have been forced to devise ways of using up the whites. Two of their best solutions to the leftover problem are *Pudim Molotov* and *Suspiros* (shattery-crisp meringues); see Recipe Index.

CLOVES: **CRAVO-DE-INDIA;** although clove is one of the spices brought home to Portugal in the hold of Vasco da Gama's caravel, it has never been as popular as cinnamon. Cloves are mixed into honey and spice cakes, however, and interestingly, occasionally added to meat and fish dishes, injecting a mysterious but unmistakable tang.

COCO: Coconut; given the fact that Brazil once belonged to Portugal, it's surprising that coconut isn't better liked in Portugal. You do find it in a few of the sweets, but that's about it. (Brazilians, on the other hand, team coconut with meat, fish and fowl as well as with sugar.)

COCOA: **CACAU**.

COELHO: Rabbit; these are farm-raised, white-meated and supremely tender. Wild rabbit (*coelho bravo*) abounds in plains and uplands and is popular quarry.

COENTRO: Coriander; fresh coriander is the single most widely used herb in Portugal, but its dried seeds (and the powder ground from them) are rarely used. Fresh coriander appears to be available the year round; at least, whenever I have visited Portugal, I have seen vast bouquets of it in town and country markets, frills of it greening doorsteps, and wicker baskets full of it atop the heads of farm women. Maybe it is hothouse grown, but it looks too bushy and vibrantly green to have been raised under glass. Suffice it to say that the Portuguese have the greenest thumbs on earth and can coax anything from hardscrabble ground. Fresh coriander scents the soups of Portugal, the stews, vegetables, rice—everything, you might say, except those infamous egg sweets.

COFFEE: **CAFÉ;** see *THE COFFEES OF PORTUGAL*.

COGUMELOS: Mushrooms; these are not commonly used except in fine restaurants.

COLHER: Spoon; Portuguese cookbooks call for small quantities of ingredients, much as we used to, by the *colher de chá* (teaspoon), *colher de sopa* (soup spoon), and *colher de sobremesa* (dessert spoon).

COLORAU: A hot paprika or powdered red pep-

The Coffees of Portugal

Few people realize how richly aromatic Portuguese coffees are or how integral to daily life, but this is scarcely surprising given the fact that some of the world's finest coffees are produced in the former Portuguese colonies of Angola, Brazil and Timor. Everywhere in Portugal the coffeehouse is an institution (make that obsession) among men who congregate to talk, read and sip cup after cup of very dark coffee. Although young women are now crashing this bastion of masculinity, their mothers still gather to gossip in *casas de chá* (tearooms) or *pastelarias* (pastry shops) where both sweets and the traditional "menu" of Portuguese coffees are served:

BICA (pronounced BEE-ka): the strong-enough-to-stand-alone demitasse that's the coffeehouse staple, especially in Lisbon.

CAFÉ: The standard heady brew served everywhere. In fine restaurants, it's made at your table in little hourglass-shaped glass vacuum pots set over alcohol burners.

CARIOCA: A half-and-half mix of *café* and hot water that approximates American coffee.

GALÃO (rhymes with *allow*): Strong filter coffee mixed with hot milk, then served in a glass. *Galão Escuro*, meaning "dark," is heavier on the coffee; *Galão Claro* (light), heavier on the milk.

GAROTO: In Portuguese, *garoto* means kid, youngster, or scamp, and this hot coffee-flavored milk is what Portuguese children drink out of little glasses or demitasse cups.

Note: If you should visit Lisbon, two famous coffeehouses to try are Café Suiça, a bustling indoor-outdoor affair with chairs and tables set up on the squiggly sidewalk mosaics overlooking the Rossio Square fountain in the city center, and À Brasileira, an elegant Old Guard establishment on Rua Garrett (Lisbon's Fifth Avenue) popular among Portuguese literati.

per that accounts for both the orange color and piquant flavor of many of Portugal's pork and poultry dishes. It resembles hot Hungarian paprika, available here in specialty food shops. Use that, if possible; or approximate the flavor and heat of *colorau* by combining 1 tablespoon of sweet paprika with ¼ to ½ teaspoon of cayenne pepper.

COLORAU-DOCE: Paprika; how intensely red and flavorful Portuguese sweet paprika is! The best substitute is fine Hungarian sweet rose paprika, obtainable in specialty food shops.

COM LEITE: With milk, as in coffee or tea.

COM LIMÃO: With lemon, as in tea.

COMPOTA: Jam; the Portuguese make lovely jams, jellies and conserves from an impressive harvest of homegrown fruits: cherries, peaches, figs, oranges, strawberries, quinces, plums and apricots.

CONGRO: Conger eel; it's much appreciated in Portugal and is one of the principal ingredients of many *caldeiradas* (which see).

CONTA: Restaurant bill or check.

COOKIE: BISCOITO.

CORIANDER: See **COENTRO.**

CORN: **MILHO.**

CORNMEAL: **FARINHA DE MILHO;** the Portuguese rely heavily upon stone-ground cornmeal (the yellow is preferred) for a number of breads. Two of the most popular are *Broa* and *Milho Frito;* see Recipe Index.

CORVINO: Croaker.

COSTELETA: A chop (usually boneless) or cutlet.

COUVE: See Cabbage.

COUVE-FLOR: Cauliflower; the Portuguese like it boiled or pickled.

COZIDO: See Boiled.

COZINHA: Kitchen; two of the most magnificent kitchens I've ever seen are in Portugal, one in the monastery at Alcobaça (a brook trickles smack through the middle of it) and the other at the Ducal Palace in Vila Viçosa, where a blinding battery of copper kettles is on display.

CRAVO-DE-INDIA: See Cloves.

CRAYFISH: **LANGOSTINS;** those of Portugal are as delectably sweet and tender as those of France.

CREAM: **NATA;** Portuguese cream is not particularly rich, more like light cream than heavy cream, although whipping cream is certainly available.

CREME: A creamed soup.

CRU: Raw, uncooked, which is the way Portugal's wonderful ham, *presunto,* is served.

CUP: See **CHÁVENNA.**

CURRY: See **CARIL.**

CUSTARD, BAKED: **FLAN;** what makes the flans of Portugal special is that they are usually thickened with egg yolks rather than whole eggs.

CUTLET: See **ESCALOPE** or **COSTELETA.**

DESSERT: **SOBREMESA.**

DINNER: **JANTAR;** the Portuguese do not dine as late as Spaniards; in fact their dinner hours more nearly coincide with ours: 8:00 or 8:30 P.M. is the stylish hour to begin, although country people sup at least an hour earlier.

DOBRADA: Tripe, which is also known as *tripas.*

DOCE: Sweet; when you see *doces* listed on a menu, it means assorted sweets (also sometimes written as *doces varios*).

DOCES DE OVOS: Rich-as-sin egg sweets; see *THE EGG SWEETS OF PORTUGAL.*

DRINKS: See **BEBIDAS.**

DUCK: **PATO;** some Portuguese cooks with whom I've spoken have an ingenious method of defatting duck; they prick it well, then simmer it in water to cover, which seems to encourage the fat just underneath the skin to melt and run out. Once the simmered duck is tender, it is browned—an unorthodox system but one that seems to work amazingly well.

EEL: **EIRÓ.**

EGG: **OVO;** egg yolks are *gemas;* egg whites, *claras.* When it comes to cooked eggs, the terminology is thus: fried eggs (*ovos estrelados*), poached eggs (*ovos escalfados*), scrambled eggs (*ovos mexidos*), soft-boiled eggs (*ovos quentes*) and hard-cooked eggs (*ovos cozidos*).

EGGPLANT: BERINGELA

EIRÓ: Eel, a generic term. Another word for eel, usually denoting the slim, snakelike river eel of the north, is *enguia*. See THE FISH AND SHELLFISH OF PORTUGAL.

EMPADA: A savory little pie usually made of meat or *bacalhau* (salt cod). Most are half-moons fried until crisply golden in deep fat.

ENCHIDO: Sausages, in general; see THE SAUSAGES AND HAMS OF PORTUGAL.

ENGUIA: See EIRÓ.

ERVAS: Herbs; see THE PREDOMINANT HERBS, SPICES AND FLAVORINGS OF PORTUGAL on page 53.

ERVILHAS: Green peas; a popular way to cook them is to braise them with rounds of garlicky sausage; see Recipe Index.

ESCALOPE: Scallop; a thin, boneless piece of meat. In Portugal, scallops may be cut from veal, pork or beef.

The Egg Sweets of Portugal—
Doces de Ovos

These excruciatingly rich confections compounded primarily of egg yolks and sugar are believed to have been introduced to Spain and Portugal by the Moors. But it was the seventeenth- and eighteenth-century nuns of Portugal who exalted them (the reason so many bear convent names). According to Almeida Garrett, a dashing nineteenth-century Portuguese poet, rhyming contests were routinely held in convents whenever a new abbess was elected, and at such times, the nuns created egg sweets of intricate design and infinite variety. They also kept busy dreaming up new egg sweets to impress visiting dignitaries and to raise funds for the convent. Among the hundreds of *doces de ovos* made in Portugal today, these are especially popular:

ALETRIA: Thin pasta drenched with egg-yolk custard and sprinkled with cinnamon.

BARRIGAS DE FREIRA (Nun's Tummies): Cloyingly sweet mounds of egg yolks and bread crumbs dusted with cinnamon. The name of this sweet proves that the nuns weren't without a certain sense of humor.

DOM RODRIGO: An Algarve sweet, named for a local nobleman, which consists of tiny hillocks of *ovos moles* (sweet soft eggs) and *fios de ovos* (thread eggs) saturated with burnt-sugar syrup. Each *Dom Rodrigo* is twirled up in silver foil.

FATIAS: Poached loaves of stiffly beaten egg yolks and sugar (and sometimes finely ground almonds) that are sliced, then inundated with lemon or cinnamon syrup.

FIOS DE OVOS (Thread Eggs): In the old days the nuns would puncture eggshells, fill them with beaten egg yolks, and drizzle the yolks into bubbling syrup, producing strands as fine as angel's hair. A tedious process. Today there are little cans with four to five pointed spouts to make short shrift of the job. Thread eggs are used both as an ingredient in and a decoration for a variety of egg sweets.

continued on next page

The Egg Sweets of Portugal—
Doces de Ovos

FLAN: This, of course, is baked custard, but in Portugal it is more apt to be thickened with egg yolks than whole eggs. Sometimes it's caramelized, sometimes not, and often it's spiked with Port. See Recipe Index.

LAMPREIA DE OVOS (Lamprey of Eggs): The lamprey (eel) is so beloved by the Portuguese that they make a festive egg sweet in its image. The base is almond paste and egg yolks, the decoration *fios de ovos* or thread eggs.

MORGADO: A generic word for a whole category of Algarve egg sweets, most of them containing ground almonds and often figs as well. See Recipe Index.

OVOS MOLES (Sweet Soft Eggs): This silky paste of egg yolks, sugar and rice cooking water or rice flour originated in the convents of the northern coastal town of Aveiro and is today the foundation of the majority of Portugal's egg sweets.

PALHA DE ABRANTES (Straw from Abrantes): These little egg-thickened rounds of almond paste are topped by thread eggs (or "straw").

PAPOS DE ANJO (Angel's Cheeks): Tiny rounded molds of egg yolks and sugar smothered with sugar syrup.

PASTÉIS: Another generic word that includes a variety of pastries filled with egg sweets. There are also savory *pastéis*.

QUEIJADAS: A family of tarts with egg-thickened fillings, sometimes containing cheese (*queijo*, which explains their name), and often enriched with finely ground blanched almonds. Among the most famous are the *Queijadas de Sintra;* see Recipe Index.

SOPA DOURADA (Soup of Gold): Cubes of buttered toast or sponge cake tossed in egg-yolk-thickened syrup; see Recipe Index.

SUSPIROS (Sighs): These are nothing more than baked meringues and one of the few egg sweets made without egg yolks, although the meringues are often sandwiched together with *ovos moles* (sweet soft eggs). See Recipe Index.

TIGELADAS: Egg custards baked in shallow individual earthenware dishes at such high heat that they brown intensely and become almost sponge-cake firm. In some areas *tigeladas* are flavored with vanilla, in others with cinnamon and/or lemon.

TOUCINHO DO CÉU (Bacon from Heaven): According to the best information available, this translucent egg-yolk-rich flan of pumpkin and ground almonds, which originated in the Trás-os-Montes town of Murça, at first contained bacon. Its celestial goodness presumably prompted the nuns to add "from heaven." The historic town of Guimarães near Porto also claims to be the source of *Toucinho do Céu,* and indeed, its version is memorable; see Recipe Index.

TROUXAS DE OVOS (Bundles of Eggs): Poached tissue-thin sheets of beaten egg yolk rolled up like little bundles of hay and submerged in sugar syrup.

Note: Because of our growing concern about both calories and cholesterol, I include in this book recipes only for those egg sweets that I consider outstanding. Most egg sweets, may the Portuguese forgive me, offer little more than "your basic sugar flavor," and require more time and attention than most busy cooks can muster.

ESPADA: Scabbard fish; see *THE FISH AND SHELLFISH OF PORTUGAL*.

ESPADARTE: Swordfish; see *THE FISH AND SHELLFISH OF PORTUGAL*.

ESPARGO: See Asparagus.

ESPARREGADO: Greens (usually spinach or turnip greens), sautéed with garlic in olive oil, then puréed; see Recipe Index.

ESPECIARIAS: Spices; see *THE PREDOMINANT HERBS, SPICES AND FLAVORINGS OF PORTUGAL* on page 53.

ESPETADA: Skewered, grilled chunks of beef. This Portuguese "shish kebab" originated on the island of Madeira among farmers who, as they worked their fields, would break off young branches of bay laurel, thread pieces of beef onto them, then lay them in smoldering coals to cook. Today, wrought-iron skewers are used, and in order for the meat to absorb the necessary bay fragrance, it is marinated for many hours with a cluster of bay leaves; see Recipe Index.

ESPINAFRES: Spinach; it's richly green and tender, less crinkly than our spinach, and ubiquitous. The way country cooks prepare it is to sauté it with garlic in olive oil or meat drippings. Often they combine spinach with turnip greens, and sometimes they toss in a handful of watercress or sorrel for zip.

ESTALAGEM: A privately owned inn, as opposed to a *pousada,* which is government-run. You will find *estalagems* in every city, town and village of Portugal. They are often the best places to eat because their cooks, invariably local, specialize in the regional cooking.

ESTUFADO: Stewed; or the stew itself.

ÉVORA: See *THE CHEESES OF PORTUGAL*.

FACA: Knife.

FARINHA: Flour; the white flour of Portugal comes from hard wheat containing a high percentage of gluten, which accounts for the sturdiness and chewiness of the truly wonderful Portuguese bread.

FARINHEIRA: See *THE SAUSAGES AND HAMS OF PORTUGAL*.

FATIA: Slice.

FATIAS: One of the popular egg sweets of Portugal; see *THE EGG SWEETS OF PORTUGAL*.

FAVA: The fava or broad bean; country people pick them young and eat them pods and all, especially in the northerly Trás-os-Montes Province.

FEIJÃO: See Bean.

FENNEL: **FUNCHO;** when Prince Henry's navigators stepped ashore on the island of Madeira early in the fifteenth century, the air was so filled with the sweetness of fennel that they named the place *Funchal.* The capital of the Madeira archipelago, Funchal is today a city of more than 100,000 people that spills down the green mountains to embrace a horseshoe harbor. Fennel still grows wild in Madeira, but it is not so widely used in cooking as it once was.

FERMENTO: Yeast; Portuguese women use cake yeast for making bread or for starters, which they keep from one batch of dough to the next. Our dried yeast works very well, however, and is what I have used in the recipes in this book.

FIAMBRE: Boiled ham; see *THE SAUSAGES AND HAMS OF PORTUGAL*.

FIGADO: Liver; beef, mutton and pork livers are the most commonly used, but their flavors are too intense for most American palates.

FIGO: Fig; big sprawling fig bushes grow all along the Algarve coast, many of them half wild. But the natives gather them dutifully, dry them, grind them to paste with nuts, and shape them into sweetmeats—holdovers, surely, of the five-hundred-year Moorish occupation.

FILETE: Fillet; a thin, boneless piece of meat or fish.

FIOS DE OVOS: See *THE EGG SWEETS OF PORTUGAL.*

FISH: **PEIXE;** see *THE FISH AND SHELLFISH OF PORTUGAL.*

FLAN: Baked custard; see *THE EGG SWEETS OF PORTUGAL.*

FLOUR: **FARINHA.**

FORK: **GARFO.**

FORNO: Oven; when you see *no forno* on a menu, it means that the food was baked, often in a brick or stone oven.

FORTE: Strong, as in coffee or tea.

FRACO: Weak, as in coffee or tea.

FRAMBOESA: Raspberry; you don't often see fresh raspberries in Portugal, except in luxury hotels and restaurants.

FRANGO: A young broiling or frying chicken.

FRESCO: Fresh.

FRIGIDEIRA: Frying pan or skillet; this word is perhaps the most confusing to appear on any Portuguese menu. For example, *bifes na frigideira* quite logically suggests cold beef. *Not so!* translated literally, it means *beef in a frying pan,* i.e., panbroiled or fried beef.

FRIO: Cold, and the way most Portuguese, as well as Americans, like their *cerveja* (beer).

FRITO: Fried; the Portuguese dote upon fried foods almost as much as the American southerner, and they prepare them with equal skill.

FRUTAS: Fruits; *frutas doces* are candied or preserved fruits; *frutas sêcas,* dried fruits such as raisins or currants.

FUMADO: Smoked; you'll have to search far and wide to find more delicious smoked hams than those of Portugal.

FUNCHO: See Fennel.

GALÃO: See *THE COFFEES OF PORTUGAL.*

GALINHA: Stewing fowl or hen.

GAMBAS: Prawns (the common Mediterranean variety); often, as soon as you settle at the table of a fish restaurant, you'll be brought a big bowl of unshelled prawns and a bottle of *piri-piri* (hot pepper) sauce. If you don't want them, say so at once; otherwise you'll be charged for them.

GAME: See **CAÇA.**

GARFO: Fork.

GARLIC: **ALHO;** anyone not fond of garlic will have a rough time in Portugal because cooks are prodigious in their use of it. Indeed, at country markets you see women buying garlic by the braid, not by the bud or head.

GAROTO: See *THE COFFEES OF PORTUGAL.*

GAROUPA: Grouper.

GELADO: Ice cream.

GELO: Ice; if you want your drinks without ice, learn to say *"sem gelo."*

GEMA: Egg yolk; see Egg.

GENGIBRE: Ginger; like cloves, ginger is not as lavishly used in Portugal as cinnamon, although it, too, was one of the spices made available by Vasco da Gama's opening up of the trade routes to the Indies.

GIBLETS: **MIÚDOS;** Portuguese cooks use these in stocks, sauces, soups and gravies, but even more

The Fish and
Shellfish of Portugal

Washed on two sides by the Atlantic and coursed by no less than a dozen major rivers, Portugal is blessed with an abundance of fish and shellfish. Among the best are:

FISH—*Peixe*

ANCHOVAS (anchovies) . . . ATUM (tuna—these giants used to be caught in waters off the Algarve, but fishermen must now go deep into the Atlantic for their catch; *bifes de atum* are tuna steaks) . . . BACALHAU (dried salt cod; see page 37) . . . BARBO (barbel; a fish that swims the rivers of the Alentejo) . . . BESUGO (sunfish) . . . CARAPAU (horse mackerel, a small, oily fish abundant and much beloved in the Algarve) . . . CHERNE (stone bass) . . . CONGRO (conger eel) . . . CORVINO (croaker) . . . EIRÓS (eels) . . . ENGUIAS (slender snakelike eels popular around the lagoon town of Aveiro near Porto) . . . ESPADA (scabbard fish; there are two varieties of this big, flat, eellike fish—gleaming silver ones, which you'll see in the markets of Lisbon and Cascais coiled into boxes like strips of aluminum, and sinister-looking black ones, all head and teeth, which swim the waters of Madeira; both types are lean and white but a bit coarse of texture) . . . ESPADARTE (swordfish; *espadarte fumado,* or smoked swordfish, is the specialty of the little fishing town of Sesimbra near Lisbon and by all means try it if you should see it on a menu—it's superb!) . . . GAROUPA (grouper) . . . LAMPREIA (a fat eel that spawns in the rivers of northern Portugal and is considered a delicacy; it is in season only in the early spring) . . . LINGUADO (sole) . . . PARGO (sea bream) . . . PESCADA (hake; "the noble fish of Portugal") . . . PESCADINHA (whiting) . . . RAIA (skate) . . . ROBALO (sea bass) . . . SALMÃO (salmon) . . . SALMONETE (red mullet; these fine-fleshed white fish are the specialty of Setúbal, where they are grilled with the tart local oranges) . . . SARDA (mackerel) . . . SARDINHAS (sardines; everyone's favorite and best between early April and November when they are fat and sweet) . . . SARGO (porgy) . . . SÁVEL (shad; those found in the Tagus above Lisbon are superior) . . . TAINHA (gray mullet) . . . TAMBORIL (monkfish) . . . TRUTA (trout; those pulled from the clear, rushing rivers of the northerly Minho and Trás-os-Montes provinces are unusually fine-fleshed and tender).

SHELLFISH—*Mariscos*

AMÊIJOAS (tiny, buttery, thin-shelled clams) . . . CAMARÕES (shrimp) . . . CARACÓIS (snails; these, like *escargots,* are from the land but cooked like shellfish) . . . CHOCO (cuttlefish) . . . GAMBAS (prawns) . . . LAGOSTA (lobster) . . . LAGOSTINS (crayfish) . . . LAPAS (limpets; these are more popular in the Azores than on the mainland) . . . LULA (squid) . . . MEXILHÕES (mussels) . . . OSTRAS (oysters) . . . PERCEVES (tiny barnacles) . . . POLVO (octopus) . . . SANTOLA (spider or spiny crab) . . . SAPOTEIRA (a large crab rather like Dungeness) . . . VIEIRAS (scallops).

often in a sort of rice pilaf; see Recipe Index for *Arroz de Forno.*

Grão-de-bico: See Chick-pea.

Grão de pimenta: Peppercorns; the black and the white are used with equal frequency in Portugal, perhaps because so much fish and chicken are eaten. (Ever conscious of appearance, a Portuguese cook is not likely to "dirty" a snowy piece of sole or of *cherne* with black pepper.)

Grapefruit: Toranja.

Grapes: Uvas; the grapes of Portugal are simply dazzling, both in their appearance and in their abundance. It's touching to see how carefully they are arranged in slatted baskets at markets, how artistically they are garnished with a few perfect grape leaves, strategically placed. It's touching, too, to watch a vendor scramble to rearrange his produce the instant a bunch of grapes is sold.

Gratinado: Gratinéed; topped with crumbs or cheese and quickly browned.

Grelhado: Grilled.

Grelos: Pungent spring greens beloved by the Portuguese. Portuguese dictionaries give "turnip greens" as a translation, but as a daughter of the Deep South, I know turnip greens when I taste them. These greens are altogether different: paler, stalkier, furled at the top like fiddleheads. In researching *grelos,* I've discovered they are the young shoots of a non-heading broccoli. The Portuguese know how to cook them perfectly—by sautéing them in a fruity olive oil with whole cloves of garlic (sometimes unpeeled for more delicate flavor). I have even seen *grelos* served with *whole* buds (heads) of garlic.

Guisado: See Braised.

Hake: Pescada; this lean, white-fleshed fish is one of the choicest that swims in Portuguese waters.

Ham: See *The Sausages and Hams of Portugal.*

Headwaiter: Chefe de mesa.

Herbs: Ervas; see *The Predominant Herbs, Spices and Flavorings of Portugal.*

Honey: Mel; in Portugal, this includes both true honey (*mel da abelhas,* or "honey of the bees") and molasses (*mel da cana* or "honey of the cane," i.e., sugarcane). Both are used in the compactly textured cakes so characteristic of Portugal—and especially of Madeira.

Hors d'oeuvre: Acepipes.

Hortelã: Mint; the mountainous North and midriff of Portugal are overrun with mint. Or so it seems to me. Local cooks make good use of the herb, snipping it into a variety of soups and stews.

Horteliça: Fresh vegetables.

Hot: Quente.

Ice: Gelo.

Ice Cream: Gelado.

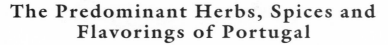

The Predominant Herbs, Spices and Flavorings of Portugal

Almonds (AMÊNDOAS), bay leaves (LOURO), cinnamon (CANELA, in both sweets and savories), fresh coriander *(coentro)*, curry (CARIL—used in minute quantities), garlic (ALHO—and plenty of it), lemon (LIMÃO), mint (HORTELÃ), olive oil (AZEITE; see page 56), olives (AZEITONAS), onions (CEBOLAS), orange (LARANJA), oregano (OREGÃO, used mostly in the Alentejo Province, where it grows wild), paprika (both hot—COLORAU —and sweet—COLORAU DOCE), parsley (SALSA), saffron (AÇAFRÃO), sweet red pepper or pimento (PIMENTÃO; the Portuguese make lavish use of *massa de pimentão,* a dry marinade used primarily for pork and chicken; see Recipe Index. *Note: You can shortcut its long-winded preparation and approximate its flavor; see the quick version on page 55.)* Other seasonings no Portuguese cook could do without are PIRI-PIRI (tiny, incendiary red peppers from Angola), tomato (TOMATE), vinegar (VINAGRE), and dry wine (VINHO SECO—both the red, *tinto,* and the white, *branco*).

JAM: See **COMPOTA.**
JANTAR: See Dinner.

KITCHEN: See **COZINHA.**
KNIFE: **FACA.**

LAGOSTA: Lobster; the lobsters netted off the Portuguese coast are spiny lobsters—without claws. The choicest of them come from waters off the craggy Peniche promontory some fifty or sixty miles north of Lisbon, but sweet-meated lobsters are also found near Cascais and Guincho, just twenty miles west of Lisbon. *A note of warning: Ask the price of lobster before ordering (it's never listed because the price varies from day to day). Lobster is invariably expensive, as a friend of mine once discovered. To his dismay, the lobster he'd just polished off cost $50—exhorbitant by any standard.*

LAMB: See **ANHO** and **BORREGO.**

LAMPREIA: See *THE FISH AND SHELLFISH OF PORTUGAL.*

LAMPREIA DE OVOS: See *THE EGG SWEETS OF PORTUGAL.*

LANCHE: A snack; also tea with all the trimmings.

LANGOSTINS: Crayfish.

LAPAS: See *THE FISH AND SHELLFISH OF PORTUGAL.*

LARANJA: Orange; it's surprising to see oranges growing so abundantly in Portugal, which is, after all, on a latitude with Pennsylvania. But oranges flourish as far north as Porto. The best of them, however, are the small tart oranges from orchards around Setúbal. They're made into a tart *marmelada* or *doce de laranja* so good you want to eat it with a spoon (many Portuguese do).

LEEK: See **ALHO FRANCÊS.**

LEGUMES: Vegetables.

LEITÃO: Suckling pig; one of the wonders of Portugal is the little town of Mealhada directly north of Coimbra on the road to Porto. Here, lined up along both sides of N-1, the major north-south route, are fifteen (at last count) restaurants specializing in spit-roasted suckling pig *(leitão assado)*. Two of the most famous are Pedro dos Leitões and Meta dos Leitões, just next door to each other. If you have never tasted suckling pig, this is the place to do so. The skin of the piglets is as light and crisp as parchment and the flesh meltingly succulent.

LEITE: Milk; Portugal was never much of a dairy country, but on recent trips I've noticed impressive herds of black-and-white Holsteins, prolific producers of low-butterfat milk.

LETTUCE: See **ALFACE.**

LIMÃO: Lemon; the lemons of Portugal are as big as oranges and almost as sweet. They grow on the peninsula directly south of Lisbon and also in the Algarve.

LIMÃO VERDE: Lime.

LINGUADO: Sole.

LINGUIÇA: See *THE SAUSAGES AND HAMS OF PORTUGAL.*

LISTA DOS VINHOS: The wine list.

LIVER: See **FIGADO.**

LOMBO: Loin of pork, beef, lamb, veal or mutton.

LOURO: Bay leaf.

LULA: Squid.

LUNCH: See **ALMOÇO.**

MAÇA: Apple.

MAÇAPÃO: Marzipan or almond paste; Portuguese cooks make their own by blanching almonds, grinding them very fine, mixing with sugar, and stirring slowly over low heat until thick. Marzipan is the foundation of nearly half of Portugal's sweets. And in the Algarve, where groves of almonds march over the red-brown hills, women shape marzipan into miniature fruits, animals and flowers of stunning detail. Every *confeitaria* (candy shop) sells them.

MAIZE OR CORN: **MILHO.**

MAL PASSADO: Medium-rare meat; truly rare is *muito mal passado* (and not something many Portuguese enjoy).

MANJERICÃO: See Basil.

MANTEIGA: See Butter.

MARGARINA: Margarine; it's popular, not so much because of any concern about cholesterol (how *could* there be, with a diet so rich in egg sweets!) but because it is usually cheaper than butter.

MARISCOS: Shellfish; see *THE FISH AND SHELLFISH OF PORTUGAL.*

MARMELADA: Marmelade, but especially a thick caramel-colored quince (marmelo) paste. Food historians believe this to be the original marmelade.

MARZIPAN: See **MAÇAPAO.**

MASSA: Paste or *pâté.*

MASSA DE PIMENTÃO: A paste made of roasted sweet red peppers, crushed garlic and olive oil, which is used as a dry marinade for meats in the Alentejo Province; see Recipe Index. It's possible to make a quick version by blending 1 tablespoon of sweet Hungarian paprika with 1 crushed clove of garlic and 1 tablespoon of robust olive oil.

MEAT: See **CARNE.**

MEDRONHO: "Strawberry tree" or Arbutus, the fruit of which is made into *aguardente* (which see).

MEL: See Honey.

MELÃO: Melon, especially cantaloupe or honeydew melon, which ripen splendidly on the vine in the hot Portuguese sun.

MENU: EMENTA.

MERENDEIRAS: See *THE CHEESES OF PORTUGAL.*

MESA: Table.

MEXILHÕES: Mussels; Portuguese mussels are smaller than ours, sweeter, and not quite as abundant. They go into *caldeiradas* and other fish stews, and in the Algarve are cooked in a *cataplana.*

MIGA: Crumb; see *AÇORDAS AND MIGAS.*

MILHO: Corn.

MILHO FRITO: A rich fried corn bread that is the traditional accompaniment to *Carne de Vinho e Alhos*, chunks of pork marinated with garlic and dry white wine; see Recipe Index.

MILK: LEITE.

MINCED: PICADA.

MINT: See **HORTELÃ.**

MIÚDOS: See Giblets.

MOLHO: Sauce. See page 92 for *Molho Maionese*, an olive-oil mayonnaise.

MORANGO: Strawberry.

MORCELA: See *THE SAUSAGES AND HAMS OF PORTUGAL.*

MORGADO: See *THE EGG SWEETS OF PORTUGAL.*

MORNO: Warm, like the warm milk used for making yeast breads.

MOSTARDA: Mustard; Portuguese cooks use dried (English) mustard occasionally. Prepared mustard, as we know it, isn't yet a kitchen staple in Portugal.

MUSHROOMS: COGUMELOS.

MUSSELS: See **MEXILHÕES.**

MUTTON: See **CARNEIRO.**

NABIÇAS: Turnip greens; better-liked than the turnips themselves, the greens are sautéed quickly in oil or drippings with garlic, then wreathed around platters of meat.

NABO: Turnip; these are commonplace among farm people, who boil them and turn them in meat drippings or mash them with potatoes.

NAS BRASAS: Charcoal-grilled; see **BRASA.**

NATA: Cream.

NOZ: Nut, especially walnut; the loveliest candies made in Portugal, to my taste at least, are the *Nozes* of Cascais—little balls of *ovos moles* (egg yolks and sugar cooked until stiff), crowned with a single perfect walnut, then dipped into caramelized sugar, which hardens into the thinnest and crackliest of coatings. You can find them in fine *confeitarias* in Lisbon, Sintra, and of course Cascais.

NOZ-MOSCADA: Nutmeg; another of the East Indian spices the Portuguese use sparingly.

OCTOPUS: See **POLVO**.

ÓLEO ALIMENTAR: Vegetable oil; sunflower oil, widely used today in combination with the more expensive olive oil, is *óleo de girassol*.

OLIVE OIL: See **AZEITE** and box below.

OLIVES: See **AZEITONAS**.

ONION: See **CEBOLA**.

ORANGE: See **LARANJA**.

OREGÃO: Oregano; a wild oregano grows on the plains of the Alentejo, and cooks there frequently use it to season meats, soups and vegetables.

OSTRAS: Oysters; they are not as abundant in Portugal as clams or mussels, and those that do come to market seem to be snapped up by the restaurant chefs.

OVO: See Egg.

OVOS MOLES: See *THE EGG SWEETS OF PORTUGAL*.

PADARIA: Bakery; if you should ever drive about the Portuguese countryside, I urge you to follow your nose to the nearest village bakery and to buy a loaf or two for picnicking. It's unlikely that you will ever eat better bread than these robust, yeasty loaves, with substance enough to give your jaws a real workout. To accompany the bread, you'll need only a chunk of local cheese—a *Serra*, perhaps, or a *Serpa*—some olives, a few gloriously ripe tomatoes, some slices of *presunto* (ham) and, of course, a bottle of the local wine. The smallest village store can supply the makings of a picnic, and Portugal provides hundreds of scenic stopping places, or *miradouros*, accommodatingly set atop mountains and promontories—wherever, in fact, you most itch to pull off the road and enjoy the view.

PAIO: See *THE SAUSAGES AND HAMS OF PORTUGAL*.

The Robust Olive Oil of Portugal

Is "robust" the way to describe Portugal's olive oil? I think so, although others have called it "rank." Certainly Portuguese olive oil (*azeite* or *azeite de azeitonas*) is intensely aromatic. With good reason. The Portuguese do not, as is done elsewhere, rush the olives from tree to press. Their December harvests are merry and casual affairs, *festas* with friends and neighbors gathering in the orchards to beat the branches with sticks and rain the olives down upon the ground, where they are left to age (fester?) for two to ten days. This intensifies the olive flavor, as does running the pressed oil off into hot water (cold water, i.e. *cold-press*, produces more delicate oil). *Note: Portuguese olive oils (albeit milder ones than would be used in Portugal), can be bought here in many Latin American groceries and specialty food shops. If you find none, substitute any fruity Spanish, Italian or Greek olive oil.*

PALHA DE ABRANTES: See *THE EGG SWEETS OF PORTUGAL*.

PANADO: See Breaded.

PANELA: Kettle; one of Portugal's most nourishing soups is an odds-and-ends "muddle" called *Sopa da Panela;* see Recipe Index.

PÃO: Bread; Portuguese bread, to my taste, is the best in the world. Countrywomen still bake their own, and village bakers still shove wooden paddles full of plumply risen loaves into brick or stone ovens filled with clouds of steam.

PÃO-DE-LÓ: Sponge cake; what makes Portuguese sponge cakes different is their high proportion of egg yolks. They are deeply yellow and, unlike American sponge cakes, rarely contain any vanilla or lemon rind. The Portuguese not only eat *Pão de Ló* out of hand, but also use it as the foundation of a seemingly endless parade of sweets.

PÃO-DOCE: The heavenly Portuguese sweet bread that is baked in many Portuguese-American communities as well as in Portugal itself. Because of the bread's richness (no stinting on eggs or butter), it is used in Portugal primarily as a feast or festival bread. See Recipe Index.

PÃO TORRADO: Toast.

PÃOZINHO: Roll; Portuguese rolls are delicious because they're often nothing more than the usual hardy bread dough shaped into little rounds or ovals.

PAPOS DE ANJO: See *THE EGG SWEETS OF PORTUGAL*.

PAPRIKA: See **COLORAU** and **COLORAU DOCE**.

PARGO: Sea bream.

PARSLEY: **SALSA;** the variety most often used in Portugal is the flat-leafed Italian parsley.

PASTÉIS: See *THE EGG SWEETS OF PORTUGAL*.

PASTELARIA: Pastry shop; even the smallest Portuguese village has a pastry shop that fills its windows with an irresistible assortment of little tarts and bite-size sweets.

PATO: See Duck.

PEACH: **PÊSSEGO;** Portugal produces plump peaches full of flavor, but they are more often boiled into conserves than eaten fresh (except, of course, in fine restaurants, where it's fascinating to watch a waiter spear a fresh peach with a fork, then spiral off its peel for you with a sharp knife).

PEANUTS: **AMENDOIMS**.

PEAR: **PERA;** Portugal grows its own, often on espaliered trees that bear so heavily that the boughs all but break under the load of fruit.

PEAS (GREEN): See **ERVILHAS**.

PEIXARIA: Fish market; do step inside one of Portugal's big fish markets to see the best of what fishermen's nets have fetched up only hours earlier.

PEIXE: Fish; see *THE FISH AND SHELLFISH OF PORTUGAL*.

PEPPER: See **PIMENTA, PIMENTÃO,** and **GRÃO DE PIMENTA**.

PEQUENO ALMOÇO: Breakfast (literally, "little lunch").

PERCEVES: Tiny barnacles, scarcely bigger than beans, which the Portuguese pick out of the shells with long pins. Most Americans find their flavor too intensely marine to be enjoyable.

PERDIZ: Partridge; one of the best game birds in Portugal.

PERNA: Leg, as in *perna de borrego* (leg of lamb).

PERU: Turkey; the birds are reserved for special occasions in Portugal. They are somewhat smaller than our turkeys, more flavorful, too, perhaps because they are allowed to scratch around in the ground for food. When it comes to stuffing turkey, good Portuguese cooks are more likely to make a rich bread paste and to pat it just underneath the breast skin than to fill the body cavity. Do try the roast turkey recipe in the poultry chapter; I predict you'll find it the best turkey you've ever eaten.

PESCADA: See Hake, and also *THE FISH AND SHELLFISH OF PORTUGAL*.

PESCADINHA: Whiting.

PÊSSEGO: See Peach.

PETISCOS: Dainty little tidbits, often served with drinks.

PICADA: Minced.

PICANTE: Peppery, hot and spicy.

PIMENTA: Pepper.

PIMENTÃO: Capsicum, i.e., a pepper, especially a sweet pepper. Sweet red pepper (*pimentão-doce vermelho*) is more commonly used in Portuguese recipes than sweet green (or bell) pepper (*pimentão-doce verde*). The red peppers of Portugal are a deep and dazzling scarlet; they are also supremely sweet. The Portuguese roast them, peel them, and drizzle them with fruity olive oil to eat as a salad. They also make a paste of roasted red peppers, garlic and olive oil to use as a dry marinade for meats; see **MASSA DE PIMENTÃO.**

PINEAPPLE: See **ANANÁS.**

PIRI-PIRI: An explosive little red pepper from Angola, widely used in Portuguese cooking. (Crushed dried red chili peppers make an appropriate substitute.) The Portuguese are so fond of *piri-piri* that they mince it, mix it with olive oil, let it steep for weeks, and have it always on hand. If a bottle of murky-looking liquid automatically arrives at your table when you order prawns or shrimp, better taste it before upending the bottle. It is probably *piri-piri* sauce and packs enough power, someone once said, to blow a safe. See page 91 for a home-made recipe.

PLATE: PRATO; the "daily special" is *prato do dia.*

PLUM: See **AMEIXA.**

POLVO: Octopus; an image that shall forever remain in my memory is of a fisherman tenderizing a small octopus by slapping it against the stone retaining wall of the Albufeira waterfront. I went off to photograph the gaudily painted boats lounging on the fishermen's beach, and when I returned, the man was still at it—slap, slap, slapping the tentacled thing against the wall. I've always wondered if it was the octopus I had seen him with the first time around. If so, he gave it a good hour's pounding.

PORCO: Pork; the hogs of Portugal live a good life. In the Alentejo they are put into the cork orchards to root for acorns. In the North, where the smoky-sweet, dry-cured *presuntos* (hams) are produced, women actually cook corn and potatoes for their hogs. They feed them chestnuts, too, and more acorns, and wheat. Small wonder Portugal's hams are so fine and sweet of flesh.

POSTA: A large piece; *bacalhau*, for example, is often cooked and served *em posta*, meaning in a single large slab. I frankly prefer minced *bacalhau* because I find the single piece tough, stringy, unpleasant to eat (and the very devil to get out of one's teeth). Beef is also grilled *em posta*, and there is no place better to try it than at a little restaurant called Gabriela inside the old fortified river town of Miranda do Douro, in the far reaches of the Trás-os-Montes. This beef is juicily tender and aromatic of the wine, garlic and bay leaves with which it has marinated.

POTATO: See **BATATA.**

POULTRY: See **AVES.**

POUSADA: A government inn; the term has an ominous ring—conjuring images of cots, dreary rooms and communal baths—that is altogether misleading. The *pousadas* of Portugal are positively princely! Many, indeed, are housed in royal castles and furnished with museum-caliber antiques. There are now more than thirty *pousadas* scattered about the country. My own favorites, starting in the North and working south are: Pousada de São Teotónio in the border town of Valença do Minho (a low-slung modern inn on a bluff overlooking the Minho River and the green folds of Galicia, Spain; the chef here is top-notch) . . . Pousada de Dom Dinis, in Vila Nova de Cerveira (a sequestered *pousada* village with separate blocks of big, beautifully furnished rooms, many of them with private sun terraces) . . . Pousada da Oliveira, in the historic town of Guimarães (a cluster of sixteenth-century town houses made into an inn of immense charm; the dining room looks onto the town's medieval square, and the Minho specialties it serves are as well prepared as any *pousada* dishes anywhere) . . . Pousada do Castelo, in Óbidos (this first of Portugal's castle *pousadas* perches atop one of the country's prettiest walled towns; the *pousada* has six rooms only and is very difficult to get into, but non-residents can go for lunch and dinner—and do, in droves, because the *pousada* serves robust regional food) . . . Pousada do Castelo de Palmela, in Palmela (a sky-high castle just forty-five minutes south of Lisbon, with twenty-seven modern bedrooms and a splendid dining room) . . . Pousada de São Filipe, in Setúbal (a sixteenth-century castle set at the edge of a sea cliff overlooking the Atlantic Ocean; again, the *pousada* chef is superb) . . . Pousada dos Lóios, in Évora (a fifteenth-century monastery with thirty-one up-to-the-minute rooms that were once monks' cells; the cloister is now the dining room; the food consists of deftly prepared Alentejo specialties) . . . Pousada da Rainha Santa Isabel, in Estremoz (Portugal's most palatial *pousada*, each room individually decorated with seventeenth- and eighteenth-century antiques; the dining room is an imposing marble hall with ceilings that vault out of sight; the food is kingly, too, and features such Alentejo classics as *Sopa de Grão* (Chick-pea Soup) and *Sopa Dourada* (one of Portugal's more imaginative egg sweets); see Recipe Index. Finally, there's a brand new little jewel, the Pousada do Castelo de Alvito in a sumptuously renovated fifteenth-century castle in the merry Alentejo market town of Alvito.

PRATO: See Plate.

PRAWNS: See **GAMBAS**.

PRESUNTO: See THE SAUSAGES AND HAMS OF PORTUGAL.

PÚCARA: An earthenware jug in which fowl and game are cooked. Do try the *Frango na Púcara* (Jugged Chicken); see Recipe Index.

PUMPKIN: See **ABÓBORA**.

QUEIJADA: A little cheese tart; see THE EGG SWEETS OF PORTUGAL.

QUEIJO: Cheese; see THE CHEESES OF PORTUGAL.

QUENTE: Hot.

RABAÇAL: See THE CHEESES OF PORTUGAL.

RABBIT: See **COELHO**.

RAIA: Skate or stingray, a fish much enjoyed in Portugal.

RAMO: Branch; a parsley branch is *ramo de salsa*.

RAMO DE CHEIROS: See Bouquet garni.

RASPBERRY: **FRAMBOESA**.

REACHEADO: Stuffed.

RECHEIO: Stuffing.

REFOGADO: When making soups, stews, and fricassees, the Portuguese use a special technique for cooking the onions and garlic at the outset. They sauté them lightly in robust olive oil (or sometimes a combination of olive and vegetable oil with butter or meat drippings) for five to six minutes, just until the onions begin to look glassy and golden. They then turn the heat down low, cover the pan, and let the onions and garlic "sweat" or steam twenty minutes or more until very soft and sweet. This onion paste is called a *refogado* or *cebolada*.

REQUEIJÃO: See THE CHEESES OF PORTUGAL.

RICE: See **ARROZ.**

ROBALO: Sea bass; very popular.

ROJÕES: This is a term used in the north of Portugal, mainly the Minho and Trás-os-Montes, to connote small chunks of stew meat (usually pork) that are braised or stewed and served with a garnish of vegetables—potatoes, onions, and often pickled carrots and cauliflower as well. See Recipe Index.

ROSEMARY: See **ALECRIM.**

ROUPA-VELHA: Translated literally, this means "old clothes." It is the Portuguese term for "leftovers." Few people, I think, can best the Portuguese when it comes to producing a full and satisfying meal out of cupboard gleanings.

SAFFRON: **AÇAFRÃO.**

SAGE: **SALVA;** not one of the more popular herbs in Portugal, although you see plenty of it growing there.

SAL: Salt; when something is salty, it's *salgado.* The Portuguese use a fairly heavy hand with salt, perhaps because they're accustomed to the intense saltiness of *bacalhau.* If you visit Portugal and must watch your sodium intake, learn to say *sem sal*— without salt.

SALADA: Salad; if there is a weakness in the cooking of Portugal, it is in the category of salads and some vegetables. As I have mentioned (see **ALFACE**), there is little variety in lettuces and salad greens. Still, there are other good salads to be found in Portugal: Roasted Sweet Peppers marinated in oil and vinegar with wild oregano (see Recipe Index)

and, even more universal, red ripe tomatoes, full of bouquet, sliced thin, trickled with olive oil, then sprinkled with salt and pepper.

SALMÃO, SALMONETE: See *THE FISH AND SHELLFISH OF PORTUGAL.*

SALPIÇÃO: See *THE SAUSAGES AND HAMS OF PORTUGAL.*

SALSA: Parsley.

SALVA: Sage.

SANTOLA, SAPOTEIRA: See *THE FISH AND SHELLFISH OF PORTUGAL.*

SARDA: Mackerel.

SARDINHA, SARGO, SÁVEL: See *THE FISH AND SHELLFISH OF PORTUGAL.*

SAUSAGE: See *THE SAUSAGES AND HAMS OF PORTUGAL.*

SCALLOPS: **VIEIRAS;** these have all but vanished from Portugal although on rare occasion they do appear on pricey restaurant menus and are simply, exquisitely prepared.

SEASONING: **TEMPERO.**

SERPA: See *THE CHEESES OF PORTUGAL.*

SERVIÇO INCLUÍDO: Service included; it always *is* included in the bill in Portuguese hotels and restaurants, together with tax. Still, you are expected to leave a few escudos. Most people simply round the bill—*conta*—upward to the nearest even number. If service has been exceptional, I usually tip 5 to 10 percent.

SHELLFISH: **MARISCOS;** see *THE FISH AND SHELLFISH OF PORTUGAL.*

SHRIMP: See **CAMARÃO.**

SNAILS: **CARACÓIS:** see *THE FISH AND SHELLFISH OF PORTUGAL.*

SOBREMESA: Dessert.

SOPA: Soup, especially a thick soup brimming with vegetables.

SOPA DOURADA: See *THE EGG SWEETS OF PORTUGAL.*

SORREL: See **AZEDA.**

The Sausages and Hams of Portugal

Pork-curing and sausage-making are cottage industries in Portugal—and not just on farms. Villagers often keep a hog or two, butcher them in the fall, then lay down hams to cure and stuff yards of casings with blends of pork and spices known only to members of the family. Still, certain pork products are widely available commercially and highly prized throughout the country. Among them:

ALHEIRA: In the beginning this was not a pork sausage at all, but one made of chicken, partridge, rabbit and bread so cleverly disguised by garlic, hot peppers and paprika that no one was the wiser. It was invented nearly five hundred years ago during the Inquisition by Marranos (Jews claiming to be "New Christians") who, instead of leaving Portugal, fled to the remotest corner of it—the Trás-os-Montes—where they could quietly follow their own dietary laws and faith. Today, *alherias* do often contain pork and are best when boiled or grilled and accompanied by potatoes.

AZEDO: Another sausage from the Trás-os-Montes, this one is known as "the king of sausages." It's made of beef, assorted pork parts (including bacon, head and feet), hot peppers and paprika.

BANHA: Lard or rendered pork fat; the favored cooking medium in the north of Portugal where olive oil is often highly acidic. Lard may be used in combination with olive oil, however, or with butter. Unlike our bland commercial lards, *banha* has distinct pork flavor.

CHOURIÇO: This is probably Portugal's most popular sausage. It's even made by Old-Country methods in some of America's Portuguese communities. A dry sausage similar to the more widely available Spanish *chorizo* (which may be substituted for it in recipes), *chouriço* is very garlicky, red-brown with paprika, and sold in links about ten inches long and one and a half inches in diameter. In the *fado* houses of Lisbon (*fado* is Portugal's soul music), grilled *chouriços* are so much a staple that they are known as "*fado* sausage."

FARINHEIRA: A thin rope of garlicky pork sausage from the Alentejo Province that is filled out with either bread crumbs or flour. The Portuguese like it boiled or fried.

FIAMBRE: A pale, lightly smoked boiled ham much like America's packinghouse hams. It is not very popular among the Portuguese (more so among tourists) who prefer *presunto* (which see).

LINGUIÇA: This dry sausage is not, as has been written, made of tongue. It consists of coarsely chopped pork shoulder (both the lean and the fat), plenty of garlic and paprika. It's shape, rather like a long and slender *lingua* (tongue) explains the name. You can find it in the many Portuguese-American communities on both the Atlantic and Pacific coasts.

MORCELA: A blood sausage similar to England's black pudding that is integral to many Portuguese stews and meat and vegetable recipes.

PAIO: A large sausage made of chunks of pork tenderloin, lightly smoked and encased in string netting. It is especially popular in the Alentejo and Algarve.

PRESUNTO: A mahogany-hued, richly smoked ham that is a match for the finest

continued on next page

The Sausages and Hams of Portugal

Parma (prosciutto), Bayonne or Westphalian hams. It is dry-cured in a thick paste of salt, garlic, paprika and dry red wine for about a month, then smoked over smoldering embers of oak (and sometimes pine) for about a week. The choicest *presunto* comes from the Trás-os-Montes town of Chaves, although the people of nearby Valpaços insist theirs is superior. I won't quibble. Another superb *presunto* comes from the Algarve mountain spa of Monchique; its hams are a little sweeter than the more

famous Chaves hams and, to my taste, less salty. The Portuguese use *presunto* liberally in cooking, but they also like it sliced tissue-thin, then teamed with dead-ripe figs, pineapple or melon.

SALPICÃO: Pork tenderloin that has been cured three to four days in dry wine, salt and garlic, then lightly smoked. Its flavor is more that of a pickled meat than a smoked one.

TOUCINHO: Smoked bacon, exquisitely lean and nutty.

SPICES: **ESPECIARIAS;** see *THE PREDOMINANT HERBS, SPICES AND FLAVORINGS OF PORTUGAL* on page 53.

SPINACH: See **ESPINAFRES.**

STEW: See **ESTUFADO;** also *AÇORDAS AND MIGAS.*

STRAWBERRY: **MORANGO.**

STUFFING: **RECHEIO.**

SUCKLING PIG: See **LEITÃO.**

SUGAR: See **AÇUCAR.**

SUSPIROS: See *THE EGG SWEETS OF PORTUGAL.*

SYRUP: See **XAROPE.**

TABLE: **MESA;** a *vinho de mesa* is a table wine.

TACHO: A large shallow pan or baking dish; a *tacho de barro* is a large clay or earthenware casserole that is essential to every Portuguese kitchen. You see these laid out by the acre (or so it seems) at the Barcelos market held every Thursday in the historic river town of Barcelos. There are round casseroles with and without covers; square and rectangular baking dishes in a range of sizes to match those of our aluminum baking pans; there are little individual ramekins, all of them hand-shaped, hand-glazed, and hand-painted. Yet most of them cost mere pennies. For example, I recently bought a 13 × 10 × 2-inch baking dish for about $2. But what a thing to have to lug all the way back to New York!

TAINHA: Gray mullet.

TAMALHO: Thyme; like sage, it can be seen growing in Portugal, but it is not as popular a kitchen herb as fresh coriander or parsley.

TAMBORIL: Monkfish.

TASCA: Café, bistro or taverna; these little mom-and-pop restaurants are delightful places to eat because everything is strictly fresh and cooked to order. There's nothing fancy about the food, but it is often prepared with consummate skill. You'll find many *tascas* in Lisbon, especially in the Bairro Alto section just above (for Lisbon *is* perpendicular!) the fashionable Rua Garrett ("Fifth Avenue").

TEA: See **CHÁ**; tea with biscuits or pastries is *lanche* (as is a snack).

TEMPERO: Seasoning.

TENRO: Tender.

TIGELA: A flat little earthenware baking dish; a *tigelada* is a richly browned egg sweet baked in the *tigela*. See *THE EGG SWEETS OF PORTUGAL.*

TOMAR: See *THE CHEESES OF PORTUGAL.*

TOMATADA: A rich tomato sauce integral to nearly every tomato-based recipe; it is made by the *refogado* process (which see).

TOMATE: Tomato; if richer, redder, more *tomatoey* tomatoes grow outside of Portugal, I have yet to see them. I'm convinced that the reason so many Portuguese recipes rely upon tomatoes is that this key ingredient is perfection.

TORANJA: Grapefruit.

TORRADA: Toast (and no bread makes better toast than Portuguese bread).

TORTA: A torte or cake, often rolled up jelly-roll style; see Recipe Index.

TOUCINHO: Bacon; see *THE SAUSAGES AND HAMS OF PORTUGAL.*

TOUCINHO DO CÉU: Bacon of Heaven; maybe the best of Portugal's many egg sweets. See Recipe Index.

TRIPAS: Tripe; Portugal's most famous tripe recipe—justifiably, in my opinion—is tripe done the Porto way, baked slowly in the company of sausages, ham and white beans. See Recipe Index.

TROUXAS DE OVOS: See *THE EGG SWEETS OF PORTUGAL.*

TRUFA: Truffle; in years past, these were commonly found in Estremadura, the coastal province in which Lisbon is located. I am told that truffles of respectable size and excellent flavor are still occasionally found there.

TRUTA: Trout; for a country so small, Portugal has an unbelievable number of rivers, brooks and streams. Those of the northern Trás-os-Montes Province, Portuguese friends tell me, are the best for trout. Certainly this is the corner of the country where cooks prepare trout with respect and flair. See Recipe Index.

TUNA: **ATUM.**

TURNIP: **NABO.**

TURNIP GREENS: See **NABIÇAS**; also **GRELOS.**

UVAS: See Grapes.

VACA: Beef; the way it's written on menus, however, is *carne de vaca.*

VAGENS: Green or runner beans; one of the most widely grown and appreciated vegetables in

Portugal. The majority of Portuguese like their beans simply boiled so that at table they can drizzle them with olive oil, vinegar and, yes, sometimes a little *piri-piri* (hot red pepper) sauce, too.

VANILLA: See **BAUNILHA.**

VEAL: See **VITELA.**

VEGETABLES: **LEGUMES.**

VERMICELLI: See **ALETRIA.**

VIEIRAS: See Scallops.

VINAGRE: Vinegar; cider vinegar is what comes to the table in little glass cruets to be sprinkled over beans, tomatoes and sweet peppers. But the more acetic white (distilled) vinegar is more commonly used in cooking.

VINHO: Wine; see the following chapter on the Wines of Portugal.

VINHO DA CASA: The house wine; it's frequently quite good and, in the smaller towns, nearly always produced by a local cooperative.

VINHO E ALHOS: A tart marinade of white wine and garlic used to season pork.

VITELA: Veal; most Portuguese veal is not veal at all but baby beef. Its flesh is red rather than pale-pink, meaning that the calf has gone off mother's milk and began to nibble grass. The flavor of such meat is not objectionable; it just isn't veal. Or beef, either, for that matter. The cuts of *vitela* that show up time and time again on *pousada* menus are cutlets and very thin chops, which *pousada* chefs bounce in and out of spitting-hot skillets lightly glossed with garlic-scented olive oil.

WARM: **MORNO.**

WATER: See **ÁGUA** and box below.

WATERCRESS: See **AGRIÕES.**

The Beer and Bottled Waters of Portugal

For a country so small, Portugal fairly bubbles with hot springs (the government publishes a leaflet describing forty-four major spas), and the waters of many of them are bottled and widely distributed throughout the country. The mineral waters *(águas minerais)* I especially like are LUSO (still, or *sem gas*), ÁGUA CASTELLO (carbonated, or *com gas*), MONCHIQUE (still), VIMEIRO (both still and bubbly), CARVALHELOS (sparkling) and VIDAGO (sparkling).

As for beer *(cerveja)*, there are two outstanding labels: SAGRES (a *cerveja prêta* or dark beer is available, as well as a lovely mellow lager) and CRISTAL (both lager and bock). An excellent lager is also made on the island of Madeira. CORAL, it's called.

XAROPE: Syrup; most of Portugal's egg sweets are drenched with syrup, either plain sugar syrup, cinnamon syrup or lemon syrup. It's as if the cook couldn't incorporate enough sugar into a dessert to satisfy her own sweet tooth—let alone the country's. Actually, the syrup serves another purpose: It keeps these potentially dry desserts moist and glistening. I must confess that the lineup of egg sweets on the dessert trolleys of Portugal *looks* irresistible. But nearly all of them, alas, taste like the sugar syrup in which they repose.

YEAST: See **FERMENTO.**

The Wines of Portugal

By Pasquale Iocca,
Portuguese Trade Commission

Since joining the European Community in 1986, Portugal has been hurtling toward the twenty-first century at near orbital speed. And nowhere is this modernization more dramatic than in the wine industry. Gone are the days when Portuguese wines were sold by brand name with rarely a mention of region or grape. Estate bottling has come of age. And at long last the unique qualities of Portuguese grapes and grape-growing regions are being recognized.

Portugal's oldest wines—the Ports and Madeiras—are the best known. Port, or *Porto* as the Portuguese call it, was demarcated in the mid–eighteenth century, a hundred years before the French came up with *appellation contrôlée*. Madeira was the favorite tipple of Colonial America. Around the turn of the twentieth century, several other wine regions (Dão and *vinho verde* to name two) were named. Portugal then took a long snooze from which it has only now awakened. In 1985, there were just ten official Portuguese wine regions. Today there are more than fifty.

Port

The original Port, a dry red table wine first made two thousand years ago in the mountains of the Upper Douro River valley, was known to the Greeks, Phoenicians and Romans. But Port's popularity today, particularly among the English, dates to the seventeenth century when, during a squabble with the French, the British banned Bordeaux. Port, then still a dry red table wine, became the substitute. Its transformation into the luscious dessert wine we know today was a gradual process triggered by an exceptionally good year—1820.

That year the elements conspired to produce a magical wine—rich, full and sweet. The English clamored for more, so producers, to preserve the natural grape sugar and emulate the sweetness of that singular wine, began adding increasing amounts of brandy to stop the fermentation early. Today the alcohol level of Port is raised to about 20 percent and the residual sugar fixed at from 9 to 11 percent.

Small amounts of Port are still made the old Roman way. The grapes, grown on stony, steeply terraced slopes, are gathered by hand in slatted baskets, run downhill, dumped into large stone troughs (*lagars*), then stomped to the beat of a drum and wheeze of a concertina (although the accompaniment today may be rock and roll blasting out of a boombox).

Colorful as this method is, 99 percent of today's Port is made by machine. Temperature-controlled stainless-steel tanks that employ automatic maceration now simulate the foot-crushing. Surprisingly, the quality is better than ever because the vinification is controlled, every step of the way, by highly skilled wine makers.

Traditionally, about a hundred different red grapes were used to make Port. Today most vintners are concentrating on the five best varieties: *Touriga Nacional,* exuding scents of cassis and violets; *Tinta Roriz,* known for its power and mature fruit aromas; *Tinta Barroca,* feminine and elegant; *Tinto Cão,* deeply sensuous; and *Touriga Francesa,* with its heady bouquet of roses.

For centuries all Port "wintered over" in the Upper Douro after the fall harvest, then, each spring, was shipped sixty miles downriver to be aged and bottled at Vila Nova da Gaia (Porto's left bank). But after 1986, when new legislation made it legal to grow, age and bottle Porto in the Upper Douro, many vineyard owners began producing estate-bottled "*Quinta Portos.*" So, to the names of respected shippers like Taylor-Fladgate, Cockburn, Fonseca, Graham, Warre, Ferreira and Ramos-Pinto such fine new estate producers as Quinta do Côtto, Quinta da Romaneira and Quinta do Infantado must now be added.

All Ports are of two main types: those bottled young with a lot of fruit, red color and power, and those left in cask to lose fruitiness and color and acquire delicacy.

Of the first type, Vintage Port is the finest. Its essence is power, depth of fruit and the ability to develop for decades. Bottled two years after the harvest in the very best years, a vintage port must be approved in blind tastings by the Instituto do Vinho do Porto's (Port Wine Institute's) demanding panel of experts. It is one of nature's great gifts; indeed, a bottle of 1834 Vintage Port opened in 1993 was still heavenly!

Ten to fifty years is more realistic for ideal drinking, and recent vintages to search for are 1945, 1955, 1960, 1963, 1966, 1970, 1975, 1977, 1983, 1985, 1987 and 1991.

Other Ports with a fruity character are Late-bottled Vintage, released at four to six years; Vintage Character, a blend of about the same age; and Ruby Porto, bottled at three years, whose charm is its spicy, fresh vibrancy.

As for the second type of Port—the cask-aged—Tawny (with an indication of age) is tops: ten-year-old Tawny, for example, or twenty-, thirty- or forty-year-old. Look for velvety textures and complex flavors that suggest dried fruit, nuts and caramel. Colheita is Tawny Port from a single year.

A Tawny (without an indication of age) is usually just three years old and owes its pale color and refinement to short skin-juice contact during fermentation or to the addition of White Port. (White Ports range from dry or medium-dry [superb as aperitifs] to a syrupy dessert wine called Lágrima.)

The French, who drink more Port than anyone else, are partial to Tawnies, understandable given their generally mild climate and sophisticated cuisine. The English, on the other hand, with their cold, rainy climate and meat-and-potatoes diet, prefer to warm themselves by the fire with a robust Vintage Port. Americans, whose consumption of Port has quadrupled over the past decade, seem to like them all. Nothing, they're discovering, ends dinner more exquisitely than a well-aged Stilton, Gorgonzola, Portuguese Serpa or São Jorge paired with a glass of fruity Port. Or a creamy Portuguese Queijo da Serra or Azeitão, or a dead-ripe Brie or Camembert accompanied by a fine Tawny.

Madeira

The wonder of Madeira, a volcanic chip lazing in the Atlantic three hundred miles west of Morocco, is that it produces any wine, let alone the noble Madeiras, which range from dry to intensely sweet. The man who started it all was Portugal's visionary fifteenth-century Prince Henry-the-Navigator. Once his explorers had claimed this lush semitropical island, Prince Henry ordered that cuttings of Sicilian sugarcane be planted there, also Malmsey grapes from the Greek island of Crete. To clear the land in a hurry, the colonists set fire to the forests.

The ash laid down by that conflagration (it smoldered, legend tells us, for seven years) fused with the bedrock basalt producing a porous, red-ochre soil called *tufa*. That, together with Madeira's balmy climate, accounts for the unique character and astonishing longevity of Madeira wines. Luscious on the tongue, they have a crisp underlying acidity that refreshes with the tingling wallop of a Granny Smith apple.

Almost from the beginning, Madeira wines were sought after. So much so that when Portugal fell under Spanish rule (1580 to 1640), the Spaniards embargoed Madeiras lest they compete with their own sherries. Soon after the Portuguese regained control of their country, Catherine of Bragança married Charles II of England. Two years later, in 1662, Charles II captured New Amsterdam and renamed it New York for his brother, the Duke of York. He also named the borough of Queens in honor of Queen Catherine, his Portuguese wife.

Queen Catherine, it turns out, was indirectly responsible for the great popularity of Madeira wine in Colonial America. Madeiras were the only European wines exempted from her husband's 1665 export ban, meaning they could be shipped direct—and duty-free—to "English Plantations overseas." Due to this lucky circumstance, Americans had great wines thrust upon them. And they soon became connoisseurs.

The glasses raised to toast the signing of The Declaration of Independence were filled with Madeira as were those served at the inauguration of George Washington. George and Martha Washington were accustomed to drinking a pint of good Madeira every evening with dinner, and Thomas Jefferson, in the first year of his presidency, uncorked more than three thousand bottles of Madeira for White House guests.

America's supply of Madeira was abruptly cut off in the mid nineteenth century as disease ravaged island vineyards. Half a century later when Madeira was available once again, Americans had switched to sherry. Sadly, Madeira has never regained its popularity here although the wines are better than ever.

There are four classic types of Madeira, all named for the grapes from which they're made:

Sercial, the driest, is blessed with a sunny golden color and a bouquet of dried almonds and apples. It is excellent as a chilled aperitif. Try it, too, with shellfish.

Verdelho, medium-dry, typically smells of toasted coffee and vanillin. Drunk with soup since Colonial times, it is particularly good with the Madeira Onion Soup on page 98. It also partners well with baked Virginia ham.

Bual, medium-sweet, exudes aromas of toffee and fudge. It is *the* perfect wine to go with all things chocolate, also with ripe, runny cheeses.

Malmsey, honey-sweet, gives off a complex bouquet with caramel, hazelnut and butterscotch predominating. It is magnificent with desserts, especially poached pears or prunes sauced with crème Anglaise or caramelized apple pastries like Tart Tatin.

Madeiras called Finest, Choice, Rich and Rainwater are made from the Tinta Negra Mole grape in imitation of the classic types.

Moscatel de Setúbal

Legend has it that the Setúbal Peninsula twenty miles south of Lisbon was settled by Tubal, one of Noah's sons. The Phoenicians came this way two thousand years ago, bringing with them the Muscat of Alexandria grape, which could be fermented into smooth, sweet wines. The Phoenicians didn't last. But the wines did. According to the court records of Louis XIV, Muscat wine from Setúbal was a staple in the royal cellar. No small compliment.

Fortified with brandy up to 18 percent alcohol with 9 to 10 percent residual sugar, today's Setúbal muscatels are unique among dessert wines. Once fermentation is complete, the grape skins are returned to the wine and left till the following spring. The result? Wines of startlingly vivid bouquet with hints of orange, almond and wildflowers. In the U.S., look for muscatels from J.M. da Fonseca and J.P. Vinhos. Some are without vintage date, others are dated, ranging in age from six to sixty years, and still others, blended wines, show only the age of the youngest wine in the blend, which is twenty years.

Vinho Verde

Portugal's northwesternmost province, the Minho, is an intensely verdant area known for its young, fresh *vinho verde* (green wine). Zesty, crisp and fruity thanks to the granitic soil and cooling Atlantic breezes, *vinho verde* has a lovely pale straw color with glints of emerald. With an average alcohol content of 9 percent, it's an "easy drinking" wine, a splendid aperitif or accompaniment to fish and shellfish.

With one hundred thousand growers in the Minho, much of the wine is blended into good standard brands such as Casal García, Vinha Verde, Tamega and Gatão. There's a trend, however, toward estate bottling and the Association of Vinho Verde Growers and Bottlers, formed in 1985, already boasts a hundred members. Some good estate *vinhos verdes* now available in the U.S. include Casa de Sezim, Solar das Bouças, Quinta de Azevedo, Quinta de São Cláudio, Tormes, Paço do Teixeiró and Quinta de Luou.

More attention is also being paid to *vinho verde* grape varieties. The Quinta da Aveleda makes a wine entirely from Loureiro grapes (aromas of laurel and quince), another from Trajadura (hints of tropical fruit and pears) and a third wine, Grinalda, that teams the two.

The most prestigious *vinho verde* grape variety, Alvarinho, is grown only in the far northerly subregion of Monção, which abuts Spain. Alvarinho wines have an alcohol content of 11 to 12 percent (high for *vinho verde*) and though dry, they display a bouquet reminiscent of Riesling. Some outstanding examples sold here are Palácio da Brejoeira, Quinta da Pedra, Morgadio da Torre, Quinta de Alderiz, Forum Prior do Crato and Soalheiro.

All of the wines named so far are white. But there is also red *vinho verde*. Tart, fresh and aggressive, it's a good match for spicy Thai or Szechuan food. The Portuguese like it with pork stew, grilled *bacalhau* (dried salt cod) and sardines, pouring it with unerring aim into small ceramic cups from three feet in the air to bring out its natural fizz.

Douro

Although Port gets most of the press, the Douro also produces superior red and white table wines. Ferreira's legendary red, Barca Velha, compares favorably with the world's best as does Quinta do Côtto "Grande Escolha" from Montez Champalimaud. Less exalted, but very good, are Vinha Grande and Esteva from Ferreira and Vila Régia from Sogrape, the company that created Mateus many years ago. Sogrape recently launched a fine Douro white and red called Mateus Signature in honor of their founder, Fernando Guedes. A splendid new Douro red called Quinta de la Rosa and a white called Alto da Guia are both worth tracking down.

Sparkling wines made by the Champagne method also come from the Douro. The firm of Raposeira has made lovely *bruto* (bone dry) and *meio-seco* (medium-dry) sparklers at the historic hilltop town of Lamego for generations. A new and special element was added recently when California's famous sparkling wine producer, Schramsberg, set up shop at Alijó in partnership with a Portuguese firm. Fruity, crisp and elegant, their new bubblies are already on sale in Portugal and the U.S. under the name *Vértice*.

Dão

When this mountainous area directly south of Porto was demarcated in 1907, its wines were second only to Port in quality and prestige. With its long growing seasons and cool autumns, the Dão produced grapes that fermented naturally and perfectly. Small producers took great pride in their vineyards and insisted that their grapes be crushed by foot. In the 1960s, however, Dão wines began to be mass produced and fell from favor. The whites were hard, devoid of bouquet, the reds unyielding. The region remained in decline until the mideighties, when restrictive laws were repealed and funds flooded in from Portugal's new European Community partners, all in an effort to upgrade the vineyards, build new wineries and return the Dão wines to greatness.

Today, white Dãos made from Encruzado, Assario and Cerceal grapes show superb body and crispness as well as elegant aromas of tropical fruits and flowers. Reds produced from the Touriga Nacional, Tinta Roriz, Alfrocheiro and *Jaen* are generous, soft and rich and simply burst with the mingled bouquets of cassis, mulberries and blackberries.

Look for red and white wines from Sogrape's splendid new Dão estate, Quinta das Carvalhais, also for these brands made on the property from selected nearby vineyards: Duque de Viseu and Grão Vasco. Other outstanding Dão estates now exporting to the U.S. are Casa da Insua, Casal de Tonda, Quinta do Serrado and Quinta de Saes.

Bairrada

Lying midway between Porto and Lisbon, this flat clay region is celebrated for its austere red wines made from the Baga grape, which develop complexity and finesse as they age. Here 60 percent of Portugal's sparkling wines are also made—whites, rosés, even reds. This last was developed to go with roast suckling pig (*leitão assado*), the local specialty. First-rate dry vintage-dated rosés are also made from the Baga grape, notably Nobilis from Sogrape and Rosé Seco from Aliança.

Caves Aliança has been a major exporter to America for a number of years, and its wines are easy to find. Caves São João, an outstanding vintner, also pioneered in shipping to the U.S., but for several years now its wines have been difficult to find. Newer on the scene are the worth-a-search estate wines of *Luis Pato* and *Quinta do Carvalinho*.

Colares, Bucelas, Carcavelos

These three demarcated regions are lumped together because all were important at the turn of the century, all came perilously close to extinction but are now showing signs of regeneration.

Bucelas, a tart, almost lemony white table wine produced near Lisbon, was beloved by Thomas Jefferson, the duke of Wellington and Charles Dickens. Until ten years ago, only one winery produced it. Today there are three: Caves Velhas, Quinta do Avelar and Quinta da Romeira.

Colares, an unusual table red grown on sandy soil near the Atlantic Ocean twenty

On Reading Portuguese Wine Labels

How the Wines Are Classified:

DOC (Denominação de Origem Controlada or Denomination of Controlled Origin): The top-category wine regions, the most important of which are Porto, Douro, Dão, Vinho Verde, Bairrada and Madeira. Formerly known as Regiões Demarcadas or R.D. (Demarcated Regions), this term still occasionally appears on wine labels.

IPR (Indicação de Proveniência Regulamentada or Indication of Regulated Provenance): Some thirty-five regions have earned this prestigious designation, which was created within the last five years. Some prominent ones are Alenquer, Lafões, Cartaxo, Almeirim, Redondo, Borba, Reguengos and Portalegre.

VQPRD (Vinhos de Qualidade Produzidos em Regiões Determinadas or Wines of Quality Produced in Determined Regions): An EEC concept used to identify wines that are prototypical of their specific regions (determining factors are grape varieties, soil, climate, viticultural and wine-making techniques). All DOC and IPR wines have the right to use this designation, but VQPRD is most often seen on the labels of IPR wines as an extra guarantee of quality.

Vinho Regional (Regional Wine): Another indication of typicality, but broader, geographically, than VQPRD. Since May 1992, eight large new wine regions have been declared: Terras do Sado (including all of the Setúbal Peninsula), Alentejo, Rios do Minho, Trás os Montes, Beiras, Algarve, Ribatejo and Estremadura. Not the most prestigious category, and yet many of Portugal's finest wines are being released under this designation.

Vinho da Mesa (Table Wine): This term assures that a wine is Portuguese, nothing more. *Vinhos da mesa* are not allowed to carry vintage years.

Other Wine Terms:

Adega: Originally a wine cellar or cave but often used now simply to indicate a wine producer.

Branco: A white wine.

Bruto: A dry sparkling wine.

Casta: Grape variety.

Casta Predominante: Predominant grape variety.

Colheita: The year of vintage.

Engarrafado por: Bottled by.

Engarrafado na Região: Bottled in the region of origin but not at any particular vineyard.

Escolha: Choice or selection. The term *Grande Escolha* is sometimes used for top wines.

Garrafa: A wine bottle; *meia-garrafa* means a half-bottle.

Garrafão: A five-liter jug of table wine of basic quality.

Garrafeira: Literally a wine cellar but also a legal term applied to Portuguese red wines. *Garrafeira* means that before its release, a wine has undergone lengthy aging in bulk (two years) and in the bottle (one

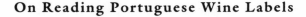

On Reading Portuguese Wine Labels

year). Usually, a *garrafeira* is the top wine of a given producer, but its quality depends on the standards of that producer.

Quinta: A farm, estate or vineyard, roughly the equivalent of the French *château.*

Produzido por: Produced by.

Reserva: A reserve wine that has met certain legal requirements. The adjectives *especial* and *particular,* often tacked onto *reserva,* are meaningless embellishments.

Seco: Dry, a term most often seen on white wine labels. *Meio-seco* or half-dry usually means the wine (most often *vinho verde* or sparkling wine) is off-dry or slightly sweet.

Tinto: Red wine.

Tinto Velho: Literally "old red," this indicates a mature-style wine but not a well-aged one.

Vinha: Vineyard.

Vinho: Wine.

Vinho Generoso: A fortified wine from a DOC region such as Port, Madeira or Moscatel de Setúbal.

Vinho Espumante: Sparkling wine made by one of several natural methods.

Vinho Espumoso: Artificially carbonated sparkling wine.

miles west of Lisbon, was, until fifty years ago, one of the world's great wines. But in recent years both the quality and quantity of Colares plummeted. One firm, however, has replanted its vineyards and aims to restore Colares to its rightful place among fine Portuguese reds.

Carcavelos, the sweet, topaz-colored, fortified wine produced near Lisbon that caused a sensation at Christie's first wine auction in 1769, could pass out of existence. The last producer of commercial size shut down several years ago. But there is hope. Three new producers are gearing up, and lovers of Carcavelos are keeping fingers crossed.

Alentejo

Portugal's bold, broad cork-and-olive country, covering almost a third of the land, is also now a region of fine wines, Portugal's southernmost. Red wines, the glory of the area, are full-bodied, displaying ripe fruitiness when young and elegant complexity when mature. Some are still made in clay amphoras reminiscent of Roman times. Or foot trodden in stone *lagars* as in the Port wine region. But others are made in modern-as-tomorrow wineries. First they are fermented in stainless steel, then, for greater complexity and longevity, transferred to small oak casks to age.

Although wines from the *cooperativas* at Portalegre, Redondo, Reguengos de Monsaraz, Granja and Borba are worth seeking out, the Alentejo is singularly blessed with fine estates producing stylish wines. The Rothschild family (of Château Lafite fame) recently invested in Quinta do Carmo, a regal property near Évora built in the seventeenth century by King João IV.

At the José de Sousa estate, "Tinto Velho" is made the age-old way with amphoras and foot-crushing in *lagars*. By contrast, the giant *Esporão* estate turns out a quarter of a million cases a year utilizing the most advanced technology. Other noteworthy Alentejo wines include *Morgado do Reguengo*; *Redondo VQPRD* (see *On Reading Portuguese Wine Labels*) from the Rocquevale firm, Tapada do Chaves, and Mouchão. These last two are superb hand-crafted wines, but production is so small you'll be lucky to find them as far afield as Lisbon.

Other Regions, Other Wines

Portugal has so many newly identified regions and so many imaginative young wine-makers it would take a book to cover them all. These few, however, deserve special mention here.

Terras do Sado is the new regional name for table wines from the Setúbal Peninsula, the area that also produces the celebrated Moscatel de Setúbal discussed earlier. The Periquita grape is widely planted here, and the firm of J.M. da Fonseca has been producing a light red table wine of the same name for more than a hundred years. It's distinctive, delicious. Thanks to new technology, Fonseca is approaching cutting-edge quality at its Pasmados and Quinta de Camarate estates as well as with a whole series of Garrafeira wines (see *On Reading Portuguese Wine Labels*). The other major producer here with a state-of-the-art winery is J.P. Vinhos. It produces an impressive range of estate wines not only from Portuguese grape varieties (Tinto da Anfora, Herdade de Santa Marta, Catarina) but also from such foreign "giants" as Cabernet Sauvignon (sold as Quinta da Bacalhôa) and Chardonnay (Cova da Ursa).

Alenquer, just north of Lisbon, is the only other Portuguese region producing Cabernet and Chardonnay on a commercial scale. The label to look for: Quinta de Pancas. One of its wines took first prize as the best reasonably priced Cabernet Sauvignon at the Wine America '93 exposition in New York.

Ribatejo, the province bracketing the Tagus River north and east of Lisbon, and particularly the Falcoaria estate and Quinta da Lagoalva de Cima here, are making splendid, aromatic table wines with a mix of Periquita, Trincadeira, Touriga Nacional, Alvarelhão and Syrah grapes.

Ninety-nine percent of the Portuguese wines are made from grapes unique to Portugal, varieties unknown to most wine lovers. But these grapes produce stunning wines. Taste them—you'll see.

PART TWO

THE ✳ BEST ✳ OF
PORTUGUESE
COOKING

Appetizers and Condiments

✳

Acepipes e Condimentos

FERREIRA'S OLIVE-SAUTÉED ALMONDS
Amendôas à Ferreira

The venerable Port wine firm of A. A. Ferreira also produces its own fruity olive oil and almonds. These crisp, richly browned almonds are traditionally served with white or tawny Port before lunch or dinner.

Makes 1 pound

1	**pound unblanched almonds**
1½	**cups olive oil**
½	**teaspoon salt**
¼	**teaspoon cayenne pepper**

Blanch the almonds 1½ minutes in boiling water; drain, plunge into cold water, then slip off the skins. Spread the almonds out on several thicknesses of paper toweling and pat dry. Transfer to fresh paper toweling and let dry 24 hours. Heat the oil in a 10-inch iron skillet over moderate heat about 2 minutes or until an almond, dropped into the oil, sizzles gently. Add half of the almonds to the oil and sauté, stirring often, 4 to 5 minutes over moderately low heat until the color of light caramel. Dump the almonds into a colander set over a heatproof bowl; shake to drain off as much oil as possible, then drain on paper toweling. Return the oil to the skillet and fry and drain the remaining almonds the same way. Sprinkle with salt and cayenne and toss well; store in an airtight canister. *Note: The sautéing oil can be strained and used to dress vegetables or salads.*

ROSINHA SANTOS'S CHEESE WAFERS
Biscoitos de Queijo da Rosinha Santos

Rosinha Santos is no bigger than a minute, a merry, energetic woman who has cooked for Ferreira wine executives and visiting dignitaries for forty years. These supremely short and snappy cheese wafers of hers are traditionally passed with apéritifs of white or tawny Port in the executive dining room beside the Douro River in Vila Nova de Gaia (Porto's "Left Bank," where all the major Port wine lodges are.) Rosinha makes her wafers with a sharp yellow Portuguese cheese unavailable here. I have substituted Parmesan, the next best thing *provided* the Parmesan is freshly grated.

Makes about 6½ dozen

2½   cups sifted unbleached all-purpose flour
¾   teaspoon cayenne pepper
¼   teaspoon salt
½   pound (2 sticks) unsalted butter, cut into slim pats
½   pound Parmesan cheese, freshly and finely grated

Preheat oven to moderate (350°F.). Combine the flour, cayenne, and salt in a large shallow bowl. With a pastry blender, cut in the butter until the mixture is the texture of coarse meal. Add the cheese and rub into the flour-butter mixture gently with your fingertips until a small bit of the dough, when pinched together, will hold its shape. Roll into ¾-inch balls, place 1½ inches apart on ungreased baking sheets, then flatten into rounds ¼-inch thick by pressing with a flat-bottomed glass that has been dipped into flour. (You'll have to keep dipping the glass into flour to keep the dough from sticking to it.) Bake uncovered 10 to 12 minutes until pale tan. Transfer the wafers at once to wire racks to cool, then store airtight.

FRESH FIGS WITH SMOKED CURED HAM
Figos com Presunto

Gnarled fig bushes sprawl down the Algarve's lower mountain slopes and lounge upon the sea cliffs, their branches grazing the ground in midsummer under heavy burdens of fruit. Not surprisingly, good Algarve cooks have devised dozens of ways to use figs both fresh and dried. This popular appetizer is to my mind singularly delicious, as are the two variations that follow. All use *presunto,* Portugal's smoky-sweet, mahogany-hued ham from the Trás-os-Montes Province, sliced tissue-thin and then, as artistic Portuguese cooks so often do, shaped into wreaths, petals, or full-blown flowers. *Note: I have substituted prosciutto for Portugal's wonderful—but, alas, unavailable—*presunto. *It's texture, color, and flavor are similar.*

Makes 4 servings

4   large ripe figs
½   pound thinly sliced prosciutto
4   teaspoons olive oil
½   teaspoon freshly ground black pepper (about)

Wash the figs well, then divide into eighths, cutting from the stem to within about ⅜ inch of the bottom, so that you can spread the wedges out like petals. On each of 4 salad plates, arrange 5 to 6 slices of prosciutto spoke-fashion to resemble flower sepals. Drizzle lightly with olive oil and sprinkle with pepper. Place a fig in the center of each; then spread the wedges out like opening flowers. Let stand at room temperature 1 to 2 hours; then serve at the start of an elegant meal.

VARIATIONS:

Melão com Presunto (Melon with Smoked Cured Ham): Presentation is everything here. Slice a whole, ripe honeydew melon straight across 1½ inches thick. Remove seeds and strings from the center of each slice and cut off the rind. Place a slice on each of 4 salad plates (save any remaining melon to enjoy later); then roll the prosciutto into 20 full-blown roses, allowing 2 to 3 slices for each rose. Cluster 3 roses in the hole in the center of each melon; then place the remaining 2 artfully around the edge. Sprig with mint and serve as a first course.

Ananás com Presunto (Pineapple with Smoked Cured Ham): Cut the top and bottom off a small ripe pineapple; stand the pineapple on end and, slicing straight down, remove all prickly skin. With the point of a sharp knife, dig out all "eyes." Now lay the pineapple on its side and slice 1-inch thick; with a 1½-inch round cutter, remove the core from each slice. Arrange a pineapple ring on each of 4 salad plates (save any remaining pineapple to enjoy later). Roll the slices of prosciutto into 4 large full-blown roses, allowing 3 to 4 slices for each rose, and 12 smaller roses, allowing 2 to 3 slices for each. Place a large rose in the center of each pineapple ring; then place the 3 smaller roses decoratively around the edge. Sprig with lemon verbena or mint and serve as a first course.

PICKLED FRESH TUNA
Escabeche de Atum

To have the proper balance of flavors, the tuna must marinate in the refrigerator at least 24 hours. Although it can be served as the main course of a light meal, it is often served at the start of a meal in Portugal. *Note: Because of the tartness of the marinade, the recipe does not need salt.*

Makes 4 to 6 servings

- 2 pounds fresh boneless tuna
- 4 large garlic cloves, peeled and slivered
- ⅓ cup olive oil

MARINADE:

- 3 small yellow onions, peeled and sliced thin
- 2 large garlic cloves, peeled and minced
- 1 large lemon, sliced very thin
- 2 large bay leaves, crumbled
- ¼ cup chopped fresh coriander
- 2 tablespoons minced parsley
- 1 teaspoon freshly ground black pepper
- ⅔ cup olive oil
- ⅓ cup cider vinegar

Slice the tuna ½-inch thick, then cut into 1½-inch squares; set aside. Sauté the garlic slivers in the ⅓ cup olive oil in a large heavy skillet over lowest heat 25 minutes; with a slotted spoon, remove and discard the garlic. Sauté the tuna pieces in the garlic-oil in 2 to 3 batches, allowing about 2 minutes per side. Arrange one third of the tuna one layer deep in a 9 × 9 × 2-inch baking dish, then top with one third *each* of the onions, minced garlic, lemon slices, bay leaves, coriander, parsley, and pepper; repeat the layers twice, pour in the olive oil and vinegar, cover, and chill at least 24 hours. Serve cold with cocktails, as a first course, or as the main course of a light lunch.

ESCABECHE OF PARTRIDGES OR CORNISH HENS
Perdizes de Escabeche

If partridges are available to you, by all means use them for this recipe. If not, substitute fresh—*not frozen*—Cornish hens. I find this *escabeche* a refreshingly light entrée for hot-weather meals. And I've served it at the start of more substantial dinners, as indeed do the Portuguese. The recipe's a great favorite among families whose men like to hunt—which, to judge by the lines of pickup trucks on the road in early autumn, each filled with prize hunting dogs, must include every affluent family in the land. Once while I was staying at Portugal's most palatial *pousada,* the Rainha Santa Isabel in Estremoz, the room next to mine was occupied by retrievers who, it turned out, were better behaved than many hotel neighbors I've had.

Makes 6 appetizer servings, 4 main-course servings

½	cup olive oil
⅓	cup distilled (white) vinegar
12	large garlic cloves, peeled and halved
1	large yellow onion, peeled and sliced thin
4	large bay leaves, crumbled
4	large parsley branches
12	black peppercorns
⅔	cup water
½	teaspoon salt
2	partridges or fresh Cornish hens, each weighing about ¾ pound, cleaned and dressed and disjointed
¼	teaspoon freshly ground black pepper
4	tablespoons minced parsley
2	tablespoons cider vinegar (about)

In a large heavy saucepan set over moderately low heat, bring the olive oil, distilled vinegar, garlic, onion, bay leaves, parsley branches, peppercorns, water, and salt to a bubble; cover and simmer 10 minutes. Add the partridges, re-cover, and simmer slowly 30 to 35 minutes, just until the birds are cooked through. Transfer all to a large, shallow, heat-proof dish (preferably nonmetallic) and cool to room temperature. Cover and chill at least 24 hours.

About 45 minutes before you're ready to serve, set the *escabeche* on the counter. As soon as the chill is off and the marinade has softened (it will have jelled in the refrigerator), sprinkle the *escabeche* with the black pepper, minced parsley, and cider vinegar. Toss lightly, taste, and if the mixture is not tart enough to suit you, drizzle with a little additional cider vinegar and toss lightly again. Serve at room temperature.

CODFISH BALLS
Bolinhos de Bacalhau

If there were a contest to determine Portugal's most popular hors d'oeuvre, the codfish ball would win hands down. Many fine Lisbon restaurants offer plates of them to nibble with cocktails, as do stylish hostesses. Elsewhere about the country, women roll the codfish mixture into two-inch *bolos* (balls) and serve them as the main dish of a family meal. *Note: Because salt cod must be soaked well, you should begin this recipe the day before you serve it.*

Makes 4 main-dish servings, or enough hors d'oeuvre for 6 to 8

½	pound dried salt cod
2	medium Maine or Eastern potatoes, peeled and cubed
1	medium yellow onion, peeled and minced
1	large garlic clove, peeled and minced
4	teaspoons olive oil
2	tablespoons finely minced parsley
1	large egg, separated
⅛	teaspoon cayenne pepper
⅛	teaspoon freshly ground black pepper
	Vegetable shortening or oil for deep-fat frying

Soak the salt cod in the refrigerator 24 hours in several changes of cold water. (Keep the bowl covered so that the whole refrigerator doesn't smell of fish.) Drain the cod, rinse, and drain well again. Place in a small saucepan, add enough cold water to cover, and bring to a simmer over moderate heat. Adjust the heat so that the water barely trembles, cover, and simmer the cod 15 to 20 minutes until tender. Meanwhile, boil the potatoes in enough water to cover about 20 minutes until soft; drain well, return pan to low heat, and shake well to drive off all excess moisture. When the cod is tender, drain well, then flake with a fork, removing any bones and bits of skin; mince fine and reserve.

In a small heavy skillet set over moderate heat, sauté the onion and garlic in the olive oil about 5 minutes until limp; mix in the parsley and set off the heat. Mash the potatoes, then mix in the reserved minced cod, onion mixture, egg yolk, cayenne, and black pepper. Whisk the egg white to soft peaks, then fold into the cod mixture, cover, and refrigerate until ready to shape the balls. (It's best not to hold the mixture too long because it's apt to absorb moisture and soften too much to shape.)

Place the shortening in a deep-fat fryer, insert a deep-fat thermometer, and set over moderately high heat. Shape the cod mixture into 1- or 2-inch balls; then, as soon as the fat reaches 370°F., fry in batches, about 4 large balls at a time or 6 to 8 small ones, until golden brown—1 to 2 minutes. As the balls brown, lift with a slotted spoon to several thicknesses of paper toweling to drain; then set uncovered in a very slow oven (250°F.) to keep warm while you fry the balance. Raise and lower the burner heat as needed to keep the temperature of the deep fat as near to 370°F. as possible. Serve the codfish balls piping hot, or, as they do in Portugal, serve at room temperature—they are especially good this way.

GARLIC PÂTÉ
Pasta de Alho

The Pousada de São Filipe, a delightful government inn located in a sixteenth-century cliff's-edge castle overlooking the port of Setúbal and the Atlantic Ocean, used to have a wonderful country cook who was well into her seventies. It was she who whipped up this ingenious pâté, which was brought to your table in a little terra-cotta crock the instant you sat down. Its foundation was a translucent local cheese unavailable here, so I've taken the liberty of substituting ripe Brie.

Makes 1¾ cups

2   large buds (entire heads) of garlic (4 to 5 ounces in all)
1   pound cold ripe Brie, trimmed of white rind, then cut into 1-inch cubes
½   teaspoon cayenne pepper
3   tablespoons olive oil
1   tablespoon hot water

Preheat the oven to slow (300°F.). Bundle the whole, unpeeled buds of garlic in a double thickness of aluminum foil, then twist each loose end into a gooseneck, sealing in the garlic. Place in the oven and roast for 1 hour; remove from the oven and cool to room temperature. Place the Brie in the top of a double boiler, set over hot water, and let soften 8 to 10 minutes (do not allow the water to boil or the cheese may string and separate). Meanwhile, peel the garlic, clove by clove, and drop into an electric blender cup or a food processor fitted with the metal chopping blade; add the pepper, olive oil, and water and buzz 30 seconds nonstop to purée. Scrape down the sides of the blender cup or work bowl and buzz 30 seconds longer. Now add the softened cheese and incorporate, using 8 to 10 quick on-offs of the motor. Transfer to a small bowl and, if the mixture seems slightly lumpy, whisk hard by hand (further machine-beating at this point may make the pâté rubbery). Store airtight in the refrigerator and serve with *Pão Torrado* (page 93). *Note: Let the pâté come to room temperature before serving.*

BLACK OLIVE PÂTÉ
Pasta de Azeitonas Pretas

Another wonderful pâté from Setúbal's Pousada de São Filipe. Make sure that the olives you use for it are fleshy, gutsy ones—the Greek Kalamatas, for example.

Makes 1½ cups

1	**pound large ripe olives, pitted**
1	**large bud (entire head) of garlic (2 to 3 ounces in all)**
¼	**teaspoon freshly ground black pepper**

Preheat the oven to slow (300°F.). Meanwhile, spread the olives out on several thicknesses of paper toweling, top with several more thicknesses of paper toweling, then roll up tight and set aside (this is to rid the olives of as much moisture as possible so that the pâté won't be soupy). Wrap the whole, unpeeled bud of garlic in a double thickness of aluminum foil, then twist each loose end into a gooseneck, sealing in the garlic. Place in the oven and roast for 1 hour; remove from the oven and cool to room temperature. Now peel the garlic, clove by clove, and drop into an electric blender cup or a food processor fitted with the metal chopping blade; add the olives and pepper, and purée by buzzing 15 seconds nonstop. Scrape down the sides of the blender cup or work bowl with a rubber spatula, buzz another 15 seconds, then scoop all into a small bowl and cover tight. Store in the refrigerator until about ½ hour before serving. Mound into a small decorative bowl and serve as a cocktail spread with *Pão Torrado* (page 93) or crisp crackers.

SWEET RED PEPPER PASTE
Massa de Pimentão

This vermilion paste is a popular dry marinade used in Portugal to season a variety of meats and poultry before they are cooked. To make it, countrywomen layer sliced sweet red peppers and coarse salt in a shallow terra-cotta bowl and let them stand two to three days. I've found a way to short-cut the procedure by mellowing the peppers in the oven. This paste, by the way, makes a splendid cocktail spread for melba toast or a dip for broccoli flowerets or zucchini sticks. The Portuguese, of course, use it strictly as a seasoning.

Makes about 1¼ cups

8   medium sweet red peppers, washed, cored, seeded, and cut lengthwise into strips about 1-inch wide
2   tablespoons kosher or coarse salt
2   large garlic cloves, peeled and minced
⅓   cup olive oil (about)

Arrange a layer of pepper strips in the bottom of a shallow bowl no more than 9 inches in diameter; sprinkle with ¾ teaspoon of the salt; now add 7 more layers of pepper strips, sprinkling each with ¾ teaspoon salt. Let stand uncovered at room temperature for at least 12 hours. Drain off excess liquid.

Turn on the oven to its keep-warm setting (250° to 275°F.). Place the bowl of peppers, still uncovered, in the oven and roast 2 to 2½ hours, stirring occasionally, until all juices have been absorbed. Remove the peppers from the oven and cool to room temperature. Now peel the skin from each pepper strip and discard. Place the garlic and pepper strips in the work bowl of a food processor fitted with the metal chopping blade or in an electric blender cup and add about half the oil; buzz non-stop about 30 seconds, scrape down the work bowl sides, and buzz 30 seconds longer. Now, with the motor running, drizzle in enough of the remaining oil to make a paste slightly softer than whipped butter. Churn 60 seconds nonstop until absolutely smooth. *Note: If you have neither food processor nor blender, you'll have to grind the garlic and peppers to paste as the Portuguese women do—with a mortar and pestle. You must then add the olive oil very slowly, drop by drop at first, beating hard to incorporate.*

Transfer the red pepper paste to a small jar with a tight-fitting lid and store in the refrigerator. Dip into the paste as needed, letting whatever you remove from the jar come to room temperature before using.

HOT RED PEPPER SAUCE
Molho de Piri-piri

Portugal's navigators of the fifteenth and sixteenth centuries were responsible for disseminating many Old World foods to the New, and vice versa. *Piri-piri* peppers, for example, were brought from one Portuguese colony, Brazil, to another, Angola, where they became so integral to the local cuisine that they were ultimately known as "Angolan peppers." The peppers are tiny but they are filled with fire, which Portuguese cooks learned to capture by mincing the pods and steeping them in oil and vinegar. The resulting sauce has become a staple in kitchens and dining rooms throughout Portugal.

Piri-piri peppers are not obtainable in this country, so you will have to substitute one of the readily available chili peppers: the long, twisted cayenne pods, for instance; the torrid, scarlet New Mexico chilies; the all but flammable chili *pequins*, even round cherry peppers. To look properly Portuguese, the sauce should be made with red peppers, although you may substitute the green jalapeños in a pinch. The heat of these chilies varies considerably, so taste the pepper before using. If it is so hot it brings tears to your eyes, use about 2 peppers in the recipe below; if it is only moderately hot, use 3 to 4; and if it is merely tepid, 5 to 6—plus a healthy shot of liquid hot red pepper seasoning, if needed to heat things up. The sauce should be about as hot as Tabasco.

Makes about 1½ cups

2 to 6	chili peppers (or dried chili pequins), depending upon their hotness (see above)
1	teaspoon kosher or coarse salt
1	cup olive oil
⅓	cup cider vinegar

Stem the peppers and coarsely chop (include the seeds); place in a 1-pint shaker jar along with the salt, olive oil, and vinegar. Cover tight, shake well, then store at room temperature. The sauce will keep well for about a month. Shake the sauce every time you use it. *Note: For mellower flavor, roast the peppers uncovered for 15 minutes at low oven heat (300°F.), cool until easy to handle, then slip off the skins. Otherwise, prepare as directed.*

MAYONNAISE
Molho Maionese

With a food processor or blender, this intensely olive-flavored mayonnaise is easy to make. Stored tightly covered in the refrigerator, it will keep well for about a week. Use as you would any mayonnaise.

Makes about 1½ cups

1½	teaspoons dry mustard
½	teaspoon salt
¼	teaspoon cayenne pepper
1	tablespoon lemon juice
1	tablespoon cider vinegar
2	tablespoons half-and-half cream
2	large egg yolks
1⅓	cups olive oil

Place the mustard, salt, cayenne, lemon juice, vinegar, cream, and egg yolks in an electric blender cup or a food processor fitted with the metal chopping blade. Snap the motor on and off several times just to blend the ingredients. Now, with the motor running, add the olive oil in a very fine stream, pausing now and then to scrape down the blender cup or work bowl sides with a rubber spatula. Continue adding the olive oil, still in a fine stream, churning all the while, until all the oil has been incorporated. Now buzz 30 seconds nonstop. Transfer the mayonnaise to a 1-pint jar with a tight-fitting lid and store in the refrigerator.

PORTUGUESE TOAST
Pão Torrado

This is really a sort of melba toast and you should make it, if at all possible, with *Pão de Forma* (page 228). Failing that, use a small *baguette* of French bread.

Makes about 4 dozen pieces

½   pound *Pão de Forma* or French *baguette*
⅓   cup olive oil

Preheat the oven to slow (300°F.). Slice the bread about ¼-inch thick; then, if using the *Pão de Forma,* cut into pieces 2 to 2½ inches long and 1½ inches wide. Arrange the pieces of bread on baking sheets, then brush well with olive oil. Bake uncovered for 25 minutes until golden brown. Remove from the oven, cool to room temperature, then store airtight. Serve with *Pasta de Azeitonas Prêtas* (page 89), *Pasta de Alho* (page 88), or any pâté or cocktail spread.

Soups

✳

Sopas

CHICKEN WITH MINT, RICE AND LEMON
Canja

This clear, refreshing chicken soup is popular all over Portugal. It originally contained rice, but modern cooks seem to prefer tiny seed-shaped pasta.

Makes 4 to 6 servings

1   whole chicken breast (½ to ¾ pound), split
1   medium yellow onion, peeled and cut in thin wedges
4   parsley sprigs
4   strips lemon zest (the colored part of the rind), each about 2 inches long and ½-inch wide
1   sprig fresh mint
2   quarts rich chicken broth (preferably homemade)
⅓   cup raw rice or *semini* (little seed-shaped pasta), cooked by package directions
1   teaspoon lemon juice
¼   cup coarsely chopped mint
    Salt to taste
⅛   teaspoon white pepper

GARNISH:

4 to 6   lemon slices, each serrated about the edge and stuck with a small sprig of mint

Simmer the chicken breast with the onion, parsley, lemon zest, and mint sprig in the chicken stock in a covered heavy saucepan over low heat 35 to 40 minutes until cooked through. Remove chicken breast and cool. Strain the broth through a cheesecloth-lined sieve and return to the pan. Boil the stock uncovered 8 to 10 minutes to reduce slightly. Meanwhile, skin and bone the chicken breast; cut meat into large julienne, and add to the broth along with the rice, lemon juice, chopped mint, salt, and pepper. Heat 2 to 3 minutes. Ladle into soup plates, float a mint-sprigged lemon slice in each portion, and serve.

FRESH CORIANDER SOUP
Sopa de Coentro

It is absolutely imperative that this soup be made with fresh coriander, also known as Chinese parsley and *cilantro* (its Spanish name). You'll find it year-round at fancy greengroceries and specialty food shops. Although the Portuguese serve this soup hot, I also like it cold on sultry summer evenings.

Makes 6 to 8 servings

- 4 medium yellow onions, peeled and coarsely chopped
- 2 large garlic cloves, peeled and minced
- 4 tablespoons olive oil
- 4 medium potatoes, peeled and coarsely chopped
- 6 cups rich chicken broth (preferably homemade)
  Salt, as needed to taste (you may not need any, depending upon the saltiness of the broth)
- ¼ teaspoon cayenne pepper
- ¾ cup coarsely chopped fresh coriander leaves (you'll need 1 large bunch)

In a large heavy saucepan set over moderate heat, sauté the onions and garlic in 3 tablespoons of the olive oil 5 minutes until limp; add the remaining tablespoon of oil and the potatoes and stir-fry 1 minute. Add the broth, cover, and simmer 45 minutes until the potatoes are mushy. Remove from the heat and purée, about a fourth of the total amount at a time, by buzzing 60 seconds in a food processor fitted with the metal chopping blade or in an electric blender. If you have neither processor nor blender, simply force all through a fine sieve. Pour the soup into a large heat-proof bowl, stir in salt if needed, the cayenne, and the coriander. Cover and refrigerate 24 hours. Serve cold; or pour into a large heavy saucepan, set over moderate heat, and bring slowly to a simmer. Ladle into soup plates and serve hot with crusty chunks of *Broa* (page 239) or *Pão* (page 224).

GREEN SOUP
Caldo Verde

What makes this potato-thickened soup so green are hundreds of hairlike filaments of kale-like cabbage. According to Maria de Lourdes Modesto, star of a Lisbon television cooking show and author of the dazzling *Cozinha Tradicional Portuguesa,* what Portuguese women use for making *caldo verde* is the intensely green Galician cabbage (*couve gallego*), which has large, flat, tender leaves. At country markets you see women stacking the leaves, rolling them into fat "cigars," then shaving them into the finest of shreds by whisking razor-sharp knives back and forth across the rolls at breathtaking speed. At more modern markets, like Lisbon's *Mercado da Ribeira,* rolls of cabbage are fed into giant hand-cranked shredding wheels, each with a plastic bag at the back to catch the flying bits. If Portugal has a national dish, it is without doubt this lusty green soup, which originated in the Minho Province but now bubbles on stoves everywhere regardless of the season or temperature. To be truly authentic, each serving should contain a slice of *salpicão* (cured loin of pork) or *chouriço* (garlicky sausage). Obviously, because these Portuguese ingredients are often unavailable here, some concessions must be made. Collards, kale or turnip greens, I've found, make a good substitute for the Galician cabbage; spinach may be used in a pinch; even mustard greens, provided you shave them fine enough to cook quickly. As for the sausage, use a Spanish *chorizo* or Italian pepperoni if the Portuguese chouriço is unobtainable.

Makes 6 to 8 servings

1	large yellow onion, peeled and minced fine
1	large garlic clove, peeled and minced
4	tablespoons olive oil
6	large Maine or Eastern potatoes, peeled and sliced thin
2	quarts cold water
6	ounces *chouriço, chorizo,* pepperoni, or other dry garlicky sausage, sliced thin
2½	teaspoons salt (about)
¼	teaspoon freshly ground black pepper
1	pound collards, kale, or turnip greens, washed, trimmed of coarse stems and veins, then sliced filament-thin. (The easiest way is to stack 6 to 8 leaves, roll crosswise into a firm, tight roll, then slice with a very sharp knife.)

Sauté the onion and garlic in 3 tablespoons of the oil in a large heavy saucepan 2 to 3 minutes over moderate heat until they begin to color and turn glassy; do not brown or they will turn bitter. Add the potatoes and sauté, stirring constantly, 2 to 3 minutes, until they begin to color also. Add the water, cover, and boil gently over moderate heat 20 to 25 minutes until the potatoes are mushy. Meanwhile, fry the sausage in a medium-size heavy skillet over low heat 10 to 12 minutes until most of the fat has cooked out; drain well and reserve.

When the potatoes are soft, remove the pan from the stove and with a potato masher, mash the potatoes right in the pan in the soup mixture. Add the sausage, salt, and pepper, return to moderate heat, cover, and simmer 5 minutes. Add the collards and simmer uncovered 5 minutes until tender and the color of jade. Mix in the remaining tablespoon of olive oil, and taste the soup for salt and pepper. Ladle into large soup plates and serve as a main course accompanied by chunks of *Broa* (page 239).

MADEIRA ONION SOUP
Sopa de Cebola à Madeirense

Is it because Vasco da Gama found the water route to the East's treasury of spices that the Portuguese are so inventive about spicing their savory dishes? I think so. This rich onion soup, subtly scented with cloves, is from the island of Madeira, a standard port-of-call on early Portuguese voyages of discovery. It also contains raisins, as do many Moorish savories.

Makes 6 servings

2½	pounds yellow onions, peeled and sliced thin
3	tablespoons unsalted butter
2	tablespoons olive oil
6	whole cloves
1	teaspoon paprika
2	tablespoons golden seedless raisins (sultanas) or dried currants
5	cups rich beef broth (preferably homemade)
¼	teaspoon salt (about)
⅛	teaspoon freshly ground black pepper (about)
4	large egg yolks, lightly beaten
¼	cup dry Madeira (Sercial)

Sauté the onions in the butter and oil in a large heavy kettle over moderate heat about 30 minutes, stirring occasionally, until limp and golden and lightly touched with brown. Don't rush this process or the soup will not have the proper onion flavor. Add the cloves, paprika, raisins, and broth; cover and simmer 1 hour. Then uncover and simmer ½ hour longer. Season to taste with salt and pepper. *Note: The soup will be mellower if at this point you cool it, cover it, and chill it for 24 hours.* Bring slowly to serving temperature. Mix a little of the hot broth into the beaten egg yolks, stir yolks into the kettle, then cook and stir 3 to 4 minutes until slightly thickened. Mix in the Madeira and serve as the main course of a light meal. You will need only bread, salad, and a fruit dessert to accompany.

TOMATO AND ONION SOUP
Sopa de Tomate e Cebola

I first sampled this bracing soup high in the mountains of Madeira. I had sought refuge at a little crossroads inn because fog was closing in, making it impossible to drive farther on the island's corkscrewing cobbled roads. A fire crackled on the dining room hearth, families were assembled for Sunday lunch, and I sat off to one side dipping into the best tomato soup I had ever eaten. It had been made, of course, with the island's own heady ripe tomatoes. To come close to approximating the bouquet of that exquisite soup, you must use tomatoes that are bright and full of flavor. The pithy, mass-produced ones just won't do. This soup, like most, will be better if you make it one day, then add the finishing touches the next.

Makes 6 servings

4	large yellow onions, peeled and coarsely chopped
⅓	cup olive oil
8	large juicily ripe tomatoes, peeled, cored, seeded, and finely chopped, or 2 cans (1 pound each) whole tomatoes, drained
4	large garlic cloves, peeled and minced
5	cups rich beef broth (preferably homemade)
¼	pound (1 stick) unsalted butter
¼	teaspoon salt (about)
⅛	teaspoon freshly ground black pepper (about)
1 to 2	teaspoons sugar (if needed to mellow the soup)
6	small eggs
12	pieces of *Pão* (page 224), about 2 inches square and ½-inch thick, or 12 thick slices of a French *baguette* or slim loaf of Italian bread
¼	cup minced parsley

Stir-fry the onions in the oil in a heavy, broad-bottomed kettle about 15 minutes over moderate heat until limp and lightly browned. Add the tomatoes and garlic, cover, and simmer 1 hour; uncover and simmer 30 minutes, stirring occasionally, until thick and pastelike. Add the broth, 3 tablespoons of the butter, salt and pepper to taste, and if needed, the sugar. Simmer uncovered 1½ to 2 hours or until the flavors are richly blended. Cool to room temperature, cover, and refrigerate until about 1 hour before serving. Bring the soup slowly to serving temperature. Carefully break the eggs into the soup, spacing them evenly, cover, and simmer slowly for 15 minutes—just long enough to poach the eggs.

Meanwhile, brown the pieces of bread on both sides in the remaining 5 tablespoons of butter in a large heavy skillet over moderately high heat; drain on paper toweling. Ladle the soup into large shallow soup bowls, including an egg with each portion. Garnish each bowl with 2 pieces of bread and a sprinkling of parsley.

GREEN BEAN SOUP WITH MINT
Sopa de Feijão Verde com Hortelã

In the farmhouses of northern Portugal, finely sliced, unshelled young fava beans are used in this recipe in place of green beans. Although the soup itself is sieved or puréed, the beans usually aren't—except by cooks at some of the big *solares* (manor houses) and *quintas* (estates). You'll find both versions here.

Makes 6 servings

    2   medium yellow onions, peeled and coarsely chopped
    1   large garlic clove, peeled and minced
    3   tablespoons olive oil
    2   medium Maine or Eastern potatoes, peeled and coarsely chopped
    4   cups chicken broth (preferably homemade)
    1   pound tender young green beans, washed, tipped, and cut into ½-inch pieces
 1¼   cups water
    ½   teaspoon salt (about)
    ⅛   teaspoon freshly ground black pepper
    2   tablespoons coarsely chopped fresh mint

In a large heavy saucepan set over moderate heat, sauté the onions and garlic in the oil about 5 minutes, stirring often, until limp; add the potatoes and cook, stirring, 3 to 4 minutes until potatoes color slightly. Pour in the broth, bring to a simmer, adjust the heat so that the mixture bubbles gently, then cover, and simmer 40 minutes until the potatoes are very tender.

Meanwhile, cook the beans in the water with the salt in a covered saucepan over moderate heat 20 to 25 minutes until very tender; drain well, reserving both the beans and their cooking water. Add the cooking water to the onion-potato mixture. When potatoes are mushy, purée the mixture in batches by buzzing 30 seconds nonstop in a food processor fitted with the metal chopping blade or in an electric blender. If you have neither food processor nor blender, force the saucepan mixture through a food mill or fine sieve. Return all to the saucepan, add the green beans, and bring just to serving temperature. Add salt, if needed, also the pepper and mint. Ladle into soup bowls and serve as the main course of a light lunch or supper.

VARIATION:

Creme de Feijão Verde com Hortelã (Cream of Green Bean Soup with Mint):
Prepare as directed but add the green beans to the potato mixture along with their cooking water. Purée all until smooth, bring to serving temperature, and season to taste with salt and pepper. Place 2 teaspoons of coarsely chopped fresh mint in the bottom of each of 6 soup plates, ladle in the soup, and serve.

PUMPKIN SOUP
Sopa de Abóbora

The pumpkin soups familiar to most of us are lightly sugared and spiced. Not this Portuguese classic, which is aromatic of garlic and onion. This recipe is my rendition of one of the many regional recipes served at The Varanda Restaurant in Lisbon's Hotel Ritz. Portuguese "pumpkins" are small round squashes much like our butternut squash in color, texture, and flavor, so butternut squash is what I use here. Although this soup is served hot in Portugal, I find it equally delicious cold on a hot summer day. *Note: Although classified as a "winter squash," butternut squash is available year-round.*

Makes 6 to 8 servings

2   medium yellow onions, peeled and coarsely chopped
1   medium garlic clove, peeled and minced
2   tablespoons olive oil
2½   pound butternut squash, halved, seeded, cut into 1½-inch chunks, then each chunk peeled (a swivel-bladed vegetable peeler does the job nicely)
5   cups chicken broth (preferably homemade)
   Salt, if needed, to taste
⅛   teaspoon freshly ground black pepper

In a large heavy saucepan set over moderate heat, stir-fry the onions and garlic in the olive oil 5 minutes; turn heat to low, cover the pan, and let the mixture steam 20 minutes (this is what the Portuguese call making a *refogado*). Add the squash and toss well with the onion mixture; pour in the broth, bring to a simmer, adjust the heat so that the liquid bubbles gently, cover, and simmer about 1 hour until the squash is very soft. Purée the mixture in batches in a food processor fitted with the metal chopping blade or in an electric blender by buzzing 30 seconds nonstop; scrape down the work bowl or blender cup sides and buzz 30 seconds longer until smooth; return all to the saucepan. If you have neither food processor nor blender, force the saucepan mixture through a food mill or fine sieve.

Bring the soup to serving temperature over low heat, add salt as needed to taste, also the pepper. Ladle into soup bowls and serve with one of the wonderful Portuguese breads, a green salad, and a simple fruit dessert.

VEGETABLE SOUP FROM THE MINHO PROVINCE
Sopa de Legumes à Minhota

Most of the cooks at Portugal's *pousadas* are gifted local men and women who specialize in home-style soups and stews. In fact, the best country soups I've ever eaten are those served at *pousadas*. There's nothing sophisticated about them, but they will have been freshly made with the finest local produce. This particular soup is the specialty at the modern Pousada de São Teotónio, pitched high above the Minho River, overlooking the border town of Tuy and the green folds of Galicia. This recipe makes a lot, it's true, but the soup freezes well.

Makes 8 to 10 servings

2	large garlic cloves, peeled and minced
4	large yellow onions, peeled and coarsely chopped
4	large leeks, washed, trimmed, and sliced thin
¼	cup olive oil
2	cups finely shredded cabbage
1	pound turnips, peeled and coarsely chopped
1	large carrot, peeled and coarsely chopped
2	pounds Maine or Eastern potatoes, peeled and sliced thin
2	large bay leaves (do not crumble)
½	teaspoon crumbled leaf marjoram
¼	teaspoon crumbled leaf thyme
¼	teaspoon crumbled leaf rosemary
	Pinch freshly grated nutmeg
⅛	teaspoon freshly ground black pepper
1	quart rich chicken broth (preferably homemade)
6	cups water
1	medium-size carrot, peeled and cut in matchstick strips
3	cups very finely sliced cabbage
2	cups very finely sliced fresh young spinach
¼	cup minced parsley
2½	teaspoons salt

In a large heavy kettle set over moderate heat stir-fry the garlic, onions, and leeks in the oil 15 minutes until golden; add the shredded cabbage, turnips, chopped carrot, potatoes, herbs, nutmeg, and pepper and sauté, stirring now and then, 20 minutes. Add the chicken broth and water, bring to a simmer, adjust the heat so the mixture bubbles gently, cover, and cook 5 to 6 hours, stirring occasionally. Then with a potato masher, mash the potatoes and other vegetables into a rough purée.

Add the carrot matchsticks, re-cover, and simmer 2 hours. Add the sliced cabbage and simmer uncovered 45 minutes. Add the spinach and parsley and simmer uncovered 10 minutes. Stir in the salt, adjusting the amount as needed, to taste. Cool the soup to room temperature, cover, and refrigerate overnight.

Next day, bring the soup slowly to serving temperature. Ladle into large soup plates and serve with crusty chunks of *Pão* (page 224). Add a fruit dessert and you have a hearty meal.

PORTUGUESE STONE SOUP
Sopa de Pedra

This lusty, catchall country soup comes from the broad plains of the Ribatejo Province, which begins just across the Tagus River and slightly to the north of Lisbon. It's a land of spirited horses trained in dressage, of bulls and bullfighters. (The sport here is mostly fun and games because the animals, instead of being killed, are returned to pastures to graze.) As is the case with most of Portugal's good soups, *Sopa de Pedra* is popular all over the country. This particular recipe comes from the Pousada do Castelo de Palmela, one of the newest and most luxurious of the country's splendid government-run inns. Built inside the walls of an ancient mountaintop Moorish castle, the *pousada* is less than an hour's drive via *auto-estrada* from downtown Lisbon and is one of the most idyllic places to stay in Portugal.

Makes 8 to 10 servings

1   cup dried red kidney beans, washed and sorted
3   cups cold water
3   medium yellow onions, peeled and coarsely chopped
4   medium leeks, trimmed, washed, and sliced thin
3   tablespoons peanut or vegetable oil
4   medium Maine or Eastern potatoes, peeled and cut in small dice
4   medium carrots, peeled and cut in small dice

6 medium white turnips, peeled and cut in small dice
½ pound Savoy or green cabbage, cored and sliced thin
2½ quarts chicken broth (preferably homemade)
1 large bay leaf (do not crumble)
½ pound lean smoked ham, in one piece
¼ pound pepperoni or *chorizo*, in one piece
½ pound green beans, washed, tipped, and cut on the bias into ½-inch pieces
1 can (1 pound) water-pack tomatoes (do not drain)
½ cup elbow macaroni, cooked by package directions just until *al dente*, then drained
3 tablespoons minced Italian parsley
2 teaspoons salt (about)
¼ teaspoon freshly ground black pepper (about)

Soak the dried beans in the water overnight in a large heavy saucepan. Next day, bring the beans and their soaking water to a boil, cover, and cook 30 to 40 minutes, just until the beans are firm-tender. Drain the beans and reserve. In a large heavy kettle, stir-fry the onions and leeks in the oil 10 to 12 minutes over moderate heat just until golden and lightly touched with brown. Turn the heat to its lowest point and add the potatoes, carrots, turnips, and cabbage one by one as you prepare them, stirring well after each addition to the pot. Add the chicken broth, bay leaf, ham, and pepperoni, bring to a simmer, cover, and cook 20 minutes. Add the green beans, re-cover, and cook 30 to 40 minutes longer, until the vegetables are tender and their flavors well blended.

Remove the ham and pepperoni from the kettle; cut the ham into small cubes and slice the pepperoni thin; return both to the kettle. Add the tomatoes and their juice, breaking up any large clumps; also add the reserved red kidney beans. Cover and simmer 10 to 15 minutes—just long enough to mellow the flavors and bring all to serving temperature. Finally, add the macaroni, parsley, salt and pepper to taste, cover, and warm 5 to 10 minutes. Ladle into large soup plates and serve with generous wedges of *Broa* (page 239). *Note: This soup, like most, will be better if made one day and served the next.*

SOUP OF THE KETTLE
Sopa da Panela

An odds-and-ends soup that shows how clever Portuguese country women are at making a sustaining meal from a bit of this and a dab of that. This unusual dish comes from the Alentejo Province and, like so many other recipes from this farming region, is thickened with bread. It really falls into the category of *açordas* (dry soups) even though it is not called an *açorda*.

Makes 6 servings

2   ounces lean bacon, in 1 piece
1   large yellow onion, peeled and coarsely chopped
2   ounces *chouriço* (or Spanish *chorizo*) or garlicky Italian sausage, in 1 piece
3   ounces pepperoni, in 1 piece
1   whole chicken leg (drumstick and thigh) weighing about ½ pound
6   cups cold water
4   large parsley branches
½   teaspoon salt (about)
¼   teaspoon freshly ground black pepper (about)
5   ounces day-old *Pão* (page 224) or Italian bread (about ⅔ of a slim 18-inch loaf), cut in 1-inch chunks
2   tablespoons coarsely chopped fresh mint
1   tablespoon minced parsley

Score the bacon criss-cross fashion, then fry in a large heavy kettle over high heat until some of the drippings trickle out—2 to 3 minutes. Add the onion and stir-fry 8 to 10 minutes over moderate heat until limp; add the *chouriço*, pepperoni, and chicken and fry, stirring occasionally, 5 minutes. Add the water and parsley and bring to a simmer, adjust heat so the liquid bubbles gently, cover, and simmer 1½ hours. Discard the parsley; remove the bacon, *chouriço*, pepperoni, and chicken from the kettle; when cool enough to handle, halve the *chouriço* and pepperoni lengthwise, then slice thin; dice the bacon; remove the skin and bones from the chicken meat and tear the meat into bite-size pieces. Return all meats to the kettle. Mix in the salt and pepper, the bread, mint, and minced parsley. Taste and add more salt and pepper, if needed. Ladle into large soup plates and serve as the main course of a family meal. You'll need only a tartly dressed green salad and fruit dessert to complete the meal.

CHICK-PEA SOUP ALENTEJO-STYLE
Sopa de Grão à Alentejana

There are two Alentejos—Upper and Lower—lying to the east and south of Lisbon, which together comprise nearly half the area of Portugal. They are for the most part barren ground—brown, dry, and hellishly hot half the year. Yet this land is far from fallow. From the Alentejo comes the bulk of Portugal's cork and olives and unusually fine-fleshed hogs. It is fitting, then, that one of the region's best soups is an earthy one, studded with sausage. It is the porridge-thick *Sopa de Grão,* made of chick-peas and potatoes, aromatic of olive, onion, and garlic, and accented with shreds of spinach. Even though olives abound in the Alentejo, few families there can afford the luxury of cooking with olive oil. So they use the cheaper corn, peanut, or vegetable oil for most cooking jobs, then inject a fruity olive flavor by stirring a tablespoon or so of olive oil into their soups and stews at the last minute.

Makes 6 to 8 servings

2½	cups dried chick-peas, washed and sorted
2	quarts cold water
4	medium garlic cloves, peeled and minced
4	large yellow onions, peeled and coarsely chopped
3	tablespoons peanut, corn, or vegetable oil
3	medium Maine or Eastern potatoes, peeled and coarsely chopped
½	teaspoon crumbled leaf thyme
½	teaspoon freshly ground coriander seeds
1	large bay leaf (do not crumble)
1	quart beef or chicken broth (preferably homemade)
½	pound pepperoni, *chorizo,* or, if available, Portuguese *chouriço* or *linguiça*
1	cup finely chopped fresh young spinach leaves
1½	teaspoons salt (about)
¼	teaspoon freshly ground black pepper (about)
2	tablespoons olive oil

Soak the chick-peas overnight in 6 cups of the water in a large heavy kettle. Next day, add the remaining 2 cups water, bring to a gentle boil, cover, and cook 4 to 5 hours until the chick-peas are very tender. *Note: 4 to 5 hours may seem excessive, but it isn't really. Dried chick-peas are unusually hard, and for this recipe they must be cooked almost to mush so that you can purée them easily.*

Meanwhile, stir-fry the garlic and onions in the peanut oil in a second large heavy kettle over moderate heat 12 to 15 minutes until translucent and touched with brown. Add the potatoes and stir-fry 2 to 3 minutes; add the thyme, coriander, and bay leaf, turn the heat down low, and allow to mellow about 10 minutes. Pour in the broth, bring all to a gentle simmer, cover, and cook slowly alongside the chick-peas—keep the potatoes simmering the whole while; they, too, will be puréed.

As soon as you've set the two kettles to simmer, stir-fry the pepperoni in a large heavy skillet 3 to 5 minutes—just until lightly browned and most of the drippings have cooked out. Drain the pepperoni well, reserving 1 tablespoon of the drippings. Set the pepperoni aside. Return the 1 tablespoon of drippings to the skillet, dump in the spinach and stir-fry 2 to 3 minutes over moderate heat just until glazed and intensely green; reserve.

When the chick-peas are good and tender, purée half of them by buzzing about 60 seconds in a food processor fitted with the metal chopping blade, adding only enough kettle liquid to purée them easily. If you have no food processor, force the chick-peas through a food mill or fine sieve. Return the puréed chick-peas to the kettle in which they cooked. Now purée the potato mixture, about half of the total amount at a time, by buzzing 30 to 40 seconds in the food processor or by forcing through the food mill or sieve. Blend the puréed potato mixture into the chick-pea mixture, add the reserved pepperoni and spinach, cover, and simmer 30 to 40 minutes—just long enough to blend and mellow the flavors. Season the soup to taste with salt and pepper, then smooth in the olive oil. Ladle into soup bowls and serve with *Pão* or *Pão de Forma* (pages 224 and 228).

CHICK-PEA AND SPINACH SOUP
Sopa de Grão com Espinafres

A meatless and more frugal chick-pea soup, also from the Alentejo Province.

Makes 6 to 8 servings

1   pound dried chick-peas, washed and sorted
7   cups cold water
3   large garlic cloves, peeled and minced
3   large yellow onions, peeled and coarsely chopped
3   tablespoons vegetable oil
2   medium Maine or Eastern potatoes, peeled and coarsely chopped

  2 tablespoons minced parsley
  2 tablespoons minced fresh coriander
  1 teaspoon crumbled leaf marjoram
  1 quart chicken or beef broth (preferably homemade)
  ¾ pound tender young spinach, washed, trimmed of coarse stems and veins, then
       coarsely chopped
  2 tablespoons olive oil
  2 tablespoons cider vinegar
 1½ teaspoons salt (about)
  ¼ teaspoon freshly ground black pepper (about)

Soak the chick-peas overnight in cold water in a large heavy kettle. Next day, bring the peas and their soaking water to a gentle boil, cover, and cook 4 to 5 hours until the chick-peas are very tender. If at any time they seem to be cooking dry, add a cup or so more water. *Note: The peas must be cooked this long because they are unusually hard and must become soft enough to purée easily.*

Meanwhile, stir-fry the garlic and onions in the vegetable oil in a large heavy saucepan 12 to 15 minutes until translucent and lightly browned. Add the potatoes and stir-fry 2 to 3 minutes; add the parsley, coriander, and marjoram and let mellow over low heat 10 to 12 minutes. Pour in the broth, bring all to a gentle simmer, cover, and cook slowly alongside—and as long as—the chick-peas; the potatoes, too, will be puréed.

When the chick-peas are nearing tenderness, stir-fry the spinach in the olive oil in a large heavy skillet set over moderately high heat 2 to 3 minutes until nicely glazed and intensely green; remove from the heat and reserve. When the chick-peas are soft enough to purée, buzz half of them 60 seconds in a food processor fitted with the metal chopping blade, adding just enough kettle liquid to make the purée-ing go more smoothly. If you have no food processor, force the chick-peas through a food mill or fine sieve. Return the puréed chick-peas to the kettle in which they cooked. Now purée the potato mixture, about half of the total amount at a time, by buzzing 30 to 40 seconds in the food processor or by forcing through the food mill or fine sieve. Blend the puréed potato mixture into the chick-pea mixture, add the reserved spinach, cover, and simmer 30 minutes—just until flavors are blended. Stir in the vinegar, then season to taste with salt and pepper. Ladle into soup bowls and serve with a rough country bread.

SHRIMP SOUP
Sopa de Camarão

The name "Shrimp Soup" gives no clue to the complexity of this dish. It's made with fresh tomatoes, onions, garlic, parsley, and coriander, spiked with dry white wine, and warmed with peppers red and black. The place to try it on its own turf is at any of the posh seaside resorts just west of Lisbon—Estoril, for example, Cascais, or Guincho. This is where *Lisboetes* go for a bowl of shrimp soup because they consider Lisbon, sixteen miles inland, too far from the sea for truly fresh seafood.

Makes 6 to 8 servings

2	pounds raw medium shrimp, in the shell
2	quarts water
3	large yellow onions, peeled and coarsely chopped
2	large garlic cloves, peeled and minced
¼	cup olive oil
4	large ripe tomatoes, peeled, cored, seeded, and coarsely chopped
3	tablespoons minced parsley
2	large bay leaves (do not crumble)
¼	cup tomato paste
½	teaspoon freshly ground black pepper
½	teaspoon cayenne pepper
1	cup *vinho verde* or other dry white wine
1	teaspoon salt (about)
¼	cup freshly chopped coriander

Place the shrimp and water in a large heavy saucepan, set over moderate heat, and bring to a simmer; drain at once, reserving both the shrimp and the cooking water. In a second large heavy saucepan, sauté the onions and garlic in the olive oil 5 to 6 minutes until glassily golden; mix in the tomatoes, parsley, bay leaves, tomato paste, black and cayenne peppers; turn heat to low, cover, and simmer 25 minutes. Add the shrimp cooking water and wine and simmer uncovered for 1 hour. Meanwhile, shell and devein the shrimp and set aside.

When the tomato mixture has cooked down by about one third and its flavors are well balanced, add the shrimp and salt to taste and heat about 5 minutes. Ladle into soup plates, sprinkle each portion with freshly chopped coriander, and serve. *Note: The Portuguese way to eat this husky soup is to crumble chunks of country bread into it to bring it to about the consistency of scalloped tomatoes. Try it with* Pão *or* Pão de Forma *(pages 224 and 228) or Italian or French bread.*

CREAM OF SHRIMP SOUP
Creme de Camarão

A more refined shrimp soup than the previous one, this is served at stylish restaurants throughout the Lisbon-Cascais-Estoril-Sintra area.

Makes 6 servings

1	pound raw medium shrimp, in the shell
1½	quarts water
⅔	cup dry white wine
2	medium yellow onions, peeled and chopped
2	medium garlic cloves, peeled and minced
2	tablespoons olive oil
1	tablespoon unsalted butter
2	large ripe tomatoes, peeled, cored, seeded, and coarsely chopped
¼	cup minced parsley
1	large bay leaf (do not crumble)
5	tablespoons tomato paste
¼	teaspoon freshly ground black pepper
¼	teaspoon cayenne pepper
1	teaspoon salt (about)
½	cup heavy cream

Place the shrimp, water, and wine in a large heavy saucepan, set over moderate heat, and bring to a simmer; drain at once, reserving both the shrimp and the cooking liquid. In a second large heavy saucepan, sauté the onions and garlic in the olive oil and butter 5 to 6 minutes until limp and golden; mix in the tomatoes, 2 tablespoons of the parsley, the bay leaf, tomato paste, and black and cayenne peppers. Turn the heat to low, cover, and simmer 25 minutes. Add the shrimp cooking liquid and simmer uncovered for 1 hour. Meanwhile, shell and devein the shrimp and set aside.

When the tomato mixture has cooked down by about one third and its flavors are well balanced, discard the bay leaf, then purée in 2 to 3 batches by buzzing 60 seconds nonstop in an electric blender or food processor fitted with the metal chopping blade or by forcing all through a fine sieve. Add 8 shrimp to the last batch of soup and purée along with it. (If using a sieve, simply mince the 8 shrimp as fine as possible). Return all to the saucepan, add the salt, cream, and reserved whole shrimp, and bring slowly to serving temperature over low heat—this will take about 5 minutes. Taste for salt and add more if needed. Ladle into soup plates, sprinkle with the remaining parsley, and serve.

FISH STEW GUINCHO-STYLE
Caldeirada à Moda de Guincho

Caldeirada, I suppose, might be considered Portugal's bouillabaisse. It is a grand and glorious fish muddle that varies from town to town and depends upon what the fishermen have managed to catch. Usually it contains a fifty-fifty mix of lean and oily fish, such shellfish as clams and mussels, and often squid or octopus as well. This particular *caldeirada,* which is served at half a dozen little beach restaurants along the broad sandy shore at Guincho near Lisbon, is my own favorite. *Note: Because of the brininess of the mussels, clams, and squid, this recipe is not likely to need salt.*

Makes 6 to 8 servings

5	large yellow onions, peeled and coarsely chopped
4	large garlic cloves, peeled and minced
2	large sweet green peppers, cored, seeded, and coarsely chopped
5	tablespoons olive oil
4	large parsley branches
2	large bay leaves (do not crumble)
10	peppercorns
4	large vine-ripened tomatoes, peeled, cored, seeded, and coarsely chopped
5	tablespoons tomato paste
2	cups dry white wine
1	cup water
½	pound squid, cleaned, the body sliced ½-inch thick and the tentacles coarsely chopped
18	small littleneck clams in the shell, scrubbed and purged of grit. (To do this, cover the clams with cold water, add a tablespoon of cornmeal, and let stand at room temperature 20 to 30 minutes.)
2	pounds lean white fish. (Use two kinds—cod, for example, monkfish, hake, flounder or haddock; each fish should be in one piece.)
2	pounds oily fish. (Use two kinds—mackerel, for example, swordfish, tuna; each fish should be in one piece.)
½	pound shrimp in the shell. (If you're fussy, shell and devein the shrimp, but the Portuguese rarely do because the shells add flavor.)
18	mussels in the shell, bearded and scrubbed well
½	teaspoon freshly ground black pepper
⅓	cup freshly chopped fresh coriander, or, if unavailable, minced parsley

In a large heavy kettle set over moderate heat, sauté the onions, garlic, and green peppers in the olive oil 15 minutes; turn heat to low, cover, and steam 20 minutes. Add the parsley, bay leaves, peppercorns, tomatoes, tomato paste, wine, and water and simmer, stirring now and then, 10 minutes; add the squid and clams, cover, and simmer 30 minutes. Now lay the fish in the kettle—don't stir!—also the shrimp and mussels; sprinkle with pepper, cover, and cook gently 15 to 20 minutes, just until the mussels open and the fish flakes. Carefully stir the mixture, breaking the fish into large chunks and bringing the tomato mixture up on top. Ladle into large soup plates, sprinkle with the coriander and serve with crusty chunks of bread. (The Portuguese often crumble their bread into the *caldeirada*.)

CLAMS BULHÃO PATO
Amêijoas Bulhão Pato

Few Portuguese remember the verse of poet Bulhão Pato, but how they love this soupy recipe of his.

Makes 6 to 8 servings

6	dozen uniformly small littleneck clams in the shell, scrubbed and purged of grit. (To do this, cover the clams with cold water, add ¼ cup each salt and cornmeal, and let stand at room temperature 30 minutes.)
1½	cups boiling water
½	cup dry white wine
6	tablespoons fruity olive oil
3	medium-size cloves garlic, peeled and minced
1	cup moderately coarsely chopped fresh coriander
¼	teaspoon freshly ground black pepper

Rinse the clams, drain well and set aside. Combine the boiling water, wine and olive oil in a large, heavy, broad-bottomed kettle and bring to a boil over moderate heat. Ease the clams into the kettle, cover, and steam 5 minutes. Sprinkle with the garlic, coriander, and pepper, re-cover and steam 5 to 10 minutes, just until the clams open. Gently turn the clams several times in the kettle liquid, then serve in large soup plates topped by plenty of the liquid. Accompany with a good chewy bread.

MADEIRA SQUID STEW
Caldeirada de Lulas à Madeirense

I've always been impressed by the Portuguese gift for using spices in savory dishes so subtly that they heighten the end result without identifying themselves. This squid stew, for instance, contains both curry powder and ground ginger, but their presence is undetectable except for a certain "heat." The secret, by the way, of simmering rubbery squid into tender submission is to keep the heat low and the pot covered, and also to add a bit of acid (in this case, both tomatoes and dry white wine).

Makes 6 to 8 servings

- 2 large yellow onions, peeled and coarsely chopped
- 2 large garlic cloves, peeled and minced
- 2 medium sweet red or green peppers, cored, seeded, and cut lengthwise into thin strips
- ¼ cup olive oil
- 1 teaspoon curry powder
- ½ teaspoon ground ginger
- 2 large bay leaves (do not crumble)
- ½ teaspoon salt
- 2 large juicily ripe tomatoes, cored, peeled, seeded, and coarsely chopped
- 2 pounds small squid, cleaned, the bodies sliced ¼-inch thick and the tentacles cut into 1-inch lengths
- 1 cup dry white wine
- 2 large Maine or Eastern potatoes, peeled and cut into 1-inch chunks

In a medium-size heavy kettle set over moderate heat, sauté the onions, garlic, and peppers in the olive oil 5 to 6 minutes until limp; blend in the curry powder and ginger and mellow 1 to 2 minutes, stirring often. Add the bay leaves, salt, and tomatoes, turn the heat to low, cover, and steam 25 minutes. Add the squid and wine, adjust the heat so that the mixture bubbles very gently, cover, and simmer 2½ to 3 hours until the squid is tender. (During the final hour, place a Flame-Tamer under the kettle to keep the liquid just lazing along, not boiling away.) Add the potatoes, raise the heat to moderate (but keep the Flame-Tamer in place) so that the liquid bubbles a little more actively, re-cover, and cook 45 minutes to 1 hour until the potatoes are fork-tender. Check the kettle from time to time to see that it isn't boiling so rapidly that the juices are reducing. Ladle the *caldeirada* into soup plates and serve with chunks of Portuguese, French, or Italian bread, a cold green bean salad, and a gutsy red Portuguese wine such as Dão Grão Vasco or Colares.

FUNCHAL FISH CHOWDER
Sopa de Peixe à Moda de Funchal

What goes into this fish muddle from the island of Madeira depends upon what the fishermen's nets have fetched up. As a general rule, it's best to use a half-and-half mixture of lean and oily fish. This soup, like most, will have a more balanced flavor if you make it one day and serve it the next.

Makes 6 to 8 servings

4	medium yellow onions, peeled and sliced thin
2	large garlic cloves, peeled and minced
3	tablespoons unsalted butter
3	tablespoons olive oil
2	large bay leaves (do not crumble)
¼	cup dry Madeira (Sercial)
3	medium juicily ripe tomatoes, peeled, cored, seeded, and chopped fine
3	medium Maine or Eastern potatoes, peeled and cut into ¼-inch cubes
2	tablespoons minced parsley
4	whole cloves
¼	teaspoon cayenne pepper
2	quarts water
1	pound boned, skinned halibut, hake, haddock, whiting, or cod
1	pound boned, skinned swordfish, bluefish, or mackerel
1	tablespoon salt (about)

GARNISHES:

12	pieces *Pão* (page 224) about 2 inches long, 1½ inches wide, and ½-inch thick, or 12 slices (½-inch thick) French *baguette*
4	tablespoons unsalted butter
½	cup freshly grated Parmesan cheese
3	tablespoons minced parsley

In a large heavy kettle set over moderate heat, stir-fry the onions and garlic in the butter and oil about 15 minutes until limp and lightly browned. Add the bay leaves, wine, tomatoes, potatoes, parsley, cloves, cayenne, and water; cover and simmer slowly 1 hour. Uncover and simmer 2 hours longer or until liquid has cooked down and flavors are concentrated but well balanced. Add the fish, breaking up clumps; simmer 5 minutes only. Cool, cover, and refrigerate until about 20 minutes before serving.

Bring the chowder slowly to serving temperature; remove the bay leaves and add salt to taste. Meanwhile, prepare the garnishes: Lightly brown the bread on both sides in the butter in a large heavy skillet over moderately high heat; drain on paper toweling.

To serve, ladle the chowder into soup plates, float two slices of bread in each, scatter a tablespoon of Parmesan into each portion, and sprinkle with parsley. Pass additional Parmesan, if you like.

FISH CHOWDER IN THE STYLE OF THE AZORES
Sopa de Peixe à Moda dos Açores

Sometimes *lulas* (squid) or *polvo* (octopus) are added to this kettle of fish, although these are usually reserved for *caldeirada* (page 112), a somewhat richer fish stew that brims with both fish and shellfish. *Note: If the fish called for are unavailable, substitute any good local fish, using about equal parts lean and oily varieties.*

Makes 8 servings

4	medium yellow onions, peeled and chopped
3	large garlic cloves, peeled and minced
¼	cup olive oil
¼	cup minced parsley
2	medium bay leaves (do not crumble)
6	large juicily ripe plum tomatoes, peeled and coarsely chopped (reserve juice) or 1 can (1 pound, 12 ounces) water-pack tomatoes (do not drain)
½	pound boned and skinned haddock, cut into 1½-inch chunks
½	pound boned and skinned porgy, cut into 1½-inch chunks
½	pound boned and skinned grouper, cut into 1½-inch chunks
½	pound boned and skinned mackerel, cut into 1½-inch chunks
½	pound boned and skinned shark or swordfish, cut into 1½-inch chunks

½ pound eel, skinned and cut into 1-inch chunks
1 cup rich fish stock or bottled clam juice
⅔ cup dry white wine
3 medium Maine or Eastern potatoes, boiled, peeled, and sliced thin
2 tablespoons cider vinegar
2 teaspoons salt (about)
¼ teaspoon freshly ground black pepper (about)
⅛ teaspoon cayenne pepper (about)

In a large heavy kettle set over moderate heat, sauté the onions and garlic in the oil 5 minutes until they begin to color and turn glassy (do not brown or the mixture will turn bitter). Add the parsley, bay leaves, tomatoes and their juice and simmer uncovered 30 to 35 minutes, stirring occasionally, until flavors mellow and the mixture has thickened to the consistency of pasta sauce. Now add all the fish, pushing the pieces down into the tomato mixture. Pour in the stock and wine, cover, and simmer slowly 30 to 35 minutes until flavors blend nicely. Add the potatoes and vinegar, bring just to serving temperature, then season to taste with salt, and black and cayenne peppers. Ladle into soup plates and serve as a main course with a crisp green salad, tartly dressed, and chunks of a rough country bread such as *Pão* (page 224).

"DRY" SHELLFISH SOUP
Açorda de Mariscos

Although *Açorda de Mariscos* is said to have originated in Ericeira, a small seaside resort some thirty miles north of Lisbon, today nearly every Portuguese restaurant within the sound of the surf serves it. The bread you use for thickening the *açorda* must be a rough country variety—a Portuguese *Pão* or *Pão de Forma,* for example, or stale French or Italian bread. It is also imperative that you use fresh—not dried—coriander. Finally, use a shallow, heavy earthenware or flameproof glass baking dish to serve the *açorda,* heating it first in a very hot oven; otherwise the soup will cool before the eggs broken into it at the last minute have a chance to cook. Serve with *Pão* (page 224) and a clean, crisp, dry white wine such as a Dão, Serradayres, or *vinho verde.*

Makes 6 servings

2½	pounds raw medium shrimp, in the shell
4	quarts rich shellfish stock or 3 quarts cold water plus three 8-ounce bottles clam juice
2	large bay leaves (do not crumble)
3	medium sprigs fresh coriander
3	medium sprigs Italian parsley
¼	cup dry white wine
3	medium yellow onions, peeled and chopped
4	large garlic cloves, peeled and minced
½	cup olive oil
2 to 3	medium fresh chili peppers (depending on how "hot" you like things), washed, trimmed, and minced, or substitute ¼ to ½ teaspoon crushed dried red chili peppers
½	pound day-old Portuguese, Italian, or French bread, broken into 1-inch cubes
½	teaspoon salt (about)
¼	teaspoon freshly ground black pepper (about)
6	large eggs, at room temperature
½	cup coarsely chopped fresh coriander

Shell and devein the shrimp; cover and refrigerate. Pile the shrimp shells in a large heavy kettle, add the shellfish stock, bay leaves, coriander, and parsley sprigs and bring to a simmer over moderate heat. Cover and simmer 1 hour. Line a colander with a dish towel and set it in a very large heat-proof bowl. Pour the kettle liquid and shrimp shells into the colander; then, as soon as the shells have cooled sufficiently to handle, bundle them in the towel and wring out as much liquid as possible. Return all liquid to the kettle, add the wine, set over moderate heat, and simmer uncovered until reduced to 5 cups—about 1 hour.

Meanwhile, stir-fry the onions and 3 cloves of the garlic in ¼ cup of the olive oil in a large heavy skillet over moderate heat 8 to 10 minutes until limp and golden. Mix in the chili peppers and stir-fry 1 to 2 minutes longer. Set off the heat and allow flavors to mellow while the shrimp liquid reduces. Now place the bread chunks in a large mixing bowl, scatter the remaining garlic evenly on top, and drizzle with the remaining ¼ cup olive oil. Toss well and let stand until ready to assemble the *açorda,* tossing again now and then.

When the shrimp liquid has reduced for 45 minutes, set a shallow, heavy 3½- to 4-quart flameproof earthenware or glass casserole in the oven and turn the thermostat to very hot (450°F.); leave the casserole in the oven until you are ready to assemble the *açorda.* As soon as the shrimp liquid has reduced to 5 cups, season to taste with salt and pepper; bring to a rolling boil, drop in the shrimp, and cook about 3 minutes—just until pink. With a slotted spoon, quickly lift half the shrimp to a heated plate and keep hot. Dump the reserved onion mixture into the kettle and stir well. Wasting no time, bring the casserole from the oven and arrange the marinated bread chunks evenly in the bottom. Pour the boiling-hot shrimp mixture on top, then break in the eggs, spacing them as evenly and artfully as possible. Scatter the chopped coriander over all and garnish with the reserved shrimp. Rush the *açorda* to the table. To serve, stir the eggs, shrimp, and coriander down into the mixture and ladle into large heated soup plates.

DRY SOUP OF GARLIC AND FRESH CORIANDER ALENTEJO-STYLE
Açorda à Alentejana

When I first tasted this soup twenty-five years ago, I thought it was horrid. But I've since become a convert, a fan of this frugal bread-thickened broth, seasoned, as one wit put it, with "enough garlic to detonate a bomb." It's the classic soup of the Alentejo Province and its success depends upon the use of absolutely fresh coriander and an intensely fruity olive oil. In farm houses and country villages the bread used to thicken the *açorda* would be one of those rough, yeasty loaves baked in stone or brick ovens. If you don't want to go to the trouble of making a Portuguese bread just for this soup, use day-old French or Italian bread that's good and chewy and full of flavor.

Makes 6 servings

4	large garlic cloves, peeled and quartered
2½	cups fresh coriander leaves (measure loosely packed; you'll need a large bunch)
2	teaspoons kosher or coarse salt
⅓	cup olive oil
6	medium eggs
7	cups boiling water
6	cups day-old Portuguese, French, or Italian bread, cut into 1½-inch chunks (you'll need a loaf 15 to 18 inches long)
½	teaspoon freshly ground black pepper

Using a mortar and pestle, grind the garlic, coriander, and salt to paste. Transfer to a large heat-proof bowl and blend in the olive oil. Break the eggs, slide into the boiling water, and poach 2 minutes; lift to paper toweling to drain; reserve the cooking water, keeping it at a gentle boil. Add the bread to the bowl, sprinkle with pepper, and toss well with the coriander mixture. Now pour in the reserved egg-poaching water (there will be bits of egg white in it, but no matter) and stir gently to mix. Ease the eggs on top of the soup, distributing them evenly; then sprinkle, if you like, with more minced fresh coriander. Serve from the bowl at table, ladling into heated soup plates and topping each portion with a poached egg.

ALENTEJO-STYLE GAZPACHO
Gaspacho à Alentejana

Although the ingredients of this gazpacho are essentially those of the better known Spanish gazpacho, the proportions are quite different. Indeed, this Portuguese gazpacho contains so much bread it qualifies as an *açorda* (dry soup). It's filling, nutritious, and delicious.

Makes 6 servings

2 large garlic cloves, peeled
2 teaspoons kosher or coarse salt
½ teaspoon crumbled leaf oregano
½ teaspoon freshly ground black pepper
2 tablespoons olive oil
3 tablespoons cider vinegar
8 large vine-ripened plum tomatoes, peeled, cored, juiced, and puréed
1 cup diced, seeded, peeled cucumber
⅔ cup coarsely chopped sweet green or red pepper
3 cups 1-inch cubes of day-old Portuguese, French, or Italian bread
2 cups ice water (about)

With a mortar and pestle, crush the garlic, salt, oregano, and black pepper to paste; blend in the olive oil. Transfer to a large bowl, mix in the vinegar, tomatoes, cucumber, and sweet pepper, and let stand at room temperature 30 minutes. Add the bread and toss well. Now, stirring all the while, mix in just enough ice water to give the mixture the consistency of very soft mashed potatoes. Let stand at room temperature 30 minutes, then ladle into soup bowls and serve. Garnish, if you like, with a little finely minced sweet green and/or red pepper.

Meats

Carnes

STEAK PORTUGUESE À LA RITZ HOTEL
Bife à Portuguesa Feito à Moda do Hotel Ritz Lisboa

Most of us have the wrong idea about Steak Portuguese. It's not a slab of beef sloshed with tomato sauce, but a slice of tenderloin topped with slices of *presunto* (Portugal's prosciutto-like ham), then glossed with a clear, tart sauce aromatic of bay leaves, garlic, and shallots. At the Ritz they use beef tenderloin only, but I frankly prefer the more pronounced flavor and less buttery texture of shell steak.

Makes 4 servings

4	tablespoons unsalted butter
2	tablespoons flour
1	cup beef broth (preferably homemade)
1	cup chicken broth (preferably homemade)
3	tablespoons dry white wine
2	tablespoons distilled (white) vinegar
3	garlic cloves, peeled and minced
2	large shallots, peeled and minced
4	large bay leaves (do not crumble)
4	slices beef tenderloin or 4 shell steaks, cut ¾ inch thick
½	teaspoon freshly ground black pepper
¼	teaspoon salt
3	tablespoons olive oil or vegetable oil
8	tissue-thin slices prosciutto

In a small heavy saucepan set over moderate heat, melt 2 tablespoons of the butter, blend in the flour to make a smooth paste, then add the beef broth and cook, stirring constantly, 3 to 5 minutes until thickened and smooth. Add the chicken broth, wine, vinegar, garlic, shallots, and bay leaves and simmer slowly, uncovered, 20 to 25 minutes until reduced to the consistency of a thin gravy; add the remaining 2 tablespoons of butter and set at the back of the stove to keep warm.

Rub each steak on both sides with pepper and salt and let stand at room temperature 30 minutes. Heat the oil in a very large heavy skillet over moderately high heat 1 to 2 minutes until ripples appear on the skillet bottom. Add the steaks and brown 1½ to 2 minutes, turn, top each steak with 2 slices of prosciutto, overlapping them as needed so they don't lop over the sides of the steak, and brown 1½ to 2 minutes longer. Meanwhile, bring the reserved sauce to a simmer. *Note: The browning times given here are for rare steak; if you like yours medium-rare, allow 2½ to 3 minutes per side; if medium, about 4 minutes per side. I don't recommend that you cook the steaks beyond medium because they will lose both tenderness and juiciness.*

Transfer the steaks to heated plates and drizzle the sauce on top, dividing the total amount evenly. The favorite Portuguese accompaniment would be *Batatas Fritas* or *Batatas Palhas* (potato chips or straw potatoes; pages 208 and 209). A mellow red wine would be in order—Dão Grão Vasco, for example, Colares, or Ferreira Barca Velha.

GRILLED SKEWERS OF BEEF WITH GARLIC AND BAY LEAVES
Espetada

In the old days when men and women harvested their crops in the mountains of Madeira (to my mind, earth's most idyllic island), they skewered chunks of beef on green bay laurel sticks and grilled them over glowing coals. Today many of the island's little inns, particularly those shelved in the hills above Funchal, make a specialty of *espetada* and bring sizzling iron skewers of steak to your table. The skewers are hung from little racks, then plates of fresh-baked bread shoved directly underneath to catch every savory dripping. I include directions here for broiling *espetada* indoors and out.

Makes 6 servings

3	pounds beef tenderloin, cut into 1-inch cubes
4	large garlic cloves, peeled and slivered fine
4	large bay leaves, crumbled
⅓	cup melted unsalted butter
1	tablespoon olive oil
½	teaspoon freshly ground black pepper
½	teaspoon salt

Place all the ingredients in a shallow baking dish and toss well. Let stand at room temperature 2 hours, tossing the mixture occasionally. Or, if you prefer, marinate 24 hours in the refrigerator, then let stand 2 hours at room temperature; the flavor will be richer. Thread the beef on 6 long metal skewers, dividing the total amount evenly; heat the marinade 2 to 3 minutes, brush lightly over the *espetada,* then broil as follows:

In the broiler: Lay the skewers on a lightly greased broiler pan, place 5 to 6 inches from the heat, then broil, turning frequently, about 6 minutes for very rare, 8 minutes for rare, and 10 for medium rare. Brush frequently with the remaining marinade. Serve with crusty bread chunks for sopping up the drippings and any remaining marinade (heat it before serving).

Over charcoal: Pour the remaining marinade into a small heavy saucepan and set at the edge of a grill, adjusted so that it is about 5 inches above white-hot coals. Lay the skewered beef on the grill and broil, turning often, about 5 minutes for very rare, 7 minutes for rare, and 9 to 10 for medium rare. Ladle a little of the hot marinade over each portion, then pass the balance along with chunks of *Pão* or *Pão de Forma* (pages 224 and 228) or with chunks of French or Italian bread.

POT ROAST TERCEIRA ISLAND-STYLE
Alcatra

Terceira, the one Azorean island linked directly to the United States by air, lies just four hours (and about a hundred years) east of Boston. It's a green volcanic sliver afloat in the mid-Atlantic, an outsize nosegay of hydrangeas and Scotch broom. Its capital city, Angra do Heroísmo, is a mini-Rio set around a horseshoe harbor complete with scaled-down "Sugar Loaf" and sidewalks of squiggly mosaics. Island cooking is straightforward, based upon whatever is available. This pot roast, for example, might be made with beef. Then again, it might be made with mutton or lamb or even pork. It's name—*alcatra*—comes from *alcatre,* the Portuguese word for rump, the preferred cut of meat to pot-roast.

Makes 6 to 8 servings

¼ pound lean slab bacon, cut into small dice
2 tablespoons vegetable oil
4 pounds boned and rolled beef rump (or leg of mutton or fresh ham)
2 large yellow onions, peeled and sliced thin
3 large garlic cloves, peeled and minced
2 large bay leaves (do not crumble)
12 peppercorns
3 whole cloves
3 tablespoons tomato paste
4 cups dry white wine
½ teaspoon salt (about)

Preheat the oven to hot (400°F.). Sauté the bacon in the vegetable oil in a large heavy kettle over moderately low heat 5 to 6 minutes until all drippings cook out and only crisp brown bits remain; lift to paper toweling to drain with a slotted spoon. In the drippings, brown the beef well on all sides over moderately high heat. Lift the beef from the kettle for the time being. Dump the onions, garlic, bay leaves, peppercorns, and cloves into the kettle and sauté, stirring often over moderate heat, 8 to 10 minutes until touched with brown. Blend in the tomato paste, turn the heat down low, cover, and steam 20 minutes. Scoop half the tomato mixture into a small heat-proof bowl, return the beef and bacon to the kettle, then spoon the tomato mixture on top. Add the wine and salt and bring to a simmer.

Cover and bake 2 hours; uncover, and turn the beef over in the kettle liquid. Lower the oven temperature to moderately slow (325°F.), and bake uncovered about 1 hour longer or until tender and browned on top. *Note: If at any point the kettle should threaten to boil dry, add a little water or additional dry white wine.* Slice the meat thin and serve with boiled or roasted potatoes and a green vegetable. As for wine, the islanders would drink a rough *tinto* (red wine), so any substantial table red would be appropriate, particularly a Portuguese Dão Grão Vasco or Colares.

PORTUGUESE BOILED DINNER
Cozido à Portuguesa

A robust one-dish dinner brimming with beef, chicken, pork, and sausages as well as with a variety of vegetables. It's particularly popular in the northerly Minho and Trás-os-Montes provinces, where winters can be cruel. Portuguese women let the kettle bubble away the better part of the day, adding whatever snippets of meat and vegetables they have handy. A trip to the local charcuterie is a must, however—for *chouriço* (garlicky sausage, which in the Trás-os-Montes often contains turnips and flour in addition to pork), blood sausage, and *salpicão* (cured smoked pork loin). In order to keep their sausages soft and fresh, country cooks cover them with olive oil. Because of the unavailability here of the wonderful Portuguese sausages, I've substituted U.S. varieties.

Makes 8 servings

1	pound eye round of beef, in one piece
1½	pounds boneless pork loin, in one piece
2½	pound broiler-fryer, in one piece
½	pound sweet Italian sausages (leave whole)
½	pound hot Italian sausages (leave whole)
½	pound *chouriço* or pepperoni (leave whole)
¼	pound slab bacon, in one piece
4	large parsley branches
2	large bay leaves (do not crumble)
12	peppercorns
2	quarts water
4	large turnips, peeled and cut into 1½-inch chunks
3	large carrots, peeled and sliced ¼-inch thick
4	large potatoes, peeled, halved crosswise, then each half quartered lengthwise
1	small cabbage, trimmed and cut into slim wedges (do not remove the core)
½	pound blood sausages (leave whole), each pricked several times with a needle to prevent the skins from bursting as the sausages cook
1	recipe *Arroz à Portuguesa* (Portuguese Rice; page 214)
	Salt, if needed, to taste

Place the beef, pork, chicken, sweet and hot Italian sausages, *chouriço*, bacon, parsley, bay leaves, peppercorns, and water in a very large heavy kettle and bring to a simmer over moderately high heat. Adjust the heat so that the water bubbles gently, cover, and simmer 1½ hours. Remove all meats from the kettle and reserve; remove and discard the parsley and bay leaves. Add the turnips, carrots, and potatoes, re-cover, and simmer 20 minutes; add the cabbage and blood sausages, re-cover, and simmer 30 minutes.

Meanwhile, prepare the *Arroz à Portuguesa* as directed. Also, slice the beef and pork loin thin, disjoint the chicken, and cut the bacon into small dice. Leave the sausages whole, or if very large, cut in half. In a small heavy skillet set over moderate heat, brown the diced bacon 5 to 6 minutes, stirring constantly, until most of the drippings have cooked out and only crisp brown bits remain; reserve both the bacon bits and the drippings. About 5 minutes before the cabbage is done, return the beef, pork, chicken, and all the sausages to the kettle, just laying them on top; simmer covered for a final 5 minutes.

To serve, ladle off the broth in the kettle, add salt to taste, then serve with sturdy chunks of *Broa* (page 239). Once that course is finished, mound the rice into a large shallow earthenware casserole and drizzle with the reserved bacon drippings; cut 5 thin slices each of pepperoni and sweet and hot Italian sausages, and use to decorate the top of the rice; scatter the bacon bits over all. Now arrange the remaining sausages, beef, pork, chicken, and all vegetables as artfully as possible in a second large shallow earthenware dish. Present all at table and let guests help themselves.

VEAL CUTLETS BEIRA ALTA-STYLE
Costeletas de Vitela à Maneira da Beira Alta

In Portugal, what tends to masquerade as veal is baby beef, whose flesh has already turned red because the animal has gone off mother's milk. Still, it's possible to find a choice piece of veal in Portugal. I once had it prepared this way at the snug little Pousada de Santa Bárbara overlooking the Serra da Estrêla, which, at 6,532 feet, is the highest mountain range in Portugal.

Makes 4 servings

1½   pounds veal scallopini, pounded moderately thin
3   large garlic cloves, peeled and quartered lengthwise
½   teaspoon salt
½   teaspoon freshly ground black pepper
1   cup *vinho verde* or other
        dry white wine
2   large bay leaves (do not crumble)
2   large eggs, lightly beaten with 2 tablespoons *vinho verde* or other
        dry white wine
1½   cups fine dry bread crumbs
4   tablespoons lard (hog lard, not vegetable shortening)
2   tablespoons minced parsley

Rub the pieces of veal on both sides with garlic, then with salt and pepper. Place in a large shallow baking dish, drop in the garlic, pour the wine evenly over all, then add the bay leaves. Cover and refrigerate several hours.

When ready to cook, dip the veal first into the egg mixture, then in the crumbs to coat lightly; let the pieces air-dry for 20 minutes on a wire rack (this is to make the crumb coating stick). Heat the lard in a large heavy skillet over moderately high heat until ripples appear on the skillet bottom; brown the veal in 2 to 3 batches, allowing about 3 minutes per side; as the veal is browned, transfer to a shallow baking pan lined with paper toweling and set uncovered in a very slow oven (275°F.) to keep warm while you fry the balance. Transfer to a warm platter, sprinkle with parsley, and serve.

LIVER WITH GARLIC, BAY LEAVES AND DRY WHITE WINE
Iscas

This Lisbon classic is usually made with pork liver, and if you like it, by all means use it, but increase the cooking time as needed—2 to 3 minutes per side—so that the liver is well done. I prefer calf's liver, not only because the flavor is more delicate, but also because it can be served rare or pink. Some Lisbon cooks fry the garlic with which the liver marinates along with the liver, but I like the dish better if the garlic is used only in the marinade. In Lisbon the liver is cooked in a *frigideira* (earthenware skillet), but any heavy skillet will do. The traditional way to serve *Iscas* is wreathed with sliced potatoes—either fried or boiled. *Note: Because of the tartness of the marinade and the saltiness of the bacon, you are not likely to need any salt in this recipe.*

Makes 2 (generous) to 4 servings

1	pound calf's liver, sliced very thin
4	large garlic cloves, peeled and sliced very thin
2	large bay leaves, crumbled
½	cup dry white wine mixed with 1 tablespoon white (distilled) vinegar
4	slices bacon, snipped crosswise into julienne strips
1	tablespoon olive oil
⅛	teaspoon freshly ground pepper
1	tablespoon minced parsley

Lay half the liver, one layer deep, in a 9 × 9 × 2-inch baking dish; sprinkle with half the garlic and bay leaves, then pour in half the wine mixture; add the remaining liver, garlic, bay leaves, and wine. Cover and chill 1 hour.

Fry the bacon in the olive oil in a very large heavy skillet set over moderate heat 5 to 6 minutes until browned and crisp; remove with a slotted spoon to paper toweling to drain. Raise the heat to moderately high, then brown the liver, freed of the garlic and bay leaves, in two batches, allowing just 1 to 1½ minutes per side per piece. Lift the liver to a hot platter, sprinkle with pepper, and keep warm. Pour all drippings from the skillet, strain the marinade, pour into the skillet, add the reserved bacon, and boil rapidly 1 to 1½ minutes until the liquid is reduced to a thin glaze. Pour over the liver, sprinkle with parsley, and surround, if you like, with sliced fried or boiled potatoes.

LEG OF BABY GOAT ROASTED THE BEIRA ALTA WAY
Perna de Cabrito à Moda da Beira Alta

Portugal's highest mountain range, the Serra da Estrêla (Mountains of the Star), is located in the green, rumpled Beira Alta Province. Goats graze its slopes, as do lambs, which provide both milk and meat. Because *cabrito* is difficult to find here, I have substituted lamb. The Portuguese like their meats well-done, but if you prefer yours pink, as I do, roast the lamb for ¾ to 1 hour only after the initial searing.

Makes 6 to 8 servings

	A leg of lamb weighing about 7 pounds
3	large garlic cloves, peeled and quartered
1	large bay leaf, crumbled
1	teaspoon kosher or coarse salt
1	tablespoon paprika (preferably the Hungarian sweet rose paprika)
½	teaspoon freshly ground black pepper
2	tablespoons olive oil
4	large Idaho potatoes, peeled, halved crosswise, then each half quartered lengthwise
4	large yellow onions, peeled and quartered
1	cup *vinho verde* or other dry white wine

Trim excess fat from the lamb; set lamb aside. Using a mortar and pestle, grind the garlic, bay leaf, salt, paprika, pepper, and 1 tablespoon of the oil to paste; blend in the remaining tablespoon of oil and rub the paste all over the lamb. Place in a large shallow roasting pan and let stand 1 hour at room temperature.

Twenty minutes before you're ready to roast the lamb, preheat the oven to very hot (450°F.). Roast the lamb uncovered for 20 minutes; reduce the oven heat to moderate (350°F.), add the potatoes and onions to the roasting pan, pour the wine over the lamb, and roast uncovered 1½ hours, stirring the vegetables every half hour and basting the lamb with the pan drippings. Let stand at room temperature 20 minutes before serving. Transfer the leg to a large platter, wreathe with the vegetables, and carve at table. Pass the pan drippings in a heated sauceboat.

BRAISED KID OR LAMB IN RED WINE SAUCE
Cabrito à Serrana

This is my interpretation of a wonderful *cabrito* stew I enjoyed recently at the Portucale restaurant in Porto. I have substituted lamb for kid.

Makes 8 servings

4	pounds boned lean lamb shoulder, cut into 1- to 1½-inch cubes
2	teaspoons salt (about)
½	teaspoon freshly ground black pepper (about)
1	cup unsifted all-purpose flour
6	tablespoons olive oil
2	tablespoons corn or vegetable oil
3	large garlic cloves, peeled and minced
4	medium yellow onions, peeled and coarsely chopped
2	medium carrots, peeled and coarsely chopped
1	medium sweet red pepper, cored, seeded, and coarsely chopped
2	tablespoons paprika
½	teaspoon cayenne pepper
2	large bay leaves (do not crumble)
1½	teaspoons crumbled leaf marjoram
½	teaspoon ground cumin
¼	pound prosciutto (in one piece), trimmed of fat and cut into ½-inch cubes
3	cups beef broth
2	cups robust dry red wine

Sprinkle the cubed lamb with salt and pepper and toss well; dredge in the flour. Heat 4 tablespoons of the olive oil and 1 tablespoon of the corn oil in a large heavy kettle over moderate heat 1 to 2 minutes until ripples show in the oil. Add a third of the lamb and brown well on all sides; transfer to a large heat-proof bowl. Add another third of the lamb, 1 tablespoon each of the olive and corn oil, and brown as before; transfer to bowl. Add the remaining tablespoon of olive oil and the rest of the lamb to the kettle and brown as before; transfer to bowl. Add the garlic, onions, carrots, and red pepper to the kettle and sauté in the drippings, stirring often, 10 to 12 minutes over moderate heat until the onions are limp and lightly browned. Return the lamb to the kettle along with any juices accumulated in the bowl, sprinkle in the paprika and cayenne, and toss lightly. Add the bay leaves, marjoram, and cumin, and mellow 2 to 3 minutes over moderate heat. Add the prosciutto, broth, and wine and bring to a simmer. Adjust the heat so that the mixture bubbles gently, cover, and simmer 2 to 2½ hours until the lamb is fork-tender. Taste for salt and pepper. Serve with fluffy boiled rice.

MUTTON STEW POUSADA DO INFANTE-STYLE
Carneiro Estufado à Moda da Pousada do Infante

In my thirty years of visiting Portugal, I've yet to snare a room at this cozy *pousada* set atop a sea cliff at Sagres in the southwestern corner of the Algarve. I have eaten there many times, however (the *pousada*'s kitchen is outstanding), and the dish I shall always remember best is the one I ordered on my very first *pousada* visit. If you want your stew to taste properly Portuguese, you should use mutton. If, however, you dislike mutton's gamy flavor, substitute lamb. *Note: In order for the meat to marinate sufficiently, you should begin this recipe the day before you plan to serve it.*

Makes 6 to 8 servings

2	large garlic cloves, peeled and quartered
1	teaspoon kosher or coarse salt
1	tablespoon paprika
¼	teaspoon cayenne pepper
	Juice of 1 large lemon
3	tablespoons olive oil
4	pounds boneless lean mutton or lamb shoulder, cut into 1½-inch cubes
2	ounces lean slab bacon, cut into ¼-inch dice
2	medium yellow onions, peeled and chopped
3	large bay leaves (do not crumble)
4	tablespoons minced fresh mint
1	tablespoon minced parsley
¾	cup dry red wine
1	cup water
½	teaspoon freshly ground black pepper
1	teaspoon salt (about)

Using a mortar and pestle, pound the garlic, kosher salt, paprika, and cayenne pepper to paste; blend in the lemon juice and 1 tablespoon of the oil. Rub the pieces of mutton well all over with the garlic paste, place in a large shallow bowl, cover, and refrigerate overnight.

When ready to begin cooking the stew, fry the bacon in the remaining oil in a large heavy kettle over moderately low heat 5 to 6 minutes until most of the drippings cook out and only crisp brown bits remain; with a slotted spoon, lift the bacon bits to paper toweling to drain. Brown the mutton in batches in the drippings over high heat, allowing about 5 minutes for each batch; as the meat browns, lift it with a slotted spoon to a large heat-proof bowl and reserve. Sauté the onions in the drippings 8 to 10 minutes over moderate heat until touched with brown, add the bay leaves, turn heat to low, cover, and steam 20 minutes. Add the mutton along with any juices that have accumulated in the bottom of the bowl, 3 tablespoons of the mint, the parsley, wine, water, black pepper, and salt. Bring to a simmer, adjust the heat so that the kettle liquid bubbles gently, then cover and cook 2 to 2½ hours until the mutton is fork-tender. (Lamb will take only 1½ to 2 hours.) *Note: This stew, like most, will be even better if you cool it, refrigerate it overnight, then bring slowly to serving temperature.*

Just before serving, stir in the reserved bacon bits and the remaining tablespoon of mint. Taste for salt and add more if needed. Serve hot with boiled potatoes and/or rice (the Portuguese like to serve both at the same meal), boiled carrots or turnips, lightly buttered, and of course, chunks of husky Portuguese bread. For wine, a sturdy table red such as Dão Grão Vasco or Colares would be best.

ROAST LOIN OF PORK
Lombo de Porco Assado

You should begin this recipe two days before you plan to serve it because the pork must marinate thoroughly before it is roasted.

Makes 6 servings

> 3 medium garlic cloves, peeled and sliced
> 1 teaspoon crumbled leaf marjoram
> 1 teaspoon paprika
> 1 tablespoon kosher or coarse salt
> 1 large bay leaf, crumbled fine
> ¼ teaspoon cayenne pepper
> ¼ teaspoon freshly ground black pepper
> 4 pound center-cut, bone-in pork loin
> 1 bottle (750 ml) *vinho verde* or other dry white wine

Using a mortar and pestle, mash the garlic, marjoram, paprika, salt, bay leaf, cayenne, and black pepper to a paste. Rub all over the loin of pork; then place the pork in a large shallow bowl (preferably nonmetallic), and pour in the wine. *Note: Wash your hands carefully after handling the paste because the hot pepper in it can irritate your skin. And by no means touch your face or eyes until after you've washed your hands.* Turn the pork in the wine several times, then cover, and marinate in the refrigerator for 48 hours, turning the pork several times each day.

Bring the pork from the refrigerator and let stand on the counter, still in the marinade, for 30 minutes. Meanwhile, preheat the oven to very hot (500°F.). Place the pork fat-side up on a rack in a large roasting pan and roast uncovered for 20 minutes. Lower the oven temperature to moderate (350°F.) and roast the pork about 2 hours longer or until a meat thermometer, inserted in the center of the meat and not touching bone, registers 160°F. As the pork roasts, baste several times using the marinade during the first hour or so, then pan drippings for the final hour. Remove the pork from the oven and let stand on the counter 20 minutes before serving to allow the juices to settle. Accompany with *Batatas com Coentro* (page 210) or boiled rice and a tossed salad of crisp greens.

PORK WITH CLAMS ALENTEJO-STYLE
Porco à Alentejana

This unseemly combination of pork and clams may sound like a new low in surf 'n' turf dinners, but it is in fact a Portuguese classic—and altogether delicious. *Note: Because the pork must marinate overnight, you should begin this recipe the day before you plan to serve it.*

Makes 6 servings

2½ pounds boneless pork loin, cut into 1-inch cubes
2 tablespoons *Massa de Pimentão* (page 90) or, if you prefer, a paste made of 1 peeled and crushed garlic clove, 1 teaspoon kosher salt, 1 tablespoon paprika (preferably the Hungarian sweet rose paprika), and 1 tablespoon olive oil
1 cup dry white wine
2 large bay leaves, crumbled
2 tablespoons olive oil
2 tablespoons lard (hog lard, not vegetable shortening)
1 large yellow onion, peeled and coarsely chopped
1 large garlic clove, peeled and minced
2 tablespoons tomato paste
18 small littleneck clams in the shell, scrubbed well and purged of grit. (To do this, cover the clams with cold water, add 1 tablespoon cornmeal, let stand at room temperature 20 to 30 minutes, then drain well.)
¼ teaspoon salt (about)
¼ teaspoon freshly ground black pepper (about)

Rub the pieces of pork well all over with the *Massa de Pimentão* and place in a large, shallow nonmetallic bowl; add the wine and bay leaves, cover, and marinate about 24 hours, turning the pork occasionally in the wine.

Next day, heat the olive oil and lard in a large heavy kettle over high heat until ripples appear on the kettle bottom—the fat should *almost* smoke. Lift the pork from the marinade (save the marinade to add to the kettle later) and brown in the three batches, transferring pieces to a large heat-proof bowl as they brown. When all the pork is brown, dump the onion and garlic into the kettle, lower the heat to moderate, and stir-fry 3 to 4 minutes until limp and golden. Turn the heat to low, cover the kettle, and steam the onion and garlic 20 minutes. Blend in the tomato paste and reserved wine marinade, return the pork to the kettle, adjust the heat so that the wine mixture barely bubbles, then cover and cook 1½ hours until the pork is fork-tender. Now bring the kettle liquid to a gentle boil, lay the clams on top of the pork, distributing them as evenly as possible, re-cover, and cook about 30 minutes—just until the clams open, spilling their juices.

Season to taste with salt and pepper, ladle into large soup plates, and serve with chunks of chewy Portuguese bread (*Pão* or *Pão de Centeio;* pages 224 and 236) and a crisp green salad, sharply dressed. To accompany, open a rich, round Portuguese red wine such as Dão Grão Vasco or Ferreira Barca Velha, if you are lucky enough to find a bottle of it.

PORK WITH WINE AND GARLIC
Carne de Vinho e Alhos

This Madeira specialty, now popular all over mainland Portugal, demonstrates the unusual Portuguese method of boiling meat *before* browning it. It's a procedure alien to Americans who are accustomed to browning the meat first and then cooking it in liquid. But the Portuguese reverse technique works equally well. *Note: The pork is first marinated for 2 or 3 days.*

Makes 6 servings

3	pounds boned pork loin, trimmed of excess fat and sliced ½-inch thick
1	bottle (750 ml) *vinho verde* or other dry white wine
1	cup cider vinegar
4	large bay leaves (do not crumble)
½	teaspoon crumbled leaf marjoram
6	whole cloves
¼	teaspoon salt
¼	teaspoon freshly ground black pepper
3	large garlic cloves, peeled and crushed
1	long slim loaf of French or Italian bread, sliced about 1-inch thick
4	tablespoons olive oil
4	tablespoons unsalted butter

GARNISHES:

1	medium navel orange, sliced thin (rind and all)
4 or 5	sprigs watercress

Layer the pork in a large ceramic bowl; add the wine, vinegar, bay leaves, marjoram, cloves, salt, pepper, and garlic. Cover and marinate in the refrigerator 2 to 3 days, turning the pork often in the marinade.

When ready to cook the pork, transfer it to a large heavy skillet (not iron), add the marinade, cover, and simmer over low heat ½ hour; drain the pork on paper toweling. Quickly moisten the bread slices by touching each side to the surface of the hot marinade; spread on paper toweling and let dry. Raise the heat under the marinade so that it bubbles gently, and boil uncovered to reduce while you proceed with the recipe.

In a second large heavy skillet, brown each pork slice lightly on both sides in 2 tablespoons each olive oil and butter over moderately high heat. *Note: You may think that these cooked pork slices will not brown, but they will—nicely.* Remove to a heated plate and keep warm.

Quickly brown the bread on both sides in the skillet drippings, adding more oil and butter as needed. Drain on paper toweling.

To serve, arrange the slices of bread on a platter, top with overlapping slices of pork, then spoon some of the reduced marinade on top. Garnish with orange slices and watercress. Pour the remaining marinade into a sauceboat and pass separately.

PORK CHOPS ALENTEJO-STYLE
Costeletas de Porco à Alentejana

Pork is the preferred meat of the vast Alentejo Province east and south of Lisbon—which is understandable, as the hogs here feed upon chestnuts and acorns from the cork oaks. Because of the danger of trichinosis in this country (not a problem in Portugal), I've altered the recipe somewhat so that the pork cooks thoroughly. The flavor, however, remains unchanged and purely Portuguese. *Note: You must begin this recipe the day before you serve it because the pork chops are first left to marinate for 24 hours.*

Makes 6 servings

6   loin pork chops, cut 1-inch thick (about 3 pounds)
4   teaspoons *Massa de Pimentão* (page 90) or 2 tablespoons paprika (preferably the Hungarian sweet rose paprika)
2   large garlic cloves, peeled and crushed
¼   teaspoon freshly ground black pepper
2   cups dry white wine (preferably *vinho verde*)
2   tablespoons olive oil
1   tablespoon lard (hog lard, not vegetable shortening)
    Salt, if needed, to taste

Rub the pork chops well on both sides with a mixture of the *Massa de Pimentão*, garlic, and pepper; place in a large shallow bowl, pour in the wine, cover, and refrigerate 24 hours, turning the chops in the wine several times. When ready to cook, heat the olive oil and lard in a very large heavy skillet over high heat almost to the smoking point. Add the pork chops and brown 8 to 10 minutes, turn, and brown the flip side 8 to 10 minutes. Meanwhile, place the marinade in a small shallow pan and boil uncovered until reduced by about three fourths and the consistency of a medium gravy. Add the reduced marinade to the chops, turn heat very low, cover, and cook 10 minutes. Taste for salt. Serve with rice.

CHUNKS OF PORK WITH PICKLED VEGETABLES
Rojões à Minhota

Rojões is what the people of the northerly Minho Province call pork stew meat, which in these parts is most likely to be browned, reddened with paprika, then simmered in red wine until falling-apart tender. This particular recipe comes from the chef of one of my favorite *pousadas,* the Pousada de Santa Maria da Oliveira (Inn of Saint Mary of the Olive Tree), or as it is more simply known, Pousada da Oliveira. It's located in one of my favorite Portuguese towns—Guimarães, hidden in green hills some forty miles northeast of Porto. This flower-splashed, essentially medieval town is known everywhere today as The Cradle of Portugal, because it was here, early in the twelfth century, that Portugal splintered off from Spain. Guimarães deserves a visit and the *pousada*'s lusty *Rojões à Minhota* certainly deserves a try.

Makes 6 servings

3	pounds lean boneless pork shoulder, cut into 1-inch cubes
4	tablespoons olive oil
2	large garlic cloves, peeled and minced
2	tablespoons paprika (preferably the Hungarian sweet rose paprika)
2	large bay leaves (do not crumble)
½	teaspoon freshly ground black pepper
1	cup dry red wine such as a *vinho verde tinto* (red "green wine") or Dão
½	teaspoon salt
1½	cups mixed pickled vegetables (carrots, cauliflower, green beans, etc.; you can buy these by the jar in fine food shops)

Brown the pork in 2 to 3 batches in the olive oil in a large heavy kettle over moderately high heat, allowing 10 to 12 minutes per batch; as the pork browns, lift it with a slotted spoon to a heat-proof bowl. When all the pork is brown, drain all but 1 tablespoon of drippings from the kettle; return the pork to the kettle, add the garlic, paprika, bay leaves, and pepper, and mellow over moderate heat 5 minutes, stirring occasionally. Add the wine, bring to a simmer, adjust the heat so that the wine barely bubbles, cover, and simmer 1 to 1½ hours until the pork is fork-tender. Season to taste with salt. Ladle the pork into a large deep platter, spoon some of the kettle liquid on top, then wreathe with the pickled vegetables. Serve with boiled or roasted potatoes and *vinho verde tinto* or Dão.

WHITE BEANS, PORK AND SAUSAGE TRÁS-OS-MONTES-STYLE
Feijoada Branca à Transmontana

Feijoada, to most of us, is a lusty Brazilian black-bean stew brimming with sausages, tongue, and other cuts of pork. The Portuguese make *feijoada,* too, especially those living in the northeastern corner of the country, but they use dried white beans instead of black and the highly prized local charcuterie, which includes such popular items as pig's ears and smoked trotters. I've had to substitute pork cuts easily available here, but the end result is superb. *Note: Because of the saltiness of the ham and sausages, you're not likely to need additional salt in this recipe.*

Makes 6 to 8 servings

1	pound dried great northern beans or large lima beans, washed and sorted
6	cups cold water
4	large yellow onions, peeled and chopped
4	medium carrots, peeled and sliced ¼-inch thick
3	large garlic cloves, peeled and minced
2	tablespoons robust olive oil
1	tablespoon lard (hog lard, not vegetable shortening)
¼	pound smoked ham, in one piece
¼	pound prosciutto, in one piece
¼	pound sweet Italian sausage (leave whole)
¼	pound hot Italian sausage (leave whole)
¼	pound pepperoni, in one piece
3	large parsley branches
2	large bay leaves (do not crumble)
2	large ripe tomatoes, peeled, cored, juiced, and coarsely chopped
½	teaspoon white pepper
¼	teaspoon freshly ground black pepper
¼	teaspoon cayenne pepper

Soak the beans overnight in the water. Next day, sauté the onions, carrots, and garlic in the oil and lard in a large heavy kettle set over moderate heat 12 to 15 minutes until limp and golden; turn heat to low, cover kettle, and allow all to steam 20 minutes. Add the beans and their soaking water, the ham, prosciutto, all three sausages, the parsley, bay leaves, and tomatoes; bring to a simmer, adjust the heat so the mixture bubbles gently, then cover and simmer ¾ to 1 hour until the beans are firm-tender. Discard the bay leaves and parsley. Remove the ham, prosciutto, and all sausages; cut the ham and prosciutto into small bite-size pieces and slice each of the sausages ¼-inch thick; return all to the kettle. Add the white pepper, black pepper, and cayenne, and simmer uncovered over low heat about 20 minutes, stirring from time to time, until almost all water is absorbed by the beans. *Note: If the mixture seems in danger of scorching, add a little water.* Ladle into soup plates and serve with sturdy chunks of Portuguese bread and a salad of crisp greens, tartly dressed.

PORK AND BEEF WITH BREAD AND GARLIC
Migas à Alentejana

In the Alentejo, where this filling dish is popular, cooks bounce the pork in and out of a sizzling skillet, the aim being merely to brown it well. Here, because trichinosis is a problem, I've altered the recipe somewhat so that the pork can be cooked thoroughly. It's important that the cuts of beef and pork be naturally tender ones because the *migas* must cook quickly. It is not a stew. *Note: If you don't want to go to the trouble of making the* Massa de Pimentão, *mix together 3 tablespoons sweet paprika, 2 crushed garlic cloves, 1 teaspoon kosher or coarse salt, and 2 tablespoons olive oil. Rub this mixture over the pork and beef.*

Makes 6 servings

¾	pound boneless pork loin, cut into 1-inch cubes
1¼	pounds rib eye of beef, cut into 1-inch cubes
4	tablespoons *Massa de Pimentão* (page 90)
¼	pound slab bacon, cut into small dice
2	tablespoons olive oil
3	large garlic cloves, peeled and minced
5	cups boiling water (about)
1	pound *Pão* (page 224) or day-old French or Italian bread, cut into 1-inch chunks
¼	teaspoon freshly ground black pepper
	Salt, if needed, to taste

Place the pork in one bowl, the beef in a second bowl, then add 2 tablespoons *Massa de Pimentão* to each; mix well with your hands until both the beef and pork are well coated; cover each bowl and refrigerate overnight. About 40 minutes before serving, bring the bowls out and let stand on the counter.

In a large heavy skillet set over moderate heat, render the bacon about 20 minutes until all the drippings have cooked out and only crisp brown bits remain; with a slotted spoon, lift the browned bits to paper toweling to drain, and reserve. Now pour off all drippings and reserve. Return 1 tablespoon of the drippings to the skillet and add 1 tablespoon of them to a large heavy kettle; now add 1 tablespoon olive oil to each. Set the skillet and kettle over moderately high heat and when ripples show in the oil, dump the beef into the skillet and the pork into the kettle. Stir-fry each 5 to 6 minutes until the cubes are nicely browned on all sides. Transfer the beef to a heat-proof bowl and keep warm. Add the garlic to the skillet, cover, and let mellow over lowest heat while you cook the pork. Pour 1 cup of the boiling water into the kettle, cover, and simmer the pork 10 to 15 minutes, just until cooked through. With a slotted spoon, lift the pork from the kettle and add to the bowl of beef; toss lightly.

Pour 1 cup of the boiling water into the skillet, set over high heat, and stir 1 to 2 minutes, scraping browned bits up from bottom; transfer this mixture into the kettle, along with the reserved bacon and bacon drippings. Now dump the bread cubes into the kettle and toss all together well. Gradually pour in enough of the remaining boiling water, stirring all the while, until the bread has the consistency of a moist stuffing. Add the pepper and, if needed, salt. Beat briskly with a wooden spoon until light.

To serve, mound the bread mixture in a large bowl, then surround with the browned cubes of pork and beef.

LAYERED EGG BREAD STUFFED WITH HAM, SAUSAGE AND CHICKEN
Folar Feito à Moda da
Maria Eugénia Cerqueira da Mota

On a recent visit to the Trás-os-Montes, I had the pleasure of dining at the home of Maria Eugénia Cerqueira da Mota in the little village of Valpaços. Maria Eugénia, a pharmacist whose hobby is Portuguese food history, shared many of her old family recipes, among them this *folar,* which took a top prize from RTP (the government television network). It's a long-winded recipe that requires plenty of energy—the soft, sticky dough must be worked by hand for half an hour if it is to develop the proper elasticity. Maria Eugénia makes *folar* with her own *presunto* (prosciutto-like cured ham), *salpicão* (garlicky smoked pork loin), and *linguiça* (pimiento-rich sausage made of pork shoulder). I've been forced to substitute commonly available American ingredients and, although my *folar* isn't as stellar as Maria Eugénia's, it is delicious and, I think, worth all the work.

Makes about 12 servings

DOUGH:

2	packages active dry yeast
¾	cup lukewarm water (105° to 115°F.)
9	cups sifted all-purpose flour (about)
1	teaspoon salt
9	large eggs, at room temperature
½	cup (1 stick) unsalted butter
7	tablespoons lard (hog lard, not vegetable shortening)
3	tablespoons olive oil

FILLING:

2½	to 2¾-pound broiler-fryer
½	pound *linguiça*, *chouriço* (or Spanish *chorizo*), garlicky Italian sausage, or pepperoni, sliced very thin
1	tablespoon olive oil
6	ounces smoked ready-to-eat ham, sliced thin, then cut into ½-inch squares
6	ounces prosciutto, cut into fine julienne
¼	cup minced parsley

GLAZE:

1	egg yolk whisked with 1 tablespoon cold water

For the dough: Soften the yeast in the lukewarm water. Sift the flour and salt into a very large bowl and make a well in the center; pour in the yeast mixture, then break the eggs into the well, one by one. Heat the butter, lard, and olive oil in a small heavy saucepan over low heat just until butter and lard melt; set aside to cool. Meanwhile, begin mixing the eggs and yeast into the flour with your hands to form a lumpy dough; pour in the cooled fats, then with your hands work in thoroughly. The dough will be very soft and sticky and if it is completely unmanageable (you need to be able to lift and turn the dough with your hands), knead in an additional ½ to 1 cup flour.

Now, grabbing fistfuls of dough, first with one hand, then with the other, twist it in the bowl and lift it about 18 inches above the bowl. Keep twisting and lifting the dough as energetically as possible until it becomes very smooth and elastic and leaves the sides of the bowl reasonably clean. This may take as long as ½ hour; do not despair (and if the telephone rings when your hands are covered with dough, ignore it!). Wash your hands. Then butter them well. Scrape any bits of dough clinging to the sides of the bowl down into the mass of dough, then pat the surface well to smooth it. Dust a little flour over the dough, cover it with a clean dry cloth, and set in a warm, draft-free spot to rise until doubled in bulk—about 1½ hours.

Meanwhile, begin the filling: Preheat the oven to very hot (425°F.). Unwrap the chicken heart, liver, and gizzard and tuck inside the chicken; place the bird, breast-side up, in a shallow pan, and roast uncovered for 1 hour. Meanwhile, sauté the *linguiça* in the oil in a small heavy skillet over moderately low heat 10 to 12 minutes until lightly browned; drain on paper toweling and reserve. As soon as the chicken is done, cool until easy to handle, then remove all skin and bones and tear the meat into smallish pieces; mince the giblets. Place chicken and giblets in a large bowl, add the reserved *linguiça,* the smoked ham, prosciutto, and parsley, and toss well to mix.

When the dough has risen sufficiently, raise oven heat to 450°F. Butter your hands well and punch down the dough. Working with about half the dough, pat and stretch it over the bottom and up the sides of a well-buttered 13 × 9½ × 2-inch baking pan. *Note: Because the dough is very soft, very rubbery, I find it easiest to grab a handful and pat it out flat, then grab a second handful, join it to the first, and pat that flat, so no seams or holes show. I proceed this way until I've covered the pan bottom and also worked the dough up the sides with an overhang about 1 inch all around the rim.*

Sprinkle half the filling mixture evenly over the dough, then pat half of the remaining dough over the filling in a thin, solid sheet. It's important that you press this layer of dough into the filling so that the meats will stick to it after the *folar* is baked. Sprinkle the remaining filling on top, then pat on the remaining dough in a smooth layer enclosing all. Roll the overhanging dough up and onto the top layer of pastry so that you have a neat roll all around just inside the rim of the pan. *Note: Don't let the roll of dough overhang the rim or it may overflow the pan as it bakes.* Cover the *folar* with cloth and let rise 20 minutes in a warm spot. Quickly brush the top of the *folar* and the rolled edge with the egg glaze.

Bake the *folar* uncovered for 15 minutes at 450°F., then lower the oven temperature to hot (400°F.) and bake 45 to 50 minutes longer, until the top is richly browned and the loaf sounds hollow when thumped. Cool to room temperature. To serve, cut into 3-inch squares as the main course of a light lunch or supper.

TRIPE IN THE MANNER OF PORTO
Tripas à Moda do Porto

The story goes that, in the fifteenth century, when Prince Henry-the-Navigator provisioned his ships for an assault on the Moors at Ceuta, he took all the meat of his hometown of Porto, leaving only tripe behind. Ever since, the people of Porto have been called *tripeiros* (tripe eaters). I must say that their way of preparing it is both unusual and splendid. I like it even better than Normandy's classic *tripes à la mode de Caen* because it is spicier, gutsier, and it needs no salt.

Makes 8 servings

1	pound dried great northern beans, washed and sorted
2½	quarts water (about)
3	large garlic cloves, peeled and minced
4	large yellow onions, peeled and coarsely chopped
3	medium carrots, peeled and sliced ¼-inch thick
¼	cup olive oil
2	tablespoons paprika
2	teaspoons ground cumin
1	teaspoon crumbled leaf marjoram
½	teaspoon crumbled leaf thyme
½	teaspoon cayenne pepper
¼	teaspoon freshly ground black pepper
¼	teaspoon ground cloves
½	cup chopped Italian parsley

2 large bay leaves (do not crumble)

1 can (1 pound 12 ounces) tomatoes packed in tomato purée

2½ cups dry red wine

2 pounds honeycomb tripe, washed in cool water, stripped of all fat, and cut into 1-inch squares

¾ pound *linguiça, chouriço* (or the Spanish *chorizo*), pepperoni, or other dry, garlicky sausage, sliced thin

½ pound prosciutto (in one piece), trimmed of fat and cut into small dice

Soak the beans in 6 cups of the water overnight; next day, drain the beans, reserving the soaking water; set both aside. Preheat the oven to slow (300°F.). In a large heavy kettle set over moderate heat, sauté the garlic, onions, and carrots in the oil 10 to 12 minutes until the onions are golden; blend in the paprika, cumin, marjoram, thyme, cayenne, black pepper, cloves, and parsley; drop in the bay leaves and mellow over moderate heat 3 to 5 minutes. Add the tomatoes, wine, and tripe, bring to a simmer, cover, and set on the middle shelf of the oven. Cook 3 hours, stirring every hour.

Meanwhile, measure the bean soaking water and add enough additional water to total 2 quarts. Place the beans in a large heavy saucepan, add the water, and bring to a simmer over moderate heat. Adjust the heat so that the water barely bubbles, cover, and cook the beans 40 to 45 minutes until *al dente;* drain, reserving 2 cups of the cooking water. Set both aside. When the tripe has cooked 3 hours, stir in the sausage, prosciutto, and reserved beans and cooking water. Re-cover and bake 1 to 1½ hours longer, stirring every half hour, until tripe and beans are both tender. If at any point the mixture threatens to cook dry, add a little additional water.

Serve as a main course accompanied by boiled rice, a crisp green salad tartly dressed, and chunks of bread, preferably the wonderful *Pão do Minho* (page 226).

RABBIT FOUNDER'S-STYLE
Coelho à Fundador

This hearty fricassee of rabbit is the specialty of the lovely little Pousada de Santa Maria da Oliveira in Guimarães. The chef here is one of Portugal's best *pousada* chefs, which the townspeople well know. The dining room overlooking the bustling medieval square is as popular with them as it is with tourists.

Makes 4 to 6 servings

½ pound lean slab bacon, cut into small dice
4 tablespoons olive oil
   A skinned, cleaned and dressed rabbit weighing 3½ to 4 pounds, cut into 1½-inch chunks
¾ cup yellow corn flour (not cornmeal; you'll find the flour in Latin groceries and also in health food stores)
1 large onion, peeled and coarsely chopped
2 large leeks, trimmed, washed well, and sliced thin
4 large parsley branches
2 large bay leaves (do not crumble)
½ teaspoon fennel seeds
¾ teaspoon crumbled leaf thyme
½ teaspoon salt (about)
½ teaspoon freshly ground black pepper (about)
1 cup dry red wine such as a Portuguese Dão
4 large carrots, peeled and cut into 1-inch chunks
4 large baking potatoes, peeled and cut into 1-inch chunks
8 small white onions, peeled

Preheat oven to moderately slow (325°F.). In a large heavy kettle set over moderately low heat, sauté the bacon in 2 tablespoons of the olive oil 8 to 10 minutes until all the drippings have cooked out and only crisp brown bits remain. With a slotted spoon, lift the browned bits to paper toweling to drain; pour off the drippings, spoon 4 tablespoons of them back into the kettle, and reserve the balance. Dredge the pieces of rabbit well in corn flour, shaking off excess. Set the kettle over high heat and when the drippings are so hot they *almost* smoke, begin browning the rabbit in batches—it will take 4 to 5 minutes for each to brown. As the pieces of rabbit are browned, lift to a large heat-proof bowl with a slotted spoon. Also add more drippings to the kettle—about 2 tablespoons—before you brown each new batch, and get them good and hot before adding the rabbit.

When all the meat has been browned, scrape any blackened bits from the bottom of the kettle and discard; add the remaining 2 tablespoons of olive oil to the kettle, set over moderate heat, and dump in the onion and leeks; sauté 4 to 5 minutes, stirring often, until glassy; add the parsley, bay leaves, fennel, and thyme; turn the heat to low, cover, and cook 25 minutes; pour this mixture from the kettle and reserve.

Arrange half the rabbit in the bottom of the kettle, spoon half the reserved onion mixture and bacon bits on top, then sprinkle lightly with salt and pepper. Add the remaining rabbit, onion mixture, bacon, salt, and pepper, pour in the wine, and set over moderate heat. Bring to a simmer, then cover, and set in the oven. After 45 minutes, remove from the oven and stir well, bringing the pieces of rabbit on the bottom up to the top; tuck in the carrots and potatoes, re-cover, and bake 45 minutes longer. Again remove from the oven and stir up from the bottom of the kettle; add the small white onions, re-cover, and bake 45 minutes longer until rabbit and all vegetables are tender. Taste for salt and pepper. Serve at table directly from the kettle and accompany with one of Portugal's good red table wines—Periquita, perhaps, or Serradayres, Colares, or Dão.

Poultry

✳

Aves

GRILLED OR BROILED CHICKEN
Frango Grelhado

In the old days, few Portuguese chickens were tender enough to grill or broil. But they are available now, and with so many Portuguese returning home after working overseas in Brazil, the land of *churrasco* (grilled meats), broiled and grilled chicken are becoming increasingly popular. The combination of seasonings is purely Portuguese—garlic, bay leaf, olive oil, paprika, and hot red peppers.

Makes 6 to 8 servings

> 2 large garlic cloves, peeled and sliced
> 1 large bay leaf, crumbled fine
> 2 teaspoons paprika (preferably the Hungarian sweet rose paprika)
> 1 tablespoon kosher or coarse salt
> ¼ teaspoon crushed dried red chili peppers
> ¼ teaspoon freshly ground black pepper
> 2 tablespoons olive oil
> 2 young broiler-fryers (about 2 pounds each), quartered

Using a mortar and pestle, mash the garlic, bay leaf, paprika, salt, chili peppers, black pepper, and olive oil to paste. Rub the chicken quarters well on both sides with the paste, then cover and refrigerate several hours. *Note: Wash your hands carefully after handling the paste because the chili peppers in it can irritate your skin. And by all means, refrain from touching your face or eyes until after you have washed your hands.* Remove the chicken from the refrigerator and let stand at room temperature 30 minutes. Meanwhile, preheat the broiler. Arrange the chicken quarters skin-side up on a lightly oiled broiler pan, place 6 inches from the heat, and broil 12 to 13 minutes until nicely browned; turn the chicken and brown 12 to 13 minutes longer until sizzling. Serve with a cool green salad and boiled rice. The Portuguese would drizzle the broiler drippings over the chicken and rice.

VARIATION:

Charcoal-Grilled Chicken: Season and marinate the chicken as directed. Meanwhile, build a moderately hot charcoal fire, and when coals are ashy white, set grill 6 to 8 inches above the coals. Lay chicken skin-side up on grill, and grill 12 to 15 minutes; turn and grill about 12 minutes longer until the chicken skin is richly browned.

ROAST STUFFED CHICKEN IN THE OLD PORTUGUESE MANNER
Frango Recheado à Antiga Moda Portuguesa

This traditional roast chicken is prepared in ways that sound most unusual to an American cook. It is rubbed with crushed garlic, paprika, and olive oil, marinated overnight in the refrigerator, then stuffed with a mixture of ground pork, chopped hard-cooked eggs, olives, and bread. I enjoyed the dish so much on my first trip to Lisbon many years ago that I now order it whenever and wherever I see it on the menu. The recipe varies from one part of Portugal to another, and indeed from one cook to another.

Makes 6 servings

    A roasting chicken weighing about 5 pounds, with its giblets
1 **large garlic clove, peeled and crushed**
1 **teaspoon kosher or coarse salt**
1 **tablespoon paprika (preferably the Hungarian sweet rose paprika)**
4 **tablespoons olive oil**
1 **cup dry white wine (preferably *vinho verde*)**

STUFFING:

    3   large yellow onions, peeled and coarsely chopped
    2   large garlic cloves, peeled and minced
  ¼   cup olive oil
  ¼   cup lard (hog lard, not vegetable shortening)
       The chicken giblets, minced
  ½   pound ground lean pork shoulder
    4   cups soft bread crumbs
    4   hard-cooked eggs, shelled and chopped
  ½   cup coarsely chopped pitted green olives
    1   tablespoon paprika (preferably the Hungarian sweet rose paprika)
    2   tablespoons minced parsley
  ½   teaspoon freshly ground black pepper
  ¼   cup dry Port wine
  ½   cup chicken broth (about)

Remove the giblets from the chicken, unwrap, place on a small plate, cover loosely with plastic food wrap, and refrigerate until ready to use. Pull all excess fat from the body and neck cavities of the bird and discard. Combine the garlic, salt, paprika, and 1 tablespoon of the olive oil, beating until smooth; rub this all over the bird, inside and out. Place the bird in a shallow bowl, cover, and refrigerate overnight.

Next day, prepare the stuffing: In a large heavy skillet set over moderate heat, sauté the onions and garlic in the ¼ cup olive oil and the lard 5 minutes until glassy; add the minced giblets and pork, turn heat very low, and cook, stirring to break up the chunks of pork, about 2 minutes; cover, and steam all for 20 minutes. Meanwhile, place the bread crumbs, eggs, olives, paprika, parsley, and pepper in a very large bowl and toss well to mix. When skillet mixture has cooked 20 minutes, dump on top of the bread mixture, drizzle the Port over all, and toss well. Now add just enough of the chicken broth to moisten the stuffing nicely—it should be moist, *not soggy.*

Preheat the oven to very hot (450°F.). Spoon the stuffing first into the neck cavity of the chicken and enclose by skewering the neck flap against the back of the bird. Now upend the bird and spoon the stuffing lightly into the body cavity—*don't* pack it in; skewer the opening shut, and truss the bird. Wrap any remaining stuffing in aluminum foil and refrigerate for the time being.

    Rub the bird well with 1 tablespoon of the remaining olive oil, arrange breast-side up on a rack in a large shallow roasting pan, and roast uncovered for 20 minutes. Lower the oven heat to moderate (350°F.), brush the bird well with 1 tablespoon of the remaining oil, and roast uncovered about 30 minutes per pound, brushing with the final tablespoon of oil midway through the roasting period. When the bird has only 40 minutes more to cook, pour the 1 cup white wine over it; also, lay the packet of stuffing on the rack beside the roasting pan, and bake it while the bird finishes roasting. The chicken will be done when it is richly browned and a leg moves easily in its hip socket.

Lift the bird to a large heated platter and remove all skewers and string. Open the packet of stuffing and wreathe around the chicken. Garnish, if you like, with clusters of green and black olives. Pour the pan drippings into a small heated gravy boat and pass separately. Accompany with *Feijão Verde com Coentro e Alho* (page 202) or, if you prefer, with plain buttered green beans. A very dry white wine would be in order—Dão, Serradayres, or Monopólio.

JUGGED CHICKEN
Frango na Púcara

This dish combines all the flavors I think of as Portuguese: onions, garlic, tomatoes, bay leaves, ham, olive oil. The recipe comes from the town of Alcobaça, some seventy miles north of Lisbon. Once a powerful religious center, Alcobaça is famous today for its pottery and its Cistercian Monastery, which the monks began to build in the twelfth century. The monastery kitchens are magnificent: A brook trickles through them, the domed hearths are cavernous enough to roast six oxen simultaneously, and the six-ton marble table would have delighted Henry VIII. The monks didn't invent *Frango na Púcara*, however; that distinction belongs to a cook at the old Café Aguia d'Ouro in Alcobaça, which still exists. The proper container for cooking the chicken is a terra-cotta jug much like our bean pot. Any fairly deep heavy casserole will work well. *Note: Because of the saltiness of the ham in this recipe, you are not likely to need additional salt.*

Makes 4 servings

     A small broiler-fryer weighing about 2½ pounds, with its giblets
1   **tablespoon olive oil**

12 small white onions, peeled
 3 medium garlic cloves, peeled
 5 large parsley branches
 ¼ pound prosciutto, finely diced
 2 large bay leaves (do not crumble)
 3 large ripe tomatoes, peeled, cored, seeded, and coarsely chopped
 ⅔ cup *vinho verde* or other dry white wine
 ⅓ cup tawny or ruby Port
 2 tablespoons brandy or, if available, Portuguese *aguardente*
 1 tablespoon Dijon mustard
 ¼ teaspoon freshly ground black pepper

Preheat the oven to moderate (350°F.). Rub the chicken all over with olive oil, then stuff the body cavity with 3 onions, 1 garlic clove, and 1 parsley branch; set aside. Scatter half of the prosciutto over the bottom of a 3½-quart earthenware jug or deep heavy casserole, add 2 parsley branches, 4 of the remaining onions, 1 garlic clove, all the chicken giblets, and 1 bay leaf. Now place the chicken in the jug headfirst (if using a casserole, simply set the chicken breast-side up). Tuck the remaining onions around the chicken, scatter with the remaining prosciutto, drop in the remaining garlic, parsley, and bay leaf. Combine the tomatoes, *vinho verde,* Port, brandy, mustard, and pepper, and pour evenly over all. Cover the jug and bake the chicken 1½ to 1¾ hours or until a drumstick moves easily in its socket.

Remove the jug from the oven, carefully fish out the whole onions on top, and reserve. Next, carefully drain the liquid from the jug into a large heavy skillet. Lift out the bird and place on a broiler rack. Also preheat the broiler. With a slotted spoon, lift the giblets from the bottom of the jug along with all whole onions and add both to the onions already reserved. If any onions should have landed in the skillet while you drained the jug, lift these out and reserve also. Set the skillet over high heat and boil uncovered about 10 minutes to reduce the liquid by about half. Keep an eye on the skillet and stir often; lower the heat if the mixture is reducing too fast. When it is properly reduced, turn the heat to its lowest point, and keep the liquid hot.

Meanwhile, place the chicken in the broiler, the breast 5 to 6 inches from the heat, and broil 3 to 4 minutes until nicely browned. To serve, center the chicken on a deep platter (I like to bed it on a mound of fluffy boiled rice, although this is not the Portuguese way), and wreathe with the whole onions and giblets. Spoon some of the reduced jug liquid on top and pass the rest in a heated sauceboat. To be really Portuguese, serve with thinly sliced or shredded fried potatoes.

MARIA EUGÉNIA CERQUEIRA DA MOTA'S ROAST STUFFED TURKEY
Peru Assado Feito à Moda da Maria Eugénia Cerqueira da Mota

Having roasted and written about turkeys for years, I thought I knew all there was to know about this big, beautiful American bird. Well, I was wrong. I recently learned an extraordinary way to roast turkey from a talented cook who lives in the northeastern reaches of Portugal—Maria Eugénia Cerqueira da Mota. Her method breaks almost every rule of turkey cookery that I had been taught, and it produces a bird of incomparable moistness, with skin as crackly as a potato chip. "You should never rub a turkey's skin with anything but salt," Maria Eugénia told me. "The salt seals the pores and keeps the juices in the flesh. People make a mistake in rubbing turkey with fat, in basting it with drippings, and in roasting it at a low temperature, all of which make the juices run out." What also distinguishes her roast turkey is that she smooths the stuffing—a buttery bread paste—directly underneath the skin and leaves the body cavity empty. Even though I'd just eaten Maria Eugénia's supremely succulent turkey (roasted, by the way, at 400°F. from start to finish), I remained skeptical until I tried her unorthodox method in my own kitchen. It worked, though I had to roast my turkey longer, our birds being heftier than their Portuguese cousins. Nevertheless, roasting the turkey for 2½ hours at 400°F. produced the finest, juiciest, most flavorful bird of recent memory, and it won raves from dinner guests, who are now also converts to Maria Eugénia's technique. And, so impressed was her good friend Maria de Lourdes Modesto (Portugal's Julia Child), that she included the recipe in her lavishly illustrated new book of regional Portuguese cooking, *Cozinha Tradicional Portuguesa*. What follows is my own adaptation of Maria Eugénia's recipe, adjusted to take account of American ingredients and equipment.

Makes about 10 servings

    A small fresh turkey weighing about 10 pounds
2 **pounds salt (that's right, 2 pounds)**

STUFFING:

2 **large garlic cloves, peeled and minced**
¼ **pound (1 stick) unsalted butter**

3   tablespoons olive oil
1   pound rough Portuguese, French, or Italian bread, broken into small chunks
      (this will amount to about two 15-inch loaves)
½   teaspoon salt
½   teaspoon freshly ground black pepper
3½ cups chicken broth (preferably homemade)
2   large egg yolks, lightly beaten

Remove the giblets from the turkey and reserve for *Arroz de Forno* (Baked Rice, page 214, which Maria Eugénia likes to serve with turkey); or save to use another time. Fill the neck and body cavities of the turkey with salt, then rub the skin well all over with salt. Place the turkey and remaining salt in a very large deep kettle, add enough cold water just to cover the bird, and set in a very cool spot for 3 to 4 hours. (Maria Eugénia soaks her turkey a full 24 hours, but in America's super-heated houses, that would be unwise.)

Toward the end of the soaking period, prepare the stuffing: In a large heavy kettle set over moderate heat, sauté the garlic in the butter and olive oil about 5 minutes until limp. Add the bread, salt, and pepper, and toss well; now add the chicken broth and beat hard with a wooden spoon until the mixture is pastelike; turn the heat to its lowest point, cover the kettle, and steam 15 to 20 minutes, until the bread has absorbed all the liquid. Add the egg yolks and beat hard until smooth. Remove from the heat and reserve.

Preheat the oven to hot (400°F.). Drain the turkey and rinse very well, removing every bit of salt from the neck and body cavities. It's important to rinse the bird several times in cool water, so that all traces of salt are gone. Place the bird on the counter with the neck cavity facing you. With your hands, begin working the skin free from the breast. Proceed gently, taking care not to tear the skin. It's slow going at first, but once you begin to free the skin, the job goes quickly. Loosen it all the way down the bird to within about 1 inch of the tail end, down both sides. Now, with your hands, push the stuffing bit by bit far down under the skin and continue, packing it in lightly, until the breast is covered with about a 1-inch layer. Now fill the neck cavity, skewer the neck skin flat against the back to enclose, and truss the bird.

Place the turkey breast-side up in a large shallow roasting pan (no rack needed) and roast uncovered for about 2½ hours or until the bird is richly browned and a leg moves easily in the hip joint; *do not baste*. Remove from the oven and let stand 20 minutes. Drain the drippings into a sauceboat and keep warm. Remove the trussing string and skewers and serve at once. *Arroz de Forno,* as I've mentioned, is Maria Eugénia's favorite accompaniment, together with a crisp salad of greens.

BRAISED DUCK AND RICE
Arroz de Pato

Here's an ingenious Portuguese method for ridding a duck of its excess fat: Prick the bird well, then simmer it until tender *before* browning it. The simmering also provides a rich stock in which to cook the rice. As served in Portugal (and this dish is served everywhere about the country), the pieces of duck are arranged in the bottom of a shallow terra-cotta casserole (usually rectangular), browned in a quick oven, topped with the rice mixture, then baked at moderate heat just until the rice is golden. *Note: Because of the saltiness of the ham, bacon, and sausage used, you will not need to add any salt.*

Makes 6 servings

	A duckling weighing 5 to 5½ pounds, with its giblets
5	**cups cold water**
1	**large yellow onion, peeled and sliced thin**
2	**large carrots, peeled and sliced thin**
10	**peppercorns**
¼	**pound prosciutto, in one piece**
¼	**pound slab bacon, in one piece**
½	**pound *chouriço, chorizo,* or pepperoni, in one piece**
2	**cups converted rice**
¼	**teaspoon freshly ground black pepper**
4	**tablespoons unsalted butter, melted**
1	**egg yolk beaten with 2 tablespoons cold water**

Pull all excess fat from the neck and body cavities of the duck and discard; prick the bird well all over with a sharp-pronged fork, then refrigerate until needed. Place the water, duck giblets and neck, onion, carrots, peppercorns, prosciutto, bacon, and *chouriço* in a large heavy kettle, and bring to a simmer over moderate heat. Adjust the burner heat so that the mixture bubbles gently, cover, and simmer for 1 hour.

   With a slotted spoon, lift the duck giblets and neck, the prosciutto, bacon, and *chouriço* from the kettle and reserve. Now place the duck in the kettle, breast-side up, bring the liquid to a gentle simmer, cover, and simmer 30 minutes; turn the bird breast-side down, re-cover, and simmer 30 minutes longer. Remove the duck from the broth and cool until easy to handle. Strain the broth, discarding the solids. Now skim as much fat as possible from the broth—there will be plenty of it!—so this is a job requiring patience.

Preheat the oven to very hot (450°F.). With poultry shears, cut the legs and wings off the duck. Divide the breast in half by cutting down the middle of the breastbone, then cut each half crosswise into three chunks. Remove as much meat as possible from the back of the bird. Place all pieces of meat, skin-side up, in a shallow 3-quart earthenware casserole. (It should measure about 12 × 9 inches, or 11 to 12 inches in diameter, and be 2 inches deep.) Place the uncovered casserole on the middle shelf of the oven and bake the duck until lightly browned—about 15 minutes. Remove the casserole from the oven and set aside; reduce oven heat to moderate (350°F.).

Pour 1 quart of the skimmed duck broth (reserve any extra to use in making a soup, sauce, or stew) into a large heavy saucepan and bring to a boil over high heat; add the rice and pepper, bring to a simmer, adjust the heat so that the mixture bubbles gently, then cook uncovered about 10 minutes until the level of the liquid is below that of the rice. Meanwhile, cut as much meat from the duckling neck as possible and reserve; discard the neck. Also, coarsely chop the giblets, and dice the prosciutto. Add all to the rice, cover, and cook 5 to 8 minutes longer until most of the liquid has been absorbed.

Meanwhile, dice the bacon and brown in a small heavy skillet over moderately high heat until most of the drippings have cooked out, leaving crisp brown bits—about 5 minutes. You'll have to stir the bacon frequently to keep it from burning. With a slotted spoon, lift the crisp brown bits to paper toweling to drain; discard the drippings or reserve to use another time. Slice the *chouriço* ¼-inch thick and reserve 20 slices to use in garnishing the dish. Stir the remainder into the rice along with the bacon bits.

Spoon the rice into the casserole, covering the duck completely. Drizzle the surface first with melted butter, then with the egg yolk mixture. Now arrange three rows of *chouriço* rounds decoratively on top—down both sides and down the center. Cover snugly with foil and bake 15 minutes; uncover and bake 10 to 15 minutes longer, just until the rice is faintly golden. Serve at once, directly from the casserole.

PARTRIDGES WITH CABBAGE
Perdizes com Couve

Perdiz, according to my Portuguese dictionary, is "any of various partridges." From mid-October until about Christmastime, big-city Portuguese offices seem to shut down (or at least to close for very long weekends), so that the men can head for the Beiras, Alentejo, or the Algarve's lonely heather-snarled Sagres promontory to shoot any of various partridges, quails, pheasants, and rabbits. This old Portuguese recipe is a singularly good way to deal with all manner of game birds, and even with fresh Cornish hens, because it renders them unusually succulent and tender. The cabbage leaves you use to wrap the birds should be large and intensely green. I use the outer leaves of an untrimmed common cabbage and find that they work perfectly. Portuguese cooks favor a local, dark-green, heading variety called *couve lombarda.*

Makes 4 servings

8	very large green cabbage leaves (no matter if they're tough)
6	cups boiling water plus 1 tablespoon salt
1	teaspoon salt
½	teaspoon freshly ground black pepper
4	partridges (or fresh Cornish hens), each weighing about ¾ pound, cleaned and dressed
¼	pound *chouriço, chorizo,* or pepperoni, cut into small dice
1	tablespoon olive oil
1	tablespoon unsalted butter
1	cup beef broth
½	cup white or tawny Port wine

Blanch the cabbage leaves 8 to 10 minutes in the boiling salted water in a large heavy kettle set over high heat—just until they are thoroughly pliable. Drain, cut out the large central vein from each leaf, then place each leaf between several thicknesses of paper toweling to dry. Rub the salt and pepper all over each bird, inside and out; set the birds aside. In a large heavy sauté pan set over moderately high heat, fry the *chouriço* in the olive oil and butter 3 to 4 minutes until most of the drippings cook out and only crisp brown bits remain. With a slotted spoon, lift the brown bits to paper toweling to drain. Now brown the birds well on all sides in the drippings over moderately high heat—this will take 8 to 10 minutes. Cool the birds until easy to handle; reserve all pan drippings. Preheat the oven to moderate (350°F.).

To wrap the birds, place 2 cabbage leaves, stem-end to stem-end on the counter, overlapping about ½ inch. I find it easiest to place the leaves with the overlapping ends perpendicular to the edge of the counter. Lay a bird breast-side up on top of the overlap, with its vent end facing you. Lap first the left cabbage leaf over the bird, then the right leaf, pulling as snugly as you dare. Next, do just as you would when wrapping a package, which in fact you are: Fold the loose cabbage-leaf ends, top and bottom, into points and tuck under the bird. Tie the bird with string, once end-to-end, pulling it tight; then tie around twice, a little above and a little below the center, to hold the cabbage leaves in place.

Pour half the reserved drippings into a shallow earthenware casserole large enough to accommodate all the birds in a single layer. Also scatter in half the reserved *chouriço* bits. Arrange the birds breast-side up in the casserole; combine the remaining drippings with the broth and wine and pour over the birds; sprinkle the rest of the *chouriço* on top. Cover snugly and bake 1 hour and 15 minutes.

Remove the birds from the oven, carefully remove the strings, then arrange the birds on a heated platter, and wreathe, if you like, with new potatoes, boiled in their skins, and clusters of baby carrots. Pour the pan drippings into a heated sauceboat and pass separately. The perfect wine: a light Portuguese red such as Periquita or Serradayres.

PARTRIDGES ALCÂNTARA-STYLE
Perdizes à Alcântara

In his *Guide Culinaire*, Escoffier writes that this recipe is the only good thing to have come out of France's disgraceful campaign in Portugal during the early nineteenth-century Peninsular War. Or so claims the late António M. de Oliveira Bello, first president of Portugal's Gastronomic Society, founded in 1933. In his own book, *Culinária Portuguesa*, a classic published soon after the formation of the Society and available today in facsimile edition, António Bello writes that the recipe was discovered among the records of the Convent of Alcântara near Lisbon which was pillaged by Junot's soldiers. It also proves, he insists, that truffles were known at the time in Portuguese Estremadura, adding that the truffles sometimes found there today are not to be sneered at. According to António Bello, the Duchess of Abrantès (Madame Junot, for Napoleon had made Junot the *Duc d'Abrantès*) knew of the recipe and published it in her memoirs. In the opinion of historian Matos Sequeira, the convent Escoffier refers to is the *Convento do Sacramento* in the Lisbon quarter of Alcântara, a rich Dominican Order known to have been sacked by Junot's troops. I have not been able to verify any of this in the editions of Escoffier's *Guide Culinaire* available to me, but I have no reason to doubt António Bello, who is to Portugal as Brillat-Savarin was to France. The recipe is unusually elegant, surprisingly easy to prepare once the birds are boned (my advice is to sweet-talk a butcher into doing the job for you), and equally superb hot or cold. *Note: If you are unable to obtain partridges, use fresh Cornish hens instead. Because the birds must marinate overnight in the Port wine, you should begin this recipe the day before you intend to serve it.*

Makes 4 servings

2   fresh partridges or Cornish hens, each weighing about ¾ pound, cleaned, dressed, and boned (ask the butcher to leave the wings and drumsticks intact so that the birds will have some shape)
¼   teaspoon salt
¼   teaspoon freshly ground black pepper
1   can (14 ounces) Strasbourg liver pâté with truffles
2   cups white or tawny Port wine
2   tablespoons unsalted butter
½   small black truffle, cut into fine julienne (optional)

Rub the birds lightly inside and out with the salt and pepper. Stuff the body cavities of the birds with pâté, dividing the total amount evenly and packing it in lightly. Skewer the body cavities shut (also skewer any neck skin flat against the backs of the birds), then truss. Place the birds breast-side up in a shallow casserole just large enough to accommodate them comfortably, pour in the wine, cover, and refrigerate 24 hours, turning the birds in the wine several times.

When ready to cook the birds, preheat the oven to hot (400°F.). Drain the wine from the casserole into a small heavy saucepan, add the butter, and boil uncovered over moderate heat about 20 minutes until reduced to a syrupy glaze. Pour the glaze evenly over the birds, cover the casserole, and bake 45 minutes. Lower the oven temperature to moderately hot (375°F.) and bake the birds uncovered 30 minutes longer, basting every 10 minutes with drippings, until they are richly browned and you can move a drumstick easily in its hip socket. Remove the birds to a heated platter and keep warm. Pour the drippings into a small heavy saucepan, add the truffle, if you like, and boil quickly about 5 minutes until slightly reduced. Pour the reduced drippings over the birds and serve, allotting half a bird to each person. (Split the birds lengthwise with a sharp, heavy knife). Accompany with roasted potatoes, buttered baby carrots and/or green beans. As for wine, a fine Portuguese red would be perfect: Colares, Dão Grão Vasco Reserva, or Ferreira Barca Velha.

To serve the birds cold: Baste them well with the pan drippings, transfer to a plate, cover loosely, and chill several hours. Split lengthwise and serve.

Fish and Shellfish

✳

Peixes e Mariscos

GRILLED RED MULLET SETÚBAL-STYLE
Salmonetes Grelhados à Setubalense

The best of Portuguese cooking is often the simplest—absolutely fresh harvests of land and sea prepared with a light and knowing touch. This fish dish, for example, is based upon the foods for which the Setúbal area on the peninsula directly south of Lisbon is famous: puckeringly tart oranges, olives, and fish pulled minutes earlier from the sea. I've had to make some adjustments to compensate for our lack of precisely the right ingredients: small red snappers instead of the difficult-to-find red mullet and a combination of orange and lemon to approximate the orangey tartness of those little Setúbal oranges. The presentation here, with lightly poached orange slices arranged on top of the fish, is that of the luxurious Pousada de Palmela built inside a mountaintop castle-fortress just seven miles from Setúbal. *Note: Because the fish must be grilled with split-second timing, it's best to prepare the sauce ahead of time.*

Makes 4 servings

1   large garlic clove, peeled and crushed
⅓   cup olive oil
4   small red snappers, weighing ½ to ¾ pound each, cleaned and dressed but with
    heads and tails left on

SAUCE:

¼   pound (1 stick) unsalted butter
6   tablespoons dry white wine
    Juice of 2 medium oranges
    Juice of 1 medium lemon
¼   teaspoon salt
¼   teaspoon freshly ground black pepper
2   small navel oranges, sliced thin
¼   cup minced parsley (preferably the flat-leaf Italian variety)

Steep the garlic in the olive oil at room temperature for several hours; then brush the fish well on both sides with the garlic oil, cover, and refrigerate until shortly before ready to cook. Reserve any remaining oil, letting it stand at room temperature.

For the sauce: In a small heavy saucepan set over low heat, let the butter melt, then turn a rich topaz brown. Add the wine, orange and lemon juices, salt, and pepper, and boil uncovered 15 to 20 minutes until reduced to the consistency of syrup. Set off the heat until shortly before serving.

When ready to grill the fish, preheat the broiler and set the broiler rack about 6 inches below the broiler unit. Oil a broiler pan well, then brush each fish generously on both sides with the remaining garlic oil. Lay the fish on the broiler pan and broil about 5 minutes on each side, just until the flesh almost flakes at the touch of a fork.

While the fish broil, pour the sauce into a medium-size skillet and set over lowest heat; lay the orange slices in the sauce, covering the whole skillet bottom. The instant the fish are done, carefully lift the orange slices from the skillet to a plate for the time being and stir the parsley into the orange sauce. Arrange the fish on a large heated platter, drizzle the orange sauce evenly over all, then arrange 3 orange slices, slightly overlapping, on top of each fish. Serve at once with boiled rice, a light green salad, and a really crisp dry white wine. In Portugal, the choice would be Fonseca's Branco Seco, which also comes from the Setúbal region.

RED MULLET MADEIRA-STYLE
Salmonetes à Madeirense

The red mullet popular in Madeira and mainland Portugal is rarely available here, so I've again taken the liberty of substituting red snapper. The rest of the recipe, however, is purely Madeirense. If you should visit Madeira some day, do go to the colorful morning market in the capital city of Funchal. You will see there an awesome array of produce from land and sea, displayed with painstaking attention to detail and native artistic flair.

Makes 6 servings

SAUCE:

2	large yellow onions, peeled and coarsely chopped
2	large garlic cloves, peeled and minced
3	tablespoons olive oil
2	tablespoons unsalted butter
5	large juicily ripe tomatoes, peeled, cored, seeded, and chopped fine
2	large bay leaves (do not crumble)
½	cup *vinho verde* or other dry white wine
2	tablespoons minced parsley
¼	teaspoon freshly ground black pepper
½	teaspoon salt

FISH:

6	small (about 1½ pounds each) red snapper or trout, cleaned but with head and tail left on
⅔	cup unsifted flour (for dredging)
4	tablespoons olive oil

GARNISHES:

2	tins (2 ounces each) flat anchovy fillets, drained
18	unpitted oil-cured black olives
1	large lime or lemon, sliced thin
4 or 5	watercress or parsley sprigs

For the sauce: Stir-fry the onions and garlic in the oil and butter in a large heavy skillet over moderate heat about 15 minutes until soft and lightly browned. Add all remaining sauce ingredients, cover, and simmer 1 hour; uncover and simmer 1 to 1½ hours longer, or until the sauce is about as thick as a sturdy pasta sauce and the flavors are well blended. Remove the bay leaves and discard.

For the fish: Dredge each fish well in flour, shaking off the excess. In a large heavy skillet, brown the fish gently in the oil—about 2 minutes per side. Remove to a large ovenproof platter. Ladle some of the sauce artfully over the fish (do not cover them completely). Let cool, then cover the platter with foil, and refrigerate until about 1 hour before serving. Reserve and refrigerate the remaining sauce also.

Next day—about an hour before serving—set the platter of fish on the counter; let stand 45 minutes. Preheat the oven to moderate (350°F.). Empty the remaining sauce into a small saucepan and warm over lowest heat, stirring as often as needed to keep it from sticking. Set the fish, still covered with foil, in the oven and heat 15 minutes.

To serve, spoon some of the reheated sauce on top of the fish (leave the heads and tails exposed). Decorate with crisscrosses of anchovy fillets, clusters of black olives, slices of lime or lemon, and sprigs of watercress or parsley. Pass the remaining sauce separately.

BAKED HAKE LISBON-STYLE
Pescada Assada à Lisboeta

Pescada is one of the fish most beloved by the Portuguese. You'll be convinced of that if you visit the boisterous Cascais fish market beside "fishermen's beach," where crate upon crate of these fine, white-fleshed fish are offloaded and auctioned to the highest bidder. A curiosity of the Portuguese auction is that the high price starts the action, from which bidders work their way down to a fee acceptable to the seller. This recipe and the one that follows are two particularly popular ways to prepare *pescada*.

Makes 4 servings

1	medium yellow onion, peeled and coarsely chopped
1	large garlic clove, peeled and minced
½	medium sweet green pepper, cored, seeded, and coarsely chopped

3 tablespoons olive oil
2 large bay leaves (do not crumble)
2 tablespoons minced parsley
4 large juicily ripe tomatoes, peeled, cored, seeded, and coarsely chopped
¼ cup dry white wine
Pinch ground cloves
2 tablespoons tomato paste
1 teaspoon salt
¼ teaspoon freshly ground black pepper
4 slices of hake or cod, cut 1-inch thick (about 2 pounds in all)

Sauté the onion, garlic, and green pepper in the olive oil in a large heavy skillet over moderate heat 5 to 6 minutes until limp; add the bay leaves, parsley, tomatoes, wine, cloves, tomato paste, salt, and pepper; bring to a simmer; adjust the heat so that the mixture bubbles gently, cover, and cook 30 minutes. Uncover and simmer, stirring often, 25 to 30 minutes more until the consistency of thick pasta sauce.

As the sauce nears the right consistency, preheat the oven to moderate (350°F.). Lay the pieces of hake in a buttered shallow earthenware casserole just large enough to accommodate them comfortably in a single layer. Pour the tomato sauce evenly over all, cover, and bake 15 minutes; uncover and bake 25 to 30 minutes longer or until the fish almost flakes at the touch of a fork. *Note: This may seem an inordinately long time to cook fish, but not when you consider that both the earthenware dish and the tomato sauce effectively insulate the fish from the oven's heat—at least during the first part of baking.* Accompany with *Feijão Verde com Coentro e Alho* (Green Beans with Coriander and Garlic; page 202), chunks of chewy Portuguese bread, and a crisp dry table red or white (either wine would be appropriate with this gutsy dish).

BAKED HAKE PORTUGUESE-STYLE
Pescada no Forno à Portuguesa

The title tells you nothing about this casserole of creamed *pescada* and sliced potatoes lightly scented with garlic. It's much more refined than the previous *pescada* recipe and would be served at the elegant manor houses of Sintra, Estoril, and Cascais. If you can't find fresh hake, substitute haddock or flounder.

Makes 6 servings

2	medium garlic cloves, peeled and minced
2	tablespoons unsalted butter
2	pounds hake, haddock, or flounder fillets
½	teaspoon salt
½	teaspoon freshly ground black pepper
2	tablespoons lemon juice
6	medium Maine or Eastern potatoes, boiled until tender, peeled, and sliced thin
2	tablespoons minced parsley

CREAM SAUCE:

4	tablespoons unsalted butter
5	tablespoons flour
¼	teaspoon cayenne pepper
¼	teaspoon paprika
¼	teaspoon freshly grated nutmeg
1	cup milk
2	cups light cream or half-and-half
1	teaspoon salt
2	tablespoons lemon juice
1	large egg yolk, lightly beaten

Preheat the oven to moderate (350°F.). In a small heavy skillet set over low heat, sauté the garlic in the butter, stirring often, about 5 minutes until limp and sweet. Set off the heat and reserve. Arrange half the fish in one layer in a buttered shallow 3-quart casserole; sprinkle with half the sautéed garlic, salt, and pepper, then sprinkle with half the lemon juice. Layer half the potatoes on top and sprinkle with half the parsley. Repeat all layers, ending up with potatoes and parsley as before. Set aside.

For the sauce: Melt the butter in a small heavy saucepan over moderate heat and blend in the flour, cayenne, paprika, and nutmeg. Let mellow about a minute, stirring often, then pour in the milk and cream; heat, stirring constantly, over moderately low heat until thickened, smooth, and no raw floury taste remains—about 5 minutes. Whisk in the salt, lemon juice, and egg, then pour evenly into the casserole.

Bake uncovered for about 45 minutes until bubbly and tipped with brown. Serve at once with a salad of crisp greens, sharply dressed, and either a light red table wine such as a Serradayres or, if you prefer, a really crackling dry white such as Branco Sêco or the ever reliable *vinho verde*.

TROUT BRAGANÇA-STYLE
Truta à Moda de Bragança

The old castle town of Bragança lies just about as far north and east as you can go in Portugal, too far from the Atlantic for saltwater fish. But there are quicksilver streams hereabouts and plenty of brook trout, which local cooks twirl up in thinnest slices of *presunto,* the smoky-sweet, rosy brown ham for which the Trás-os-Montes Province is noted. The *presunto* crispens in the skillet, forming the lightest of crusts for the trout, and surprisingly, its flavor does not overpower the more delicate one of the fish. Because *presunto* is unavailable here, I've had to substitute prosciutto. Make sure your butcher slices it very carefully, so that the pieces are intact and devoid of ragged edges.

Makes 2 servings

2	small brook trout weighing about ½ pound apiece, cleaned and dressed but with the heads and tails left on
1½	cups *vinho verde* or other dry white wine
2	large garlic cloves, peeled and slivered
2	large bay leaves, crumbled
¼	teaspoon freshly ground black pepper
½	cup unsifted all-purpose flour
8	tissue-thin slices prosciutto
¼	cup olive oil
3	tablespoons unsalted butter
1	tablespoon lemon juice
3	tablespoons minced parsley (preferably the flat-leaf Italian variety)

Lay the trout in a 9 × 9 × 2-inch baking dish, pour in the wine, drop in the garlic and bay leaves, cover, and refrigerate 3 to 4 hours. When ready to cook the trout,

remove from the marinade, reserving ¼ cup of it. Sprinkle the fish on both sides
with the pepper, then dredge in the flour, shaking off the excess. Now very carefully
wrap the fish, on the bias, in the ham, letting each slice overlap the previous one
slightly so that both ends and edges are anchored. Heat the olive oil and 2 tablespoons of the butter in a large heavy skillet over high heat until ripples appear on
the skillet bottom. Gently lay the trout in the skillet, lower the heat to moderate,
and brown 4 minutes; carefully turn the fish and brown 4 minutes longer. Transfer
to a heated platter and keep warm. Quickly pour off all but 1 tablespoon of the
drippings, add to the skillet the remaining tablespoon of butter, the reserved ¼ cup
marinade, the lemon juice, and the parsley, and boil hard about 2 minutes until
reduced by about half. Pour over the trout and serve at once, accompanied, if you
like, by boiled rice or potatoes and a green vegetable. As for wine, either an authoritative table white (Dão, for example) or a dry red (again a Dão is ideal).

FRESH TUNA STEAKS IN THE MANNER OF TAVIRA
Bifes de Atum à Maneira de Tavira

Tavira, a whitewashed cubistic village on the Algarve's south coast, is the "Tuna
Capital" of Portugal. Until recently, schools of the big fish swam not far offshore,
but supplies are now so depleted that the tuna fishermen must sail far into the
Atlantic for their catch—sometimes as far as the Azores or Madeira. This old Algarve recipe and the one that follows prove just how delicious fresh tuna can be.
*Note: Because the tuna steaks are marinated overnight in the refrigerator, you must begin
this recipe the day before you plan to serve it.*

Makes 4 servings

1	large garlic clove, peeled and quartered
1	teaspoon kosher or coarse salt
½	cup chopped fresh coriander or mint
½	teaspoon freshly ground black pepper
½	cup olive oil
2	pounds fresh boneless tuna, cut into 4 steaks about ¾-inch thick
½	cup dry white wine
2	tablespoons lemon juice

Using a mortar and pestle, pound the garlic, salt, 2 tablespoons of the coriander, and the pepper to a paste; blend in 1 tablespoon of the olive oil. Rub the mixture on both sides of each tuna steak and lay the steaks in a 9 × 9 × 2-inch baking dish. Mix 2 tablespoons of the remaining coriander with ¼ cup of the remaining oil, the wine, and lemon juice. Pour evenly over the tuna, cover, and marinate in the refrigerator for 24 hours.

When ready to cook, heat the remaining 3 tablespoons olive oil in a large heavy skillet over high heat until ripples appear on the skillet bottom; add the tuna and brown about 3 minutes on each side, keeping the heat high. Meanwhile, strain the marinade, warm in a small saucepan over moderate heat, and stir in the remaining ¼ cup chopped coriander. Serve sizzling hot with a little of the hot marinade spooned over each portion. Accompany with sun-ripened tomatoes, cut into wedges or rounds, and crisp slices of cucumber—both drizzled with olive oil and vinegar.

VARIATION:

Bifes de Atum Grelhado à Maneira de Tavira (Grilled Tuna Steaks Tavira-Style): In little waterfront *tascas* (bistros) all along the Algarve coast you'll smell fresh tuna grilling over white-hot coals of oak. Sometimes fishermen improvise grills on the beach and cook their catch right there, to the fascination of tourists, some of whom are lucky enough to be offered samples together with chunks of rough Portuguese bread. To grill the tuna steaks, rub them with the garlic-coriander paste and marinate in the refrigerator as directed. When ready to cook, make a hot charcoal fire, and when it burns down, leaving coals covered with white ash, adjust the grill so that it is about 6 inches above the coals. Brush the tuna steaks well with the marinade. Strain the remaining marinade into a little saucepan and set to one side of the grill so that it will heat as the tuna grills. Grill the tuna 3 to 4 minutes on each side, brushing often with the marinade, just until cooked through. Stir the remaining chopped coriander into the marinade, top each portion with a generous spoonful of it, and serve.

FRESH TUNA STEAKS MADEIRA-STYLE
Bifes de Atum à Madeirense

Simply marvelous! *Note: Because the steaks must marinate overnight in the refrigerator, you must begin this recipe the day before you plan to serve it.*

Makes 4 servings

1	large garlic clove, peeled and quartered
1	teaspoon kosher or coarse salt
½	teaspoon crumbled leaf oregano
½	teaspoon freshly ground black pepper
½	cup olive oil
2	pounds fresh boneless tuna, cut into 4 steaks about ¾-inch thick
4	large bay leaves (do not crumble)

Using a mortar and pestle, pound the garlic, salt, oregano, and black pepper to a paste; blend in 1 tablespoon of the olive oil. Rub the mixture on both sides of each tuna steak, lay the steaks in a 9 × 9 × 2-inch baking dish, drizzle with ¼ cup of the remaining oil, then tuck in the bay leaves. Cover and marinate in the refrigerator 24 hours.

When ready to cook, heat the remaining 3 tablespoons olive oil in a large heavy skillet over high heat until ripples appear on the skillet bottom; add the tuna and brown about 3 minutes on each side, keeping the heat high. Serve sizzling hot with *Salada à Portuguesa* (page 221) and an assertive dry white wine such as a Dão or, if you prefer, one of Portugal's crackling rosés.

VARIATION:

Bifes de Atum Grelhado à Madeirense (Grilled Tuna Steaks Madeira-Style): On the garden island of Madeira, tuna steaks are more likely to be grilled over hardwood coals than panbroiled. Rub the tuna steaks with the garlic paste and marinate in the refrigerator as directed. When ready to cook, make a hot charcoal fire, and when it burns down, leaving the coals covered with white ash, adjust the grill so that it is about 6 inches above the coals. Brush the tuna steaks well with oil, then grill 3 to 4 minutes on each side—just until cooked through and not an instant longer.

GRILLED SARDINES
Sardinhas Grelhadas

In his invaluable book, *North Atlantic Seafood,* Alan Davidson writes that sardines are immature pilchards and explains that the reason they are so abundant in Portuguese waters is that pilchards do not mature well in southerly climes. I doubt that any fish is more adored by the Portuguese than fresh sardines, so although they are often difficult to find here, I simply must include two favorite Portuguese recipes for preparing them. There's a season for sardines in Portugal—an unofficial one, it's true; the Portuguese consider sardines too lean and bony to eat between November and April. When they fatten and sweeten in late spring, the Portuguese wolf them down, usually tucked into chunks of *Broa* (yeast-raised corn bread). During Lisbon's Festa de Santo António on the night of June 12, which spills over onto the saint's day on June 13, little terra-cotta braziers are set out all along the Alfama's nearly perpendicular cobbled streets, and the scent of charcoal-grilled sardines fills the air. Saint Anthony is the patron saint of lovers, and it's the custom in Lisbon for boys to give their sweethearts little pots of *manjericão* (sweet basil) as valentines. Everyone is caught up in the merriment of the Festa de Santo António and if a total stranger should offer you a freshly grilled sardine, as has happened to me many times, accept it with thanks, and enjoy!

Makes 6 servings

2   pounds fresh sardines, cleaned, dressed, and boned, but with the heads and tails left on
1   cup kosher or coarse salt
3   tablespoons olive oil

Layer the sardines and salt in a 13 × 9 × 2-inch baking dish, cover, and let stand in the refrigerator 2 to 3 hours. Rinse the salt from the sardines, then brush each liberally with olive oil. Preheat the broiler, lay the sardines on a well-oiled broiler pan, place 5 inches from the heat, and broil 2 to 3 minutes on each side, until the fish almost flake at the touch of a fork. Serve hissing-hot with chunks of *Broa* (page 239) or, failing that, with French or Italian bread.

VARIATION:

Sardinhas Assadas nas Brasas (Charcoal-Grilled Sardines): Marinate the sardines in the salt as directed. Build a hot charcoal fire, and when it burns down, leaving coals covered with white ash, adjust the grid so that it is about 6 inches above the coals. Oil well a long-handled hinged grill; brush the sardines generously on both sides with olive oil, then arrange in orderly rows in the grill. Close and latch the grill, then set on the grid and broil 2 to 3 minutes per side, brushing now and then with olive oil. Serve hot with chunks of bread.

FRIED SARDINES SETÚBAL-STYLE
Sardinhas Fritas à Moda de Setúbal

In this one recipe are concentrated all the flavors I think of as being typically Portuguese—sardines, olive oil, tomatoes, onions, garlic, and bay leaves. If you have never eaten fresh sardines, you're in for a pleasant surprise. They are quite delicate, quite sweet, quite unlike their canned counterparts.

Makes 6 servings

- 2 pounds fresh sardines, cleaned, dressed, boned, and beheaded, but with the tails left on
- 1 cup unsifted all-purpose flour
- 1 cup olive oil

TOMATO SAUCE:

- 2 medium yellow onions, peeled and chopped
- 2 medium garlic cloves, peeled and minced
- 3 tablespoons olive oil
- 4 medium juicily ripe tomatoes, peeled, cored, seeded, and coarsely chopped
- 2 large bay leaves (do not crumble)
- 2 tablespoons minced parsley
- ½ cup dry white wine
- 3 tablespoons tomato paste
- ½ teaspoon salt
- ¼ teaspoon freshly ground black pepper

Dredge the sardines well with flour, then brown in 2 to 3 batches in the oil in a large heavy skillet set over high heat—this should take no more than a minute or two per side. Lift the sardines to paper toweling to drain.

For the tomato sauce: Sauté the onions and garlic in the olive oil in a large heavy saucepan over moderate heat 5 to 6 minutes until glassy; add the tomatoes, bay leaves, and parsley, turn the heat to low, cover, and steam 20 minutes. Stir in the wine, tomato paste, salt, and pepper, re-cover, and simmer 20 minutes. Now uncover and simmer 25 to 30 minutes longer until the consistency of thick pasta sauce; cool to room temperature.

Arrange the sardines in a single layer in a lightly oiled 13 × 9 × 2-inch baking dish and pour the tomato sauce evenly on top; cover and refrigerate 2 to 3 hours to allow the sardines time to marinate in the sauce.

When ready to bake, remove the sardines from the refrigerator and let stand on the counter 30 minutes. Also preheat the oven to moderately hot (375°F.). Bake the sardines uncovered 25 to 30 minutes until bubbly. Serve with chunks of rough Portuguese, French, or Italian bread, a cool green salad, and a good Portuguese red table wine such as Periquita, Colares, or Dão Grão Vasco.

CASSEROLE OF SALT COD, POTATOES AND ONION
Bacalhau à Gomes de Sá

Gomes de Sá was a restaurateur in Porto and this splendid casserole is attributed to him. It is considered by many to be Portugal's finest *bacalhau* recipe and I would agree because the flavor of the salt cod does not predominate. Most of the *pousadas* in the north of Portugal serve delicious versions of the dish, as does the Pousada do Castelo at Óbidos much closer to Lisbon. Order it whenever you see it on the menu.

Makes 6 servings

1	pound dried salt cod
6	cups boiling water
1	tablespoon unsalted butter
3	tablespoons olive oil
1	large Spanish onion, peeled and sliced thin
2	pounds California long white or new potatoes, boiled until tender, then peeled and sliced thin
⅓	cup minced parsley
¼	teaspoon freshly ground black pepper

GARNISH:

1	large hard-cooked egg, shelled and cut in thin wedges
12	medium unpitted oil-cured black olives

Soak the salt cod in the refrigerator 24 hours in several changes of cold water. (Keep the bowl covered so that the whole refrigerator doesn't smell of fish.) Drain the cod, rinse, and drain well again. Place in a large heavy saucepan, pour in the boiling water, set over moderate heat, cover and simmer 10 to 12 minutes—just until the cod flakes at the touch of a fork. Drain and rinse well, then flake the cod, removing any bits of skin or bone.

Preheat the oven to moderate (350°F.). In a large heavy skillet set over moderate heat, warm the butter and 1 tablespoon of the oil for about 1 minute. Add the onion, separating the slices into rings, and stir-fry 8 to 10 minutes until limp and golden; do not brown. Remove the onions from the skillet and set aside. Add the remaining 2 tablespoons of oil to the skillet, dump in the potatoes, and stir-fry about 5 minutes until golden. Layer half the potatoes in a well-buttered 2-quart shallow casserole or *au gratin* pan and sprinkle with a little of the minced parsley and pepper. Add one third of the onion, half the cod, and another scattering of parsley and pepper. Repeat the layering, ending with onion rings on top. Sprinkle with the remaining pepper and all but a tablespoon or so of the parsley.

Bake the casserole uncovered for 35 to 40 minutes until hissing hot and touched with brown. Garnish with wedges of hard-cooked eggs and the olives, placed artfully on top of the casserole, plus a final light scattering of minced parsley.

SALT COD POUSADA DO CASTELO-STYLE
Bacalhau à Moda da Pousada do Castelo

The Pousada do Castelo at Óbidos, the very first of Portugal's *pousadas* to be built inside a historic castle, has an outstanding kitchen. Whenever I head that way—even if it's only on a day's outing from Lisbon—I make a point of lunching at this *pousada* perched atop one of the prettiest walled towns you could hope to see. Whenever the menu lists it, I order this delightful dish of salt cod scrambled with eggs and olives. It's a variation on the classic *Bacalhau à Bras* (see next recipe), and frankly I prefer it.

Makes 4 to 6 servings

- ½   **pound dried salt cod**
- 2   **large yellow onions, peeled and chopped**
- 1   **large garlic clove, peeled and minced**
- 3   **tablespoons olive oil**
- ½   **cup pitted, oil-cured green olives (halve, if large)**
- 8   **large eggs**
- ¼   **cup water**
- ¼   **cup coarsely chopped parsley (preferably the flat-leaf Italian variety)**
- ¼   **teaspoon freshly ground black pepper**
-   **Green and/or black oil-cured olives for garnish**

Soak the salt cod in the refrigerator 24 hours in several changes of cold water. (Keep the bowl covered so that the whole refrigerator doesn't smell of fish.) Drain the cod, rinse, and drain well again. Now remove all bones and skin, and with your fingers pull the cod into small shreds; set aside.

Sauté the onions and garlic in the olive oil in a medium-size heavy skillet over moderate heat 5 to 6 minutes—just until the onions are limp and golden. Turn the heat down low, cover the skillet, and let the onions and garlic steam 10 minutes; add the cod, mix well, then re-cover, and cook over low heat 20 minutes, stirring now and then. Add the olives, and heat, stirring, 1 to 2 minutes. Beat the eggs with the water until frothy and add to the skillet along with the parsley and pepper. Cook 2 to 3 minutes without stirring; then, with a wooden spatula gently pull the cooked eggs from underneath to the top. Cook 1 to 2 minutes longer—just until the eggs are uniformly, softly set.

To serve, mound the eggs on a heated platter and garnish with a few strategically placed green and/or black oil-cured olives. To be really Portuguese, accompany with fried potatoes—preferably shoestring potatoes.

EGGS SCRAMBLED WITH DRIED SALT COD, ONIONS AND POTATOES
Bacalhau à Brás

Also called *Bacalhau Dourado* (golden cod), this recipe is a specialty of Estremadura, the sea-washed province in which Lisbon is located. There is a third variation on the theme, *Bacalhau à Lisbonense* (Lisbon-style salt cod) that is virtually the same (it merely uses less onion). To keep this dish from being overly salty, change the salt-cod soaking water more often than usual, and rinse the cod very well after you soak it. *Note: If you have a food processor with the fine julienne disc, use it for cutting the potatoes into matchstick strips, laying the potatoes in the feed tube crosswise so that the strips will be long and slim.*

Makes 4 servings

½   **pound dried salt cod**
3   **medium yellow onions, peeled and sliced thin**
2   **large garlic cloves, peeled and minced**

¼ cup olive oil
2 cups peanut or vegetable oil (for deep-frying the potatoes)
2 medium Idaho potatoes, peeled and cut lengthwise into matchstick strips
10 large eggs, beaten until frothy
¼ teaspoon coarsely ground black pepper
2 tablespoons coarsely chopped parsley (preferably the Italian flat-leaf variety)
12 large oil-cured black olives

Soak the salt cod in the refrigerator 24 hours in frequent changes of cold water. (Keep the bowl covered so that the refrigerator doesn't smell of fish.) Drain the cod, rinse thoroughly in cool water, and drain well again. Now remove all bones and skin, and with your fingers pull the cod into fine shreds; set aside.

Sauté the onions and garlic in the olive oil in a large heavy skillet over moderately low heat, stirring often, 5 to 6 minutes—just until onions are glassily golden. Turn the heat down low, cover the skillet, and allow all to steam 10 minutes; now add the cod, mix well, re-cover, and cook over low heat 25 minutes, stirring now and then.

Meanwhile, pour the peanut oil into a heavy medium-size sauté pan, insert a deep-fat thermometer, set over moderately high heat, and heat to 375°F. Pat the strips of potato as dry as possible between several thicknesses of paper toweling, then fry in four batches, separating the strips as they fry with a long-handled fork, until richly golden—3 to 4 minutes. With a skimmer or slotted spoon, lift the potatoes to paper toweling to drain. *Note: You can reuse the oil in which you fried the potatoes; simply cool it, strain it, and pour into a bottle with a tight-fitting cap. Store in a cool place (not the refrigerator) away from the light.*

When the cod has steamed 25 minutes, add half the fried potatoes and cook, stirring constantly, about 2 minutes. Add the eggs, pepper, and half the parsley, and cook over moderately low heat, stirring the eggs occasionally, 2 to 3 minutes until softly set.

Mound the egg mixture on a heated platter, sprinkle with the remaining parsley, and garnish with clusters of the remaining fried potatoes and the black olives. Serve at once as the main course of an informal lunch or supper, accompanied perhaps by *Salada à Portuguesa* (page 221) and chunks of one of the many good Portuguese breads. The perfect wine would be a crisp red Serradayres or Periquita.

SALT COD COUNT OF GUARDA
Bacalhau à Conde da Guarda

A surprisingly elegant salt-cod recipe that's a specialty at Aviz, one of Lisbon's fine restaurants. It's imperative that the cod be soaked in several changes of cold water so that it loses its saltiness and softens enough to shred with your fingers. The cod will steam in a *refogado* of sautéed onions and garlic instead of being simmered into submission in milk or water. It must then be puréed (a breeze with a food processor; in the old days, Portuguese chefs pounded the cod and onions to a paste with a mortar and pestle).

Makes 6 servings

¾ **pound dried salt cod**
4 **medium Maine or Eastern potatoes, scrubbed but not peeled**
¼ **pound (1 stick) unsalted butter**
2 **large yellow onions, peeled and coarsely chopped**
2 **large garlic cloves, peeled and minced**
¼ **teaspoon freshly ground black pepper**
¾ **cup half-and-half cream (about)**
3 **tablespoons freshly grated Parmesan cheese**

Soak the salt cod in the refrigerator 24 hours in several changes of cold water. (Keep the bowl covered so that the whole refrigerator doesn't smell of fish.) Drain the cod, rinse, and drain well again. Now remove all bones and skin, and with your fingers pull the cod into small shreds; set aside. Boil the potatoes in enough water to cover, 35 to 40 minutes until very tender.

Meanwhile, melt the butter in a large sauté pan over moderately low heat, dump in the onions and garlic, and sauté, stirring often, 5 to 6 minutes—just until onions are limp and glassy. Turn heat down low, cover the pan, and allow all to cook 10 minutes; add the cod, mix well, then re-cover and cook over low heat 20 minutes, stirring now and then. Set off the heat and reserve.

Preheat oven to moderately hot (375°F.). As soon as the potatoes can be pierced easily with a fork, drain well, peel, and quarter. Add the pepper and about ¼ cup of the cream, then mash the potatoes well with a potato masher. Continue mashing and adding more cream until the potatoes are very smooth, moist, and fluffy.

When the cod has cooked 20 minutes, place contents of the sauté pan in the work bowl of a food processor equipped with the metal chopping blade, and purée by churning 30 seconds nonstop; scrape down the sides of the work bowl and churn 30 seconds longer. Fold the cod mixture into the mashed potatoes, spoon into a buttered 2½-quart *au gratin* dish or 9 × 9 × 2-inch baking dish. Smooth the surface, then sprinkle the grated Parmesan evenly on top.

Bake uncovered for about 30 minutes or until the surface is touched with brown. Serve at once with steamed green beans dressed with olive oil, vinegar, and freshly chopped coriander.

ENCA MELLO'S CREAMED SALT COD
Bacalhau com Nata Feito à Moda da Enca Mello

Enca Mello (called *"Pequenina"* by friends because she's so pretty and petite) is a *Lisboeta* (Lisbonite) based at the Portuguese National Tourist Office in New York. She's an outstanding Portuguese cook and this recipe of hers is to my mind one of the best of all ways to prepare *bacalhau*.

Makes 6 to 8 servings

1½	pounds dried salt cod, cut in 4 pieces
1	large yellow onion, peeled and sliced thin
5	tablespoons olive oil
1½	pounds new or California long white potatoes, peeled and cut into very small dice (about ⅜ inch)
¼	cup water
1¾	cups milk
3	tablespoons unsalted butter
3	tablespoons flour
½	teaspoon white pepper
1½	cups heavy cream (or light cream or half-and-half, if you prefer)

Soak the salt cod in the refrigerator 24 hours (or better yet, 48 hours) in several changes of cold water. (Keep the bowl covered so the whole refrigerator doesn't smell of fish.) Drain the cod, rinse, and drain well again. Remove bones and skin, and with your fingers pull the cod into small shreds; set aside.

In a large heavy skillet set over very low heat, sauté the onion in 3 tablespoons of the olive oil about 15 minutes until very soft and golden, stirring now and then. Meanwhile, stir-fry the potatoes in the remaining oil in a second large heavy skillet over moderately low heat about 2 minutes until they begin to color; add the water, turn the heat to its lowest point, cover, and cook 15 minutes; set off the heat and reserve, still covered. As soon as the onions are softly golden, mix in the cod and ½ cup of the milk, cover, and cook over lowest heat, stirring occasionally, 30 minutes.

While the cod cooks, prepare a white sauce: Melt the butter in a small heavy saucepan over moderate heat and blend in the flour; add the remaining milk and heat, stirring constantly, until thickened and smooth—about 3 minutes. Blend in the white pepper and reserve.

When the cod has only 10 minutes more to cook, preheat the oven to very hot (450°F.). When the cod is done, mix in the potatoes, white sauce, and cream. Transfer to a buttered shallow 3-quart earthenware casserole or *au gratin* pan. Bake uncovered for 15 minutes, lower the oven temperature to moderate (350°F.), and bake uncovered 25 minutes longer or until bubbly and tipped with brown. Serve at once with a tartly dressed salad of crisp greens and, to complete the meal, a light dessert of fresh fruit. Portuguese wines available here that would complement the salt cod nicely would be such authoritative dry reds as Dão Grão Vasco or a well aged Colares. The Portuguese always prefer to sip *tinto* (red wine) with *bacalhau,* which they consider too rich and heavy for white wines.

SALT COD TURNOVERS
Pastéis de Bacalhau

Whenever I have a long day's drive ahead of me in Portugal, I try to stock up for a picnic by the side of the road with a chunk of cheese, loaf of bread, bottle of wine, and if I've been lucky enough to find a village shop that sells them, with these wonderful little half-moon pies made of salt cod and mashed potatoes. Recipes for them vary from region to region, but this one is fairly representative.

Makes 10 pies

4 ounces dried salt cod
2 small Maine or Eastern potatoes
1 medium yellow onion, peeled and chopped
1 small garlic clove, peeled and chopped
1 tablespoon olive oil
1 tablespoon unsalted butter
¼ cup milk or light cream
⅛ teaspoon freshly ground black pepper
  Salt, if needed to taste

PASTRY:

2 cups sifted all-purpose flour
¼ cup stone-ground yellow cornmeal
½ teaspoon salt
⅔ cup lard or vegetable shortening
6 to 8 tablespoons ice-cold water

FOR DEEP-FAT FRYING:

1 quart peanut or vegetable oil

Soak the salt cod in the refrigerator 24 hours in several changes of cold water. (Keep the bowl covered so that the whole refrigerator doesn't smell of fish.) Drain the cod, rinse, and drain well again. Now remove all skin and bones, and with your fingers pull the cod into small shreds; set aside. Boil the potatoes in enough water to cover, 35 to 40 minutes until very tender.

Meanwhile, sauté the onion and garlic in the olive oil and butter in a small heavy saucepan over moderately low heat, stirring often, 5 to 6 minutes—just until the onions are limp and glassy. Turn the heat down low, cover the pan, and allow the onions and garlic to cook 10 minutes; add the cod, mix well, then re-cover and cook over low heat 20 minutes, stirring now and then. Set off the heat and reserve.

When the potatoes are very tender, drain, peel, and mash with the milk and pepper. Beat in the cod mixture, taste for salt, and add if needed. Set aside while you make the pastry.

For the pastry: Sift the flour, cornmeal, and salt into a large shallow bowl; with a pastry blender or two knives, cut in the lard until the texture of coarse meal. Forking the mixture briskly, scatter into it just enough ice water to make the dry ingredients hang together. Shape the pastry into a ball, then roll out about ⅛-inch thick on a lightly floured pastry cloth with a lightly floured stockinette-covered rolling pin. Cut into 4-inch rounds (I use a small cereal bowl as a pattern), then place a level ¼ cup of the cod mixture on the lower half of each pastry circle. Moisten the edges of the pastry, fold the top half over the bottom, then crimp the edges with a fork to seal. Reroll any scraps, cut, fill, and fold as before.

In a large shallow saucepan or deep skillet, heat the oil to 375°F. on a deep-fat thermometer. Fry the pies, two at a time, 4 to 5 minutes until uniformly golden brown. Drain on paper toweling and serve at room temperature.

VARIATION:

Empadas de Bacalhau Assado no Forno (Baked Salt Cod Turnovers): The Portuguese don't bake these little pies, but you may prefer to bake them rather than fry them. Prepare the pies as directed, then bake 20 minutes in a hot oven (425°F.). Serve slightly warm.

CRAB IN A CART
Santola no Carro

Two of Lisbon's most elegant restaurants, Tavares and Tagide, serve a delicious cold crab salad mounded in the scarlet shells of the *santola,* or spiny crab. This particular recipe is my interpretation of the salad served at Tagide, which is in turn a variation on the one served at Tavares. (Among Tagide's owners are men who once worked at Tavares, Lisbon's oldest luxury restaurant, which opened in 1784.)

Makes 6 servings

- 1 **pound lump crab meat, picked over for bits of shell and cartilage, then flaked**
- 2 **hard-cooked eggs, shelled and coarsely chopped**
- 1 **medium scallion, trimmed and minced (include some green top)**
- 1 **tablespoon finely diced pimiento**
- 1 **tablespoon finely minced sour or dill pickle**
- 1 **tablespoon drained small capers**
- 1 **tablespoon minced parsley**
- ⅓ **cup *Molho Maionese* (page 92) or mayonnaise**

¼ cup light cream or half-and-half
2 tablespoons tawny or ruby Port
1 tablespoon Dijon mustard
½ teaspoon salt
¼ teaspoon liquid hot red pepper seasoning
⅛ teaspoon freshly ground black pepper

GARNISHES:

2 tablespoons minced parsley
6 matchstick strips of pimiento about 2 inches long and ¼ inch wide

Place crab, eggs, scallion, pimiento, pickle, capers, and parsley in a large bowl and toss lightly. In a small bowl combine *Molho Maionese,* cream, Port, mustard, salt, hot red pepper seasoning, and black pepper; pour over crab mixture and toss well to mix. Cover and refrigerate several hours to mellow the flavors. When ready to serve, spoon the crab mixture into 6 large blue-crab or scallop shells, dividing the total amount evenly and mounding the mixture up generously. Garnish by sprinkling each lightly with minced parsley, then lay a pimiento strip diagonally across the top of each. Serve at the start of a special lunch or dinner or serve as the main course of a light meal. A salad of mixed greens, loaf of bread, bottle of well-chilled *vinho verde,* and a fruit dessert will complete the menu nicely.

STUFFED CRAB AU GRATIN
Santola Recheada e Gratinada

Many years ago on one of my earliest trips to Portugal, friends took me to a restaurant just outside Porto pitched upon a low rocky cliff above the ocean. My meal there was so memorable, I took detailed notes on each dish, among them this stunning stuffed crab. The restaurant no longer exists, alas, but most of Portugal's top dining spots do serve some version of *Santola Recheada*.

Makes 6 servings

1	medium yellow onion, peeled and moderately finely chopped
1	medium carrot, peeled and finely chopped
⅓	cup moderately finely chopped sweet red pepper
1	tablespoon olive oil
1	tablespoon unsalted butter
2	tablespoons water
1	pound lump crab meat, picked over for bits of shell and cartilage, then flaked
½	cup moderately fine soft white bread crumbs
⅓	cup *Molho Maionese* (page 92) or mayonnaise
3	tablespoons moderately finely chopped oil-cured black olives
3	tablespoons tawny Port
3	tablespoons light cream or half-and-half
1	tablespoon Dijon mustard
1	tablespoon lemon juice
1	tablespoon minced parsley
½	teaspoon salt
¼	teaspoon liquid hot red pepper seasoning
⅛	teaspoon black pepper

TOPPING:

¾	cup moderately fine soft white bread crumbs
2	tablespoons grated Parmesan cheese

Preheat oven to hot (400°F.). In a small heavy skillet set over moderate heat, sauté the onion, carrot, and sweet red pepper in the olive oil and butter 2 minutes; add the water, cover, turn heat to its lowest point, and let all steam 15 minutes. Meanwhile, place all remaining ingredients except the topping in a large bowl and toss lightly to mix. Add the skillet mixture and toss well again. Mound the mixture into greased large blue-crab or scallop shells or, failing either, into 5- or 6-ounce ramekins. Combine the topping ingredients and scatter evenly on top of the crab mixture. Bake uncovered about 20 minutes until topping is touched with brown. Serve at the beginning of an elegant dinner, or serve as the main course of a light luncheon accompanied by a green salad, tartly dressed, and chunks of a delicate Portuguese bread such as *Pão de Mesa* (page 230).

SHRIMP WITH HOT RED PEPPERS
Camarões Piri-Piri

Piri-piri are incendiary little red peppers from Angola. The Portuguese can't get enough of them, so they keep bottles of *Molho de Piri-piri* (a sauce somewhat like Tabasco) on the table alongside the salt and pepper, then sprinkle this liquid fire over virtually everything—French fries, steamed greens, shellfish. Although I am not as much a fan of *piri-piri* sauce as the Portuguese, I must admit that *Molho de Piri-piri* is the perfect dunk for shrimp prepared this way, a dish that has recently become a great specialty at a number of Lisbon's top restaurants. *Note: Because* piri-piri *peppers are unobtainable here, I've substituted the more widely available long, slender, twisted cayenne pods. You can also use the scarlet New Mexico chilis, the tiny but explosive chili pequins, even the green jalapeño peppers. Just add them in stages, tasting as you go, so that the shrimp aren't so torrid they bring tears to your eyes.*

Makes 4 to 6 servings

> 2 pounds raw jumbo shrimp, shelled and deveined
> 1 large garlic clove, peeled and crushed
> 2 medium bright-red cayenne peppers, cored and minced (leave the seeds in if you can take the heat—they're where the peppers' heat is concentrated)
> ½ cup olive oil

FOR DIPPING:

> ¾ cup *Molho de Piri-piri* (page 91), or mix ¾ cup olive oil with 1 to 2 teaspoons liquid hot red pepper seasoning (depending upon how hot you can stand things)

Place the shrimp, garlic, cayenne, and olive oil in a 9 × 9 × 2-inch baking dish and toss well; cover and marinate at least 24 hours in the refrigerator. When ready to cook, preheat the broiler. Lay the shrimp on a well-oiled broiler pan and brush generously with the marinade. Broil 5 inches from the heat 2 minutes; turn the shrimp, brush well again with marinade, and broil 2 minutes longer. Serve sizzling hot with little bowls of the dipping sauce (one for each person). To cool the fire, accompany with a crisp green salad, chunks of good Portuguese bread, and a well chilled *vinho verde*.

VARIATION:

Camarões Grelhados Piri-piri (Grilled Shrimp with Hot Red Peppers): Marinate the shrimp as directed. When ready to cook, build a hot charcoal fire and when the flames have died down, leaving white-hot coals, arrange the shrimp, not quite touching one another, on 4 to 6 well-oiled long metal skewers. Adjust the height of the grill so that it is about 6 inches above the coals, lay the skewers on the grill, and cook about 6 minutes, turning often, and brushing with additional marinade. Serve with little bowls of *Molho de Piri-piri*.

CLAMS IN A CATAPLANA CASA VELHA
Amêijoas na Cataplana Casa Velha

The Portuguese ingenuity for combining pork and shellfish in a single dish dates back, it's been said, to one of the darker chapters of Iberian history—the Inquisition. *Amêijoas na Cataplana*, together with a number of other pork-shellfish combinations, were invented as a sort of culinary double-whammy to test one's Christian zeal (pork and shellfish being proscribed to both Jews and Moslems). On a recent swing through the Algarve Province, where this popular *cataplana* recipe originated, I tried to verify the theory, without success. Manuel Paulino Revéz and Esteban Medel do Carmo, assistant directors at Faro's Escola de Hotelaria e Turismo do Algarve (Algarve Hotel and Tourism School), both doubt that there's any connection between the Inquisition and the creation of Portugal's many pork and shellfish combinations. They do admit, however, that *Amêijoas na Cataplana* is a recipe so old that its genesis is clouded by the dust of ages. Whatever its origin, the gloriously soupy mélange of unshucked baby clams, ham, and sausages in garlicky tomato sauce is supremely successful. This particular version comes from Casa Velha, once one of the Algarve's top restaurants. Now closed, alas, it was located in a historic, heavily beamed farmhouse amid the umbrella pines and luxury estates of Quinta do Lago near Faro. *Note: Portuguese clams are tiny, thin-shelled, and uncommonly sweet. The best substitutes are West Coast butter clams or, failing them, the smallest littlenecks you can find. This dish need not be prepared in a* cataplana, *a hinged metal container shaped like a giant clam shell that can be clamped shut; any kettle with a tight-fitting lid works well. Finally, this is a naturally salty dish, so add no extra salt before tasting.*

Makes 6 servings

4	dozen uniformly small clams in the shell
2	gallons cold water
3	tablespoons salt
2	tablespoons cornmeal

SAUCE:

3	medium Spanish onions, peeled and sliced thin
3	large garlic cloves, peeled and minced
2	large sweet green peppers, cored, seeded, and cut in thin strips
¼	cup olive oil
1	large bay leaf, crumbled
1	can (1 pound) water-pack tomatoes (do not drain)
1	can (8 ounces) tomato sauce
2	ounces lean prosciutto, cut into small dice
¼	pound lean smoked ham, cut into small dice
¼	pound *chouriço, chorizo* or pepperoni, cut into small dice
½	cup dry white wine
¼	cup coarsely chopped Italian parsley

Scrub the clams well in cool water, pile in a large deep kettle, add the cold water, salt, and the cornmeal, which acts as an irritant that forces the clams to purge themselves of grit. Let the clams stand in the cold water about 1 hour.

Meanwhile, prepare the sauce: Stir-fry the onions, garlic, and green peppers in the oil in a large heavy skillet over moderate heat 8 to 10 minutes until limp and golden. Add the bay leaf, tomatoes, and their juice. Break up any large clumps of tomatoes, bring mixture to a simmer, cover, and cook slowly for 30 minutes; add the tomato sauce, prosciutto, smoked ham, and pepperoni, re-cover, and cook 30 minutes longer. *Note: You can make the sauce as much as two days ahead of time but do not buy the clams until the day you plan to serve the* cataplana. *The sauce should be covered and refrigerated until you are ready to proceed.*

To assemble the *cataplana,* spoon half the tomato mixture into the bottom of a very large *cataplana* (it should measure about 15 inches across) or into a large heavy

Dutch-oven type of kettle, and bring to a simmer over moderate heat. Adjust the heat so that the mixture barely boils, arrange the clams on top, spoon in the remaining tomato sauce, cover tight, and cook 10 minutes over moderately low heat—no peeking. Open the *cataplana* or kettle, pour in the wine, scatter the parsley evenly on top, then toss the clams lightly. Re-cover and cook slowly 15 to 20 minutes longer until the clams open—discard any that do not.

Carry the *cataplana* or kettle to the table, open, and ladle into large soup plates. Serve with *Pão* (page 224) or other rough country bread. *Note: Be sure to put out a large bowl for empty clam shells.*

MUSSELS IN A CATAPLANA
Mexilhões na Cataplana

Because of the natural brininess of mussels, not to mention the saltiness of the ham and sausage used in this recipe, you are not likely to need additional salt.

Makes 4 to 6 servings

2	tablespoons olive oil
¼	pound prosciutto (in one piece), trimmed of fat and cut into ¼-inch cubes
¼	pound *chouriço, chorizo,* pepperoni, or other dry garlicky sausage, sliced thin
3	medium yellow onions, peeled and sliced thin
1	small Spanish or Bermuda onion, peeled and sliced thin
3	large garlic cloves, peeled and minced
½	sweet green pepper, cored, seeded, and cut in thin slivers
2	large bay leaves (do not crumble)
2	teaspoons paprika
¼	teaspoon crushed dry red chili peppers
¼	teaspoon freshly ground black pepper
2	cans (14½ ounces each) tomatoes (drain 1 can)
⅔	cup dry white wine (preferably a Portuguese Dão or *vinho verde*)
3½	dozen small mussels in the shell, scrubbed well under cool running water, then bearded
3	tablespoons chopped Italian parsley
3	tablespoons chopped fresh coriander

Heat 1 tablespoon of the oil in a very large heavy skillet over moderate heat about 1 minute until ripples appear on the skillet bottom; add the prosciutto and *chouriço* and stir-fry 2 minutes; with a slotted spoon, lift to paper toweling to drain. Add the remaining tablespoon of oil to the skillet, dump in the onions, garlic, and green pepper, add the bay leaves, and sauté, stirring now and then, about 5 minutes until onions begin to color and turn glassy. Blend in the paprika, chili peppers, and black pepper and mellow 2 minutes over moderate heat. Add the tomatoes (also the liquid from 1 can) and ⅓ cup of the white wine, reduce heat to low, cover, and simmer 40 minutes. Stir in the reserved prosciutto and *chouriço. Note: You can prepare the recipe up to this point a day or two in advance; transfer the tomato mixture to a bowl, cover tight, and refrigerate until ready to proceed.*

To assemble the *cataplana,* spoon half the tomato mixture into the bottom of a very large *cataplana* (it should measure about 15 inches across) or into a large heavy Dutch-oven type of kettle, and bring to a simmer over moderate heat. Adjust the heat so that the mixture barely bubbles, arrange the mussels on top, spoon in the remaining tomato mixture, splash in the remaining white wine, then sprinkle with 1½ tablespoons each chopped parsley and coriander. Close tight and simmer 15 minutes; carefully open the *cataplana* or kettle, gently stir the mussels up from the bottom, and if some of them are still closed, re-cover and simmer gently 5 minutes longer—just until the mussels open and spill their juices into the tomato mixture. Discard any that do not open.

Carry the *cataplana* or kettle to the table, open, and sprinkle with the remaining chopped parsley and coriander. Ladle into large soup plates and serve with chewy chunks of *Pão* (page 224). *Note: Don't forget to put out a big bowl for the empty mussel shells.*

SCALLOPS PORTUGUESE-STYLE
Vieiras à Portuguesa

Scallops are scarce today in Portugal—almost to the point of extinction. But I do remember being served them this way twenty or twenty-five years ago in a Lisbon restaurant whose name, I'm ashamed to say, is lost in a maze of memories. I also remember how much I enjoyed the scallops and consider few recipes for them better than this one. *Note: Because of the natural brininess of the scallops, this recipe needs no added salt.*

Makes 4 servings

1	pound bay scallops
2	tablespoons olive oil
1	medium yellow onion, peeled and chopped
1	medium garlic clove, peeled and minced
2	tablespoons minced parsley
2	tablespoons tomato paste
1	teaspoon dry Port
¼	teaspoon freshly ground black pepper

TOPPING:

4	tablespoons fine soft bread crumbs
3	tablespoons freshly grated Parmesan cheese
1	tablespoon olive oil

Preheat the oven to moderately hot (375°F.). Sauté the scallops in 1 tablespoon of the oil in a large heavy skillet over high heat 3 to 4 minutes—just until they begin to color and have released their juices. With a slotted spoon, lift the scallops to a bowl and reserve. Now boil down the scallop juices 1 to 2 minutes until reduced to a glaze; add the remaining tablespoon of olive oil, the onion, garlic, and parsley, and sauté 2 to 3 minutes until onions begin to look glassy; turn the heat to low, cover, and steam 10 minutes. Blend in the tomato paste, Port, and pepper, also any juices that have accumulated in the bowl of scallops, and cook and stir 2 minutes; return the scallops to the skillet and toss lightly. Quickly mix together topping ingredients. Spoon the scallop mixture into 4 lightly buttered large scallop shells, dividing the total amount evenly. Scatter the topping on top, again dividing the total evenly.

Note: The recipe may be prepared up to this point as much as a day ahead of time. Cover each scallop shell individually with plastic food wrap and refrigerate until ready to cook.

Place the scallop shells on a baking sheet and bake uncovered for 15 to 20 minutes until bubbly and touched with brown (only refrigerated shells will need the full 20 minutes). Serve at once as the first course of an elegant dinner, or serve as the main course of a light lunch or supper, accompanied by a green salad and plenty of bread.

SCALLOPS ALGARVE-STYLE
Vieiras à Moda do Algarve

In Portugal, it is cockles that are prepared this way, but since they are rarely available here, I have taken the liberty of substituting bay scallops. The flavor is more subtle, but no less delicious. *Note: You must use fresh coriander for this recipe—the dried just hasn't the adequate lemony-nutty flavor.*

Makes 4 servings

1	pound bay scallops
2	medium garlic cloves, peeled and minced
4	teaspoons olive oil
1	tablespoon lemon juice
¼	teaspoon cayenne pepper
¼	cup freshly minced coriander

Stir-fry the scallops and garlic in the oil in a large heavy skillet over high heat 3 to 4 minutes—just until they begin to color and have released their juices. With a slotted spoon, lift the scallops to a bowl and reserve. Add the lemon juice and cayenne to the skillet and boil with the scallop juices about 2 minutes until reduced to a glaze. Return the scallops to the skillet together with any juices that may have accumulated in the bowl and toss 1 to 2 minutes over high heat. Add the coriander, toss again, and serve. Delicious with *Salada à Portuguesa* (page 221) and chunks of husky Portuguese bread.

STUFFED SQUID LISBON-STYLE
Lulas Recheadas à Lisbonense

A Lisbon hostess once told me that she stuffed two hundred baby squid for a very special party, and I wasn't, I now realize, properly impressed. Squid are slithery creatures. Their body cavities are deep, but not much bigger around than your middle finger. They are the very devil to stuff, especially if the stuffing is as moist and sticky as this one. Just resign yourself to the fact that it will take an hour, at least, to stuff the squid for this recipe, but have faith that the results are well worth the effort. This is another Portuguese recipe that combines pork and shellfish. (Yes, squid *are* shellfish. They belong to the family of cephalopods, which carry their shells internally; the cuttlebone beloved by canaries comes from certain cephalopods.) As for the pork, finely minced *presunto*, the nut-sweet, faintly smoky, air-cured Portuguese ham goes into the stuffing; I've substituted prosciutto. *Note: Because of the saltiness of the ham, bacon, and squid, this recipe is not likely to need salt.*

Makes 6 servings

1½	pounds small squid, well cleaned and the tentacles separated from the bodies
¼	pound slab bacon, cut into small dice
3	tablespoons olive oil
2	medium yellow onions, peeled and sliced thin
2	medium carrots, peeled and sliced thin
1	large garlic clove, peeled and minced
½	cup fish stock or bottled clam juice
½	cup dry white wine
3	tablespoons tomato paste
	Juice of 1 large lemon
1	bay leaf (do not crumble)

STUFFING:

1	medium yellow onion, peeled and chopped
1	small garlic clove, peeled and minced
1	small carrot, peeled and chopped
2	tablespoons olive oil
1	tablespoon bacon drippings

The squid tentacles, washed well, freed of grit, and coarsely chopped. (You'll have to use a very sharp, very heavy knife because the tentacles are extremely gelatinous.)

¼   pound prosciutto, finely minced

2   tablespoons tomato paste

2   cups fine soft bread crumbs

¼   cup dry white wine

⅓   cup water

¼   teaspoon freshly ground black pepper

1   tablespoon minced parsley

2   egg yolks, lightly beaten

Wash the squid well in cool water inside and out, pat dry on paper toweling, then cut the tops off the larger squid so that all are more or less the same size; set aside. Slice the squid trimmings about ½-inch thick and reserve. (You'll add them to the kettle.) Sauté the bacon in 1 tablespoon of the olive oil in a small heavy skillet over moderate heat 5 to 6 minutes until all the drippings have cooked out and only crisp brown bits remain; with a slotted spoon, lift the brown bits to paper toweling to drain. Pour off all bacon drippings and reserve.

Spoon 2 tablespoons of the bacon drippings into a large heavy kettle, add the remaining olive oil, and set over high heat until ripples appear on the kettle bottom. Dump in the onions, carrots, and garlic, and sauté over moderate heat, stirring often, about 5 minutes until onions begin to look glassy; add the squid trimmings, cover, and steam over low heat 20 minutes. Mix in the fish stock, wine, tomato paste, and lemon juice, drop in the bay leaf, cover, and allow to bubble lazily over low heat while you prepare the stuffing.

For the stuffing: Sauté the onion, garlic, and carrot in the olive oil and bacon drippings in a large heavy skillet over moderate heat 5 minutes until the onions begin to look glassy; add the chopped squid tentacles, turn heat to low, cover, and steam 20 minutes. Mix in the prosciutto, tomato paste, bread crumbs, wine, water, pepper, and parsley, and cook and stir 2 to 3 minutes until very thick and pastelike. Remove from the heat, cool slightly, then blend in the egg yolks.

To stuff the squid, take up small bits of the stuffing in your fingers and poke it down into the body of a squid; keep this up until you have stuffed the squid body to within about ¾ inch of the top; close the top with a toothpick (to keep the stuffing from pushing out as the squid cook). Stuff the remaining squid the same way, making sure not to pack the stuffing in and also to leave plenty of room at the top for the stuffing to expand after each squid has been closed with its toothpick.

Lay the squid on their sides in the kettle, in two layers, if necessary. Adjust the heat so that the kettle liquid just quivers, cover, and cook 1 hour. Now slip a Flame-

Tamer under the kettle, turn the heat to its lowest point, and let the squid mellow, still covered, 45 minutes longer. Carefully remove the toothpicks from all of the squid, then sprinkle the reserved bacon bits evenly over all.

Serve hot with a cool, crisp salad, chunks of robust *Pão* or *Pão de Centeio* (pages 224 and 236), and a well-rounded, full-bodied Portuguese red wine such as a Colares.

Vegetables, Rice and Salads
✳
Legumes, Arroz e Saladas

FRESH FAVA BEANS WITH CORIANDER
Favas com Coentro

If you are able to find fresh fava beans, by all means use them for this recipe. Otherwise substitute fresh or frozen Fordhook lima beans. Make no substitutions, however, for the fresh coriander. It's essential for flavor.

Makes 4 to 6 servings

2	ounces lean slab bacon, cut into small dice
1	small yellow onion, peeled and chopped
1½	pounds shelled fresh fava beans or Fordhook limas (weighed after shelling), or 2 boxes (10 ounces each) frozen Fordhook limas
¾	cup water (about)
¼	teaspoon salt (about)
¼	teaspoon freshly ground black pepper (about)
⅓	cup chopped fresh coriander

In a large heavy saucepan set over low heat, fry the bacon until most of the drippings have cooked out and only crisp brown bits remain; with a slotted spoon, transfer the bacon bits to paper toweling to drain. Add the onion to the drippings and sauté, stirring now and then, about 5 minutes until limp. Add the beans and the water, cover, and simmer 20 to 25 minutes until beans are tender and no longer taste starchy. *Note: Watch the pot closely and if the fresh beans threaten to cook dry, add a bit more water. On the other hand, if you're using the frozen Fordhook limas, reduce the amount of water to ¼ cup and cook the beans 10 to 12 minutes only.* Drain off excess water, if any, add the reserved bacon bits, the salt, pepper, and coriander, and toss lightly to mix. Taste for salt and pepper and add more of each, if needed. Serve hot with roast pork or poultry. (I even like these beans cold.)

GREEN BEANS WITH CORIANDER AND GARLIC
Feijão Verde com Coentro e Alho

There's a reason for adding the lemon juice and vinegar to the green beans *after* they've marinated. If you mix these acids in too soon, the beans will turn an unappetizing shade of brown.

Makes 6 to 8 servings

2	pounds tender young green beans, washed and tipped
3	quarts boiling water plus 1½ teaspoons salt
2	large garlic cloves, peeled and minced
⅔	cup coarsely chopped fresh coriander (the dried won't do)
5	to 6 tablespoons olive oil
1	tablespoon lemon juice
3	to 4 tablespoons cider vinegar
¼	teaspoon freshly ground black pepper (about)

Cook the beans in the boiling salted water in a large covered saucepan over moderate heat 10 to 12 minutes until tender. Meanwhile, place the garlic and coriander in a large heat-proof bowl. As soon as the beans are done, drain well, return to moderate heat, and shake the pan 30 to 40 seconds to drive off all excess moisture. Dump the hot beans on top of the garlic and coriander and let stand 10 minutes. Add 5

tablespoons of the olive oil and toss well to mix; cover and marinate in the refrigerator 3 to 4 hours or, better yet, overnight.

About 45 minutes before serving, bring the beans from the refrigerator and let
stand, still covered, on the counter. Just before serving, add the lemon juice, 3
tablespoons of the vinegar, and the pepper. Toss well, taste, and add more vinegar,
olive oil, salt, and pepper, if needed. Serve as an accompaniment to pork, poultry,
veal, or beef.

WHITE BEANS WITH TOMATO SAUCE
Feijão Branco de Tomatada

A favorite accompaniment for roast pork, these beans are popular all over Portugal.

Makes 6 servings

1	**pound dried navy or pea beans, washed and sorted**
6	**cups cold water**
1	**large Spanish onion, peeled and sliced thin**
3	**large parsley branches**
½	**pound slab bacon, in one piece**
1	**cup tomato sauce**
½	**teaspoon salt (about)**
¼	**teaspoon freshly ground black pepper (about)**

Soak the beans overnight in 4 cups of the water. Next day, place the beans and their
soaking water in a large heavy saucepan, add the remaining water, onion, parsley,
and bacon, and bring to a simmer over moderate heat. Adjust the heat so that the
liquid bubbles gently, cover, and cook about 1 hour and 15 minutes until the beans
are firm-tender. Drain the beans and discard the parsley. Remove the bacon, cut into
small dice, and reserve. Add the tomato sauce, salt, and pepper to the beans, return
to low heat, cover, and simmer 10 minutes.

Meanwhile, brown the bacon in a small heavy skillet over moderate heat until
most of the drippings cook out and the bacon is crisply golden. Stir both the bacon
and the drippings into the beans, re-cover, and cook 5 minutes longer. Taste for salt
and pepper, and add a little more of each, if needed, then serve hot.

GREEN PEAS IN THE STYLE OF PORTIMÃO
Ervilhas à Moda de Portimão

In the Algarve, these peas are served as a main dish—altogether appropriate, since the recipe contains both sausage and eggs. Algarve cooks would use the paprika-drenched *linguiça* to make the dish, or garlicky *chouriço*. Substitute a good Spanish *chorizo,* if you must, or sweet Italian sausage or pepperoni.

Makes 6 servings

- 1   medium yellow onion, peeled and coarsely chopped
- 1   small sweet red pepper, cored, seeded, and cut into matchstick strips
- ¼   pound *linguiça, chouriço, chorizo,* garlicky Italian sausage, or pepperoni, sliced very thin
- 1   tablespoon olive oil
- 1   quart shelled fresh green peas, or partially thawed frozen green peas
- 1   quart water plus 1 tablespoon vinegar
- 6   medium eggs
- ¼   teaspoon salt (about)
- ⅛   teaspoon freshly ground black pepper (about)
- 2   tablespoons minced parsley

In a large heavy saucepan set over moderate heat, sauté the onion, red pepper, and sausage in the olive oil about 5 minutes until onion is limp; turn heat to its lowest point, cover pan, and simmer 20 minutes (this is another version of the Portuguese technique of *refogado*). Add the peas, re-cover, and cook over low heat, stirring once or twice, until tender. Fresh peas may require the addition of about ½ cup water and will take 8 to 10 minutes to cook; frozen peas need only to be heated 3 to 4 minutes.

   While the peas cook, pour the quart of acidulated water into a medium skillet and bring to a simmer over moderate heat. One by one, break the eggs into a saucer, and, after stirring the simmering water into a little whirlpool, slide the egg in. Poach the eggs just 3 minutes, lift from the water with a slotted spoon, and drain on paper toweling.

   As soon as the peas are tender, season to taste with salt and pepper, sprinkle with parsley, and toss well. Mound the peas in a bowl and place the softly poached eggs strategically on top. When serving, make sure everyone gets an egg.

CARROTS SINTRA-STYLE
Cenouras à Moda de Sintra

Although the Portuguese are masters at preparing fish, poultry, and game, and although they are bread bakers and pastry chefs of uncommon skill, they do not as a rule do justice to vegetables. This splendid recipe from the lush green resort of Sintra directly west of Lisbon is a notable exception.

Makes 4 servings

1	pound medium carrots, peeled and cut into 1½-inch chunks (halve any thick portions from the tops of the carrots lengthwise)
2¼	cups boiling beef broth (preferably homemade)
4	tablespoons unsalted butter
4	tablespoons flour
¼	teaspoon freshly ground black pepper
3	egg yolks, lightly beaten with 1 tablespoon lemon juice
	Salt, if needed, to taste
2	tablespoons minced parsley

Boil the carrots in the broth in a covered heavy saucepan over moderate heat for 30 minutes until tender; drain, reserving the broth. In a small heavy saucepan set over moderate heat, melt the butter, blend in the flour and pepper, and mellow over low heat, stirring often, 3 to 5 minutes until no raw floury taste remains. Pour in the reserved broth and heat, stirring constantly, until thickened and smooth—about 3 minutes. Blend a little of the hot sauce into the egg yolks, stir back into the pan, and cook, stirring constantly over lowest heat, 2 to 3 minutes until no raw egg flavor remains. Pour the sauce over the carrots, toss lightly to mix, and warm 3 to 4 minutes over low heat. Taste for salt and add, if necessary. Sprinkle with minced parsley and serve.

SAUTÉED SPRING GREENS WITH OLIVE OIL AND GARLIC
Grelos

Grelar is the Portuguese verb meaning to bud or sprout. That is precisely what *grelos* are, spring's first sprouts of a pungent nonheading broccoli, also of turnip or mustard greens, which are available everywhere in Portugal in April and May. By all means use turnips or mustard greens for this recipe (and the younger the better). If they are not available, try delicate shoots of spinach this way. They're wonderful with roast pork, turkey, or chicken.

Makes 4 to 6 servings

2	**pounds tender young mustard or turnip greens, or spinach**
2	**large cloves garlic, peeled and minced**
3	**tablespoons olive oil**
¾	**teaspoon salt (about)**
¼	**teaspoon freshly ground black pepper (about)**

Pick over the greens carefully, removing withered leaves and all coarse stems and veins. Wash the greens in several changes of tepid water by sloshing gently up and down. Lift leaves from the rinse water by handfuls, shaking off excess water. Bundle in several thicknesses of paper toweling and let stand 10 to 15 minutes. Rebundle in dry paper toweling and store in the refrigerator overnight or until ready to cook.

Sauté the garlic in the oil in a large heavy kettle over low heat 10 to 12 minutes, stirring now and then, until soft; do not allow to brown. Dump in all the greens and toss well in the garlic oil. Now stir-fry 2 to 3 minutes over high heat, just until greens wilt and are nicely glossed with oil. Sprinkle with salt and pepper, toss well again, and taste for seasoning. Add more salt and pepper if needed. Toss well again and serve *at once*.

PURÉED GREENS WITH GARLIC, ONION AND OLIVE OIL
Esparregado

Spinach is the preferred green for this recipe, although for added zip a mixture of spinach and mustard and/or turnip greens is often used. Lisbon's top restaurants usually present *esparregado* in hollowed-out baked tomatoes or in golden baskets of deep-fried straw potatoes.

Makes 4 servings

2   **pounds tender young spinach leaves**
1   **pound tender young mustard or turnip greens, or ½ pound of each**
2   **medium yellow onions, peeled and minced**
2   **medium garlic cloves, peeled and minced**
2   **tablespoons olive oil**
1   **tablespoon unsalted butter**
½   **teaspoon salt (about)**
⅛   **teaspoon freshly ground black pepper**

Sort the spinach and other greens carefully, rejecting any leaves that are coarse or discolored. Remove tough veins and stems from the remaining leaves, then wash the leaves several times in sinkfuls of tepid water, sloshing them gently up and down so that the grit loosens and sinks to the bottom. Lift the greens by handfuls from the water and shake to remove excess. Pile the greens in a very large heavy kettle, set over moderate heat, cover, and steam about 15 minutes until very tender—you won't need to add additional water. Dump the steamed greens into a large fine-meshed sieve and press with the back of a wooden spoon to force out as much liquid as possible; leave the greens in the sieve for the moment.

    In a large heavy skillet set over moderate heat, sauté the onions and garlic in the olive oil and butter 10 to 12 minutes until limp and lightly browned. Add the greens, salt, and pepper, and toss all well. Taste for salt and add more, if needed. Mellow the greens over moderate heat, stirring often, 1 to 2 minutes. Now transfer all into the work bowl of a food processor fitted with a metal chopping blade, and purée by buzzing 30 seconds nonstop; scrape down the sides of the work bowl with a rubber spatula and buzz 30 seconds longer. If you do not have a food processor, purée the greens in batches in an electric blender or force all through a food mill. Return the purée to the skillet, set over low heat, and bring just to serving temperature. Delicious with roast pork or chicken.

VARIATION:

Esparregado nos Tomates Assados (Puréed Greens in Baked Tomatoes): Hollow out four medium, firm-ripe tomatoes, leaving walls about ⅜-inch thick. Drain the tomatoes upside-down on several thicknesses of paper toweling about 1 hour. Prepare the *Esparregado* as directed, spoon into the tomatoes and bake uncovered in a moderately hot oven (375°F.) for 15 to 20 minutes until tomatoes are tender. Serve at once.

POTATO CHIPS
Batatas Fritas

The potatoes of Portugal have a deep earthiness and intense nutty flavor. Fried in a mixture of peanut and olive oil, they're light and crisp and put our own potato chips to shame. Most *pousadas* put out little plates of freshly made *batatas fritas* for you to munch with cocktails—and replenish the supply as fast as you wolf the chips down. *Note: The oil in which you fry the potatoes can be recycled to fry other foods in later. Cool it to room temperature, strain it, pour it into a bottle, cap tight, and store on a cool dark shelf—not in the refrigerator.*

Makes 4 servings

> 4   medium Idaho potatoes
> 1   quart peanut or vegetable oil
> 1   quart olive oil
>   Salt to taste

Peel the potatoes and slice very thin. Spread the slices out on several thicknesses of paper toweling, top with more paper toweling, and pat very dry; leave the potatoes in the toweling while you heat the oil. Pour the peanut and olive oils into a deep-fat fryer, insert a deep-fat thermometer, set over moderately high heat, and heat to 375°F. Ease a handful of potatoes into the fat, separate the slices with a long-handled fork, and fry until richly golden—3 to 4 minutes. With a skimmer or slotted spoon, lift the potatoes to paper toweling to drain. Let the temperature of the fat return to 375°F. before adding each subsequent batch of potatoes and keep the deep fat as nearly at that temperature as possible by lowering and raising the burner heat as needed. Serve the chips at once, lightly salted if you wish, as an accompaniment to meat or as a cocktail snack.

VARIATION:

Batatas Palhas (Straw Potatoes): Peel the potatoes, slice very thin (about ⅛ inch) lengthwise, then stack 3 or 4 slices together, and cut lengthwise into very thin strips. *Note: If you have a food processor and its fine julienne disc, by all means use it to cut the potatoes. Lay them crosswise in the feed tube so that you get long slim strips. Portuguese women have little hand shredders with which they can cut straw potatoes almost as fast as a food processor can. It's fascinating to watch them work, whisking the potatoes back and forth across the shredder with lightning speed.*

Once all the potatoes have been cut, spread them out on several thicknesses of paper toweling, top with more paper toweling, and pat very dry. Fry in small batches as directed for potato chips, keeping the temperature of the fat as near to 375°F. as possible throughout the frying and separating the potato strands with a long-handled fork. *Note: Portuguese women not only serve straw potatoes as a vegetable, they also use them as a recipe ingredient. They are integral, for example, to* Bacalhau à Bras, *(page 182). And they are used as a garnish for platters of meat and poultry.*

CORIANDER POTATOES
Batatas com Coentro

Instead of rolling boiled potatoes in butter and minced parsley as we do, Portuguese women turn them in a mixture of olive oil and butter, then in finely minced fresh coriander leaves. Delicious! *Note: You must use fresh coriander for this recipe—the fresher the better and more fragrant.*

Makes 4 to 6 servings

12	small new potatoes of uniform size, scrubbed but not peeled
3	tablespoons olive oil
3	tablespoons unsalted butter
¼	cup finely minced fresh coriander leaves
½	teaspoon salt (about)
⅛	teaspoon freshly ground black pepper

Cook the potatoes in enough water to cover in a large covered saucepan over moderate heat until fork-tender—35 to 40 minutes; drain well, cool until easy to handle, then slip off the skins. Warm the olive oil and butter in a large heavy skillet over low heat. Add the peeled potatoes and turn in the oil mixture 1 to 2 minutes until the potatoes begin to color; sprinkle the coriander over all and turn the potatoes in the coriander 2 to 3 minutes until nicely coated. Sprinkle with salt, taste, and add a little more if needed, then sprinkle with pepper and serve.

VARIATION:

Batatas com Hortelã (Minted Potatoes): Prepare as directed but substitute 3 tablespoons finely chopped fresh mint for the coriander.

BAY-SCENTED POTATOES
Batatas com Louro

These aromatic potatoes, popular throughout Portugal, are most often served as an accompaniment to roast pork or poultry.

Makes 4 to 6 servings

2	pounds new potatoes of uniform size, scrubbed but not peeled
1	medium yellow onion, peeled and stuck with 2 cloves
2	tablespoons unsalted butter
2	tablespoons olive oil
4	large bay leaves, crumbled fine
½	teaspoon salt
¼	teaspoon freshly ground black pepper

Boil the potatoes with the onion in water to cover about 30 minutes until fork-tender. Meanwhile, melt the butter in a large heavy skillet over low heat; mix in the olive oil and crumbled bay leaves and let steep at the back of the stove while the potatoes cook. As soon as the potatoes are tender, discard the onion, drain the potatoes well, and peel. Strain the butter mixture and return to the skillet. Add the potatoes, set over moderate heat, and turn them in the bay-scented butter mixture about 5 minutes until nicely glazed and touched with brown. Sprinkle with salt and pepper and serve.

ROASTED SWEET PEPPERS
Pimentos Assados

Oregano is not a popular herb in Portugal except in the Alentejo, where it grows wild among the corks and olives. Portuguese country cooks favor sweet red peppers for this recipe, but for color I like to use a half-and-half mixture of the red and the green.

Makes 4 servings

8	large sweet red peppers, or 4 red and 4 green
4	tablespoons olive oil
4½	teaspoons cider vinegar
¾	teaspoon kosher or coarse salt (about)
½	teaspoon crumbled leaf oregano (about)
¼	teaspoon freshly ground black pepper (about)

Preheat the oven to hot (400°F.). Wash the peppers well, then lay them on their sides in a large shallow baking pan; bake uncovered 20 minutes, turn the peppers, and bake 15 to 20 minutes longer until the skins look papery and blistered; remove from the oven and cool until easy to handle. Pull the stems from the peppers, quarter each pepper lengthwise, remove all seeds, then peel off the skins; pat the peppers dry on paper toweling. Arrange a single layer of peppers in a shallow broad-bottomed bowl, drizzle with half the oil and vinegar, then sprinkle with half the salt, oregano, and pepper. Layer the remaining peppers on top, drizzle with the rest of the oil and vinegar, and sprinkle with salt, oregano, and pepper as before. Cover and marinate at room temperature 3 to 4 hours. Serve in place of salad.

STEWED WHOLE ONIONS
Cebolas Estufadas

The best onions to use for this recipe are the sweet, mild, fawn-skinned Spanish onions often erroneously called Bermuda onions. When peeling the onions, do as the Portuguese do: Slice off the root or bottom end, then peel the outer layers upward, leaving a graceful twist of skin at the top.

Makes 6 servings

6	Spanish onions (each should be about 3½ inches in diameter)
3	tablespoons olive oil
4	bay leaves (do not crumble)
1½	cups beef broth (preferably homemade)
¼	teaspoon salt
¼	teaspoon freshly ground black pepper
2	tablespoons minced parsley

Preheat the oven to moderate (350°F.). Brown the onions lightly in the oil in a large heavy sauté pan or flameproof shallow casserole set over moderately high heat 8 to 10 minutes, turning the onions constantly in the oil. Add the bay leaves and beef broth, turn the onions so that the twists are on top, sprinkle evenly with salt and pepper, cover, and bake 45 minutes. Uncover and bake about 15 minutes longer or until the onions are nicely browned and feel tender when you pierce them with a metal skewer. Remove to a heated serving dish, sprinkle with parsley, and serve. These onions are a wonderful accompaniment to almost any roast meat—beef, lamb, pork, or poultry.

PORTUGUESE RICE
Arroz à Portuguesa

What makes this rice Portuguese is its subtle flavoring of garlic and olive oil.

Makes 6 to 8 servings

3	large garlic cloves, peeled and slivered
2	tablespoons olive oil
2	tablespoons lard (hog lard, not vegetable shortening)
2	cups long-grain rice
3½	cups cold water plus 1 teaspoon salt
¼	teaspoon freshly ground black pepper

In a large heavy saucepan set over moderately low heat, sauté the garlic in the oil and lard about 15 minutes until soft and golden; lift out with a slotted spoon and discard. Add the rice to the saucepan and stir-fry about 1 minute—just until "tweedy"-look-ing. Add the salted water, raise heat to high, and bring quickly to a boil. Sprinkle in the pepper, adjust the heat so that the water bubbles *very* gently, and cook uncovered about 5 minutes, just until the water has cooked down to the level of the rice. Cover and cook 10 to 15 minutes longer, just until the rice is fluffy and all water is absorbed. Fork the rice up and serve hot with *Cozido à Portuguesa, Feijoada Branca* (pages 128 and 143), or almost any Portuguese pork or poultry recipe.

BAKED RICE
Arroz de Forno

Whenever Maria Eugénia Cerqueira da Mota of Valpaços roasts turkey (see her recipe on page 158), she uses the giblets in this rice, which bakes alongside the turkey during the last 45 minutes or so. It's quick, delicious, and very nearly foolproof.

Makes 6 to 8 servings

	The giblets of 1 turkey or roasting chicken, minced
1	medium yellow onion, peeled and chopped

3   tablespoons unsalted butter
3   tablespoons olive oil
1   teaspoon salt
½   teaspoon freshly ground black pepper
1½ cups long-grain rice
3   cups boiling water

Preheat the oven to hot (400°F.). In a large heavy saucepan set over moderate heat, sauté the giblets and onion in the butter and oil about 5 minutes until onion is golden; add the salt and pepper, turn the heat down low, cover, and let steam 20 minutes. Stir in the rice, then the boiling water. Transfer to a buttered 2-quart casserole and bake uncovered about 45 minutes until all water is absorbed and the top is lightly browned. Fork the rice up and serve.

TOMATO RICE
Arroz de Tomate

It is a favorite all over Portugal, but nowhere is this recipe better prepared than in the Alentejo Province, where tomatoes grow ripe and red and full of flavor under the summer sun. Needless to say, the tomatoes you use for this dish should be vine-ripened and filled with home-grown tomato flavor.

Makes 6 to 8 servings

2   medium yellow onions, peeled and chopped
1   medium garlic clove, peeled and minced
¼   cup olive oil
2   tablespoons bacon drippings or lard (hog lard, not vegetable shortening)
2   large juicily ripe tomatoes, peeled, cored, seeded, and coarsely chopped
3   cups beef or chicken broth (preferably homemade)
2   cups long-grain rice
½   teaspoon salt
½   teaspoon freshly ground black pepper

In a large heavy saucepan set over low heat, sauté the onions and garlic in the olive oil and bacon drippings 5 minutes until glassily golden, stirring now and then. Add the tomatoes, cover, and simmer 30 minutes. Add the broth, bring to a full rolling boil, stir in the rice, salt, and pepper; adjust the heat so that the liquid bubbles gently, cover, and cook 20 minutes or until all liquid is absorbed and the rice is tender. Fluff with a fork and serve with roast pork, chicken, or turkey.

NOURISHING RICE
Arroz de Sustância

You could make a meal of this rich rice dish and many Portuguese do. It's particularly popular in the northern coastal provinces—Beira Litoral (where much of Portugal's rice grows), the Douro, and Minho. *Note: Because of the saltiness of the broth and the prosciutto used in this recipe, you will probably not need to add any salt.*

Makes 6 to 8 servings

- 1 large yellow onion, peeled and chopped
- 1 large garlic clove, peeled and minced
- 1 large carrot, peeled and chopped
- 3 tablespoons lard (hog lard, not vegetable shortening)
- 3 tablespoons olive oil
- ¼ pound prosciutto, cut into very small dice
- 2 tablespoons tomato paste
- 3 cups beef or chicken broth (preferably homemade)
- ½ teaspoon freshly ground black pepper
- 2 cups long-grain rice

Sauté the onion, garlic, and carrot in the lard and olive oil in a large heavy saucepan over moderate heat 5 to 6 minutes, stirring often, until onion looks glassy. Stir in the prosciutto and tomato paste, turn heat to low, cover, and cook 25 minutes. Add the broth and pepper, bring to a rolling boil, then stir in the rice. Adjust the heat so that the broth bubbles gently, cover, and cook 25 minutes until all liquid is absorbed and the rice is tender. Fluff with a fork and serve as an accompaniment to roast pork or poultry.

RICE WITH PORK
Arroz de Porco

The Portuguese are ingenious at making a meal out of bits of meat and rice.

Makes 4 servings

1	cup diced pork shoulder
3	tablespoons olive oil
1	large yellow onion, peeled and coarsely chopped
1	large garlic clove, peeled and minced
1	cup converted rice
1	cup beef broth (preferably homemade)
1	cup water
½	teaspoon salt
¼	teaspoon freshly ground black pepper

In a large heavy saucepan set over high heat, stir-fry the pork in the olive oil 4 to 5 minutes until touched with brown; add the onion and garlic, reduce the heat to moderate, and sauté, stirring now and then, 3 to 4 minutes until onions are limp and golden. Add the rice and sauté, stirring often, about 2 minutes until rice begins to color. Add the broth, water, salt, and pepper; bring to a boil, then adjust heat so that the liquid bubbles gently. Cover and cook 25 to 30 minutes until the rice is fluffy and all liquid has been absorbed. Fork the rice up and serve as a family main dish.

VARIATION:

You can use leftover cold roast pork for this recipe if you like, but reduce the initial browning time to about 2 minutes. Then prepare as directed.

RICE, TUNA AND TOMATO SALAD
Salada de Arroz, Atum e Tomate

Few of us are aware that rice is one of Portugal's important crops. It's grown up and down the mainland's West Coast and is so popular everywhere that it's usually served at every meal—often in addition to potatoes. This rather sophisticated rice and tuna salad comes from Reid's Hotel in Funchal, Madeira, where of course fresh tuna would be used for the recipe. By all means use fresh tuna if it is available to you. Simply poach a pound of it in a court-bouillon 10 to 15 minutes—just until it flakes at the touch of a fork. Cool the tuna in the poaching liquid, free of skin and bones, then flake with a fork.

Makes 6 servings

1	large can (14 ounces) solid white tuna, drained and flaked
4	cups cooked unseasoned rice, cooled
2	large hard-cooked eggs, shelled and minced
1	large firm-ripe *unpeeled* tomato, cored, seeded, and moderately finely chopped
½	cup chopped pitted black olives (preferably Greek olives)
1	medium yellow onion, peeled and minced
¼	cup minced parsley
1¼	cups *Molho Maionese* (page 92) or mayonnaise
3	tablespoons lemon juice
¼	cup milk (about)
1	teaspoon salt (about)
¼	teaspoon freshly ground black pepper (about)

Mix all ingredients together well, cover, and marinate in the refrigerator at least 4 hours. Toss well again; moisten, if needed, with a little additional milk and add more salt and pepper if flavor seems bland. Serve as is, or in hollowed-out ripe tomatoes, or in avocado halves, or on crisp leaf lettuce.

SALAD OF SALT COD AND CHICK-PEAS
Salada de Bacalhau e Grão-de-bico

One of the more unusual ways in which the Portuguese prepare salt cod—and, I think, a singularly good one. It needs nothing more to accompany it than thick chunks of Portuguese bread, a crisp dry wine such as a *vinho verde* (the Portuguese would choose a red *vinho verde*), and maybe a dessert of fresh pineapple slices.

Makes 6 to 8 servings

½	pound dried salt cod (preferably the center portion)
1½	cups dried chick-peas, washed and sorted
3½	quarts water (about)
1	large yellow onion, peeled and chopped
1	large garlic clove, peeled and minced
3	hard-cooked eggs, shelled and coarsely chopped
⅓	cup coarsely chopped parsley (preferably the Italian flat-leaf variety)
1	teaspoon paprika
¼	teaspoon freshly ground black pepper
⅛	teaspoon cayenne pepper
5	tablespoons olive oil (about)
3	tablespoons cider vinegar (about)

Soak the salt cod in the refrigerator 24 hours in several changes of cold water. (Keep the bowl covered so that the whole refrigerator doesn't smell of fish.) Meanwhile, soak the chick-peas in 4 cups of the water for at least 12 hours.

Next day, place the chick-peas and their soaking water in a large heavy saucepan, add 2 additional cups of water, and bring to a simmer over moderate heat; adjust the heat so that the liquid bubbles gently, then cover, and simmer 1 to 1¼ hours until the peas are firm-tender. *Note: To reduce the risk of boil-over, keep the saucepan lid on askew.* When the peas are almost done, drain the salt cod well, rinse, and drain well again. Place in a large heavy saucepan, add the remaining 2 quarts water, and bring to a simmer over moderate heat; lower the heat so that the water just trembles, cover the pan, and cook the cod about 15 minutes or until it flakes at the touch of a fork. Drain the cod well and rinse, then free of bones and skin, flake, and place in a large heat-proof bowl.

Drain the chick-peas well and add to the bowl along with the onion, garlic, eggs, parsley, paprika, black pepper, and cayenne, and toss lightly to mix. Add the olive oil and vinegar and toss well again. Taste and add additional oil and vinegar, if needed. Cover and marinate several hours in the refrigerator. Taste once again before serving, and fine-tune the seasoning with a little additional oil and vinegar, if needed.

BLACK-EYED PEA SALAD
Salada de Feijão Frade

A filling, gutsy salad popular in the countryside around Lisbon. Stored tightly covered in the refrigerator, it will keep well for several days.

Makes 8 servings

1	pound dried black-eyed peas, washed and sorted
4	cups cold water
2	medium yellow onions, peeled and coarsely chopped
2	medium garlic cloves, peeled and minced
5	tablespoons olive oil
1	teaspoon crumbled leaf marjoram
1½	teaspoons salt
¼	teaspoon freshly ground black pepper
3	tablespoons cider vinegar
2	hard-cooked eggs, shelled
⅓	cup chopped parsley

Soak the beans in the water 1 hour in a large heavy saucepan; set over moderate heat, bring to a boil, then cover and cook 45 to 50 minutes until beans are *al dente*. Drain the beans and dump into a large heat-proof bowl; add the onions, garlic, olive oil, marjoram, salt, pepper, and vinegar, and toss lightly. Now coarsely chop 1 egg and add to the salad along with 4 tablespoons of the chopped parsley; toss well. Reserve the remaining egg; the yolk, sieved, and the white, coarsely chopped, will be used as garnish. Cover the salad and marinate several hours or overnight in the refrigerator. When ready to serve, toss the salad well. Transfer to a decorative bowl, sprinkle with sieved egg yolk in the center, frame with a circle of chopped egg white, then frame the egg white with a circle of chopped parsley.

PORTUGUESE SALAD
Salada à Portuguesa

A fairly classic combination—sweet green peppers, sun-ripened tomatoes, garlic, and cucumber, lightly dressed with oil and vinegar. It owes its unusually mellow flavor to the fact that both the peppers and tomatoes are partially roasted.

Makes 4 to 6 servings

1	small cucumber, peeled and sliced thin
1	teaspoon kosher or coarse salt
3	medium-size sweet green peppers
4	large ripe tomatoes
1	medium clove garlic, peeled and minced
¼	teaspoon freshly ground black pepper
3	tablespoons olive oil
1	tablespoon cider vinegar
2	tablespoons coarsely chopped fresh coriander (optional)

Spread the cucumber slices out on several thicknesses of paper toweling, sprinkle evenly with the salt, top with more paper toweling, then weight down while you prepare the tomatoes and peppers. (I put a heavy chopping board on top of the cucumbers, then top it with canned goods.)

Spear a pepper and turn it over a high burner flame until blackened all over; this will loosen the skin. Repeat until all peppers are blackened, bundle in paper toweling, and let stand while you roast the tomatoes. Now spear the tomatoes, one by one, and turn over the flame until the skins burst and blacken here and there— these take much less time over the flame than the peppers. *Note: If you don't have a gas range, arrange the peppers on a broiler pan, place about 4 inches from the broiler unit, and broil 2 to 3 minutes, turning often so that the skins blacken evenly. Broil the tomatoes the same way, but turn them more often and watch closely so that they aren't reduced to mush.*

When the peppers are cool enough to handle, peel off the blackened skins, core, seed, and cut lengthwise into strips about ¾-inch wide; place the peppers in a large nonmetallic bowl. Peel the tomatoes, core, cut into slim wedges, and add to the peppers along with the sliced cucumber, garlic, and pepper. Toss lightly, drizzle with the olive oil, then vinegar, and toss lightly again. Add the fresh coriander, if you have it, cover, and marinate at room temperature for 1 hour. Toss lightly again and serve. This salad is superb with freshly grilled fish or chicken and also with almost any salt-cod dish.

GREEN SALAD WITH FRESH CORIANDER
Salada Verde com Coentro

To make this salad perfect you need fresh coriander, and an oil intensely aromatic of olive.

Makes 6 servings

2	quarts mixed prepared salad greens (romaine, chicory, spinach, Boston and/or Bibb lettuce, in roughly equal proportions)
1	small garlic clove, peeled
⅓	cup olive oil
¼	cup coarsely chopped fresh coriander
½	teaspoon salt (about)
¼	teaspoon freshly ground black pepper (about)
2	tablespoons cider vinegar (about)
2	tablespoons lemon juice

Place the greens in a large salad bowl. Crush the garlic in the oil, then strain the oil through a small fine sieve. Sprinkle the coriander, salt, and pepper over the greens and toss lightly. Drizzle in the garlic-oil, then the vinegar and lemon juice, and toss well. Taste for seasoning and add more salt, pepper, and vinegar, if needed. Toss again and serve.

Breads

❋

Pães

TO IMPROVISE A BRICK-AND-STEAM OVEN

One reason the country breads of Portugal have such thick brown crusts and moist, chewy interiors is that they are baked at intense heat in brick or stone ovens filled with steam. I shall never forget visiting a village bakery,. on a blistering summer's day, just as the baker's apprentice was pouring cold water into a vent in the oven wall. It vaporized on contact, sending great clouds of steam into the oven—and raising the humidity of the bakery to near sauna proportions. You can never duplicate the texture of the breads baked in the village ovens of Portugal, but you can approximate it if you follow these easy steps:

1. Check to see that your oven temperature reading is accurate. Test with an oven thermometer of good quality. For high-temperature baking, it's critical that your oven temperature be neither too high (in which case you will burn the bread) nor too low (the bread won't develop the proper crust or texture).
2. Place three or four unglazed bricks in a large, heavy, shallow baking pan and set on the lowest oven shelf.
3. Place the rack on which you intend to bake the bread in the exact center of the oven.
4. Preheat the oven and pan of bricks a full 20 minutes at 500°F.
5. When you are ready to bake the bread, fill a metal watering can (preferably one *without* a sprinkler attachment) with ice water and drizzle the water over the hot bricks. Whisk the bread into the oven and close the door tight.
6. As the bread bakes, douse the bricks every 5 minutes with ice water and waste no time in closing the oven door.

PORTUGUESE COUNTRY BREAD
Pão

Few Portuguese farm women have their own brick ovens, so several mornings each week they carry their freshly shaped loaves to the village ovens to be baked. Most likely the bread is *Pão,* the filling, frugal favorite of every province. It contains four ingredients only and owes its chewiness to hard-wheat flour, vigorous kneading, and brick-oven baking at intense heat amid swirls of steam. The following recipe is about as close as you can come to the classic *Pão,* given American ingredients and home ovens.

Makes two 8-inch round loaves

3	packages active dry yeast
1½	cups lukewarm water (105°F. to 115°F.)
7½	cups sifted unbleached all-purpose flour (about)
2	teaspoons salt

First make a sponge: In a large warm bowl, combine the yeast with ⅔ cup of the water and 1 cup of the flour. Beat until smooth, set in a warm, draft-free spot, cover with a clean, dry cloth, and allow to rise until light, spongy, and doubled in bulk—25 to 30 minutes.

Stir the sponge down, add the remaining warm water and the salt, then mix in enough of the remaining flour, 1 cup at a time, to make a stiff but workable dough (6 cups should be about right). Turn onto a lightly floured board (use only as much of the remaining flour as necessary to keep the dough from sticking) and knead hard for 5 minutes. Shape the dough into a ball, place in a warm, greased bowl, turn the dough in the bowl so that the top is greased. Cover with a clean, dry cloth, set in a warm, draft-free spot, and allow to rise until doubled in bulk—about 1½ hours. Punch the dough down, turn onto a lightly floured board, and knead hard for 5 minutes.

Again shape the dough into a ball, place in a clean, warm, greased bowl, turn the dough in the bowl so that it is greased all over, cover with a cloth, and set in a warm, draft-free spot until doubled in bulk—about 1 hour. Again punch the dough down, turn out onto a lightly floured board, and knead hard for 5 minutes. Divide the dough in half, knead each half hard for 2 to 3 minutes, then shape each into a ball. Place each loaf in a lightly greased 8- or 9-inch layer-cake pan and dust the tops with flour. Cover with a cloth, set in a warm, draft-free spot, and let rise until doubled in bulk—about 45 minutes.

Meanwhile, improvise the brick-and-steam oven as directed on page 223, setting the oven thermostat at very hot (500°F.) and preheating the oven for a full 20 minutes. As soon as the loaves are properly risen, drizzle cold water directly onto the hot bricks. Whisk the loaves onto the center rack, arranging them so that they touch neither each other nor the oven walls. Close the oven door tight and bake the loaves 15 minutes, drizzling the bricks with cold water every 5 minutes. Lower the oven temperature to hot (400°F.) and bake the bread 15 minutes longer, again drizzling the bricks with cold water every 5 minutes. As soon as the loaves are deep-brown, firm, and hollow-sounding when thumped, remove from the oven and cool on wire racks.

To mix the dough in a food processor: Unless you have one of the extra-large and powerful machines, mix the dough in two batches lest you stall or burn out the processor motor. Begin by hand-mixing the sponge as directed, then let it rise until doubled in bulk. Scoop half of the sponge (all of it if you have a heavy-duty machine) into the work bowl of a food processor fitted with the metal chopping blade. Now add ½ of each of the remaining ingredients (all of them if using a big machine), and buzz nonstop about 60 seconds until the mixture forms a stiff dough that rides up on the central spindle. Empty the dough into a warm bowl; then processor-mix the remaining sponge and ingredients the same way, if mixing the bread in two batches. Add second ball of dough to the first and turn out onto a lightly floured board. Knead the two together hard to form a single large ball; continue kneading 5 to 10 times until smooth and elastic. Place the dough in a warm, greased bowl for the first rising and proceed as the recipe directs.

ROUGH COUNTRY BREAD OF THE MINHO PROVINCE
Pão do Minho

This chewy white loaf is the standard country bread of northern Portugal. It's slightly rougher than the simple *Pão*.

Makes two 7-inch round loaves

3   packages active dry yeast
2   cups warm water (105°F. to 115°F.)
5   cups sifted unbleached all-purpose flour (about)
1   cup unsifted gluten flour (obtainable in health-food stores)
2   teaspoons salt
2   teaspoons cornmeal

First make a sponge: In a large, warm bowl combine the yeast, ¾ cup of the water, and 1 cup of the unbleached flour; beat hard to blend. Cover, set in a warm draft-free spot, and let rise until spongy and doubled in bulk—about 30 minutes.

Stir the sponge down and mix in the gluten flour, salt, and remaining 1¼ cups water. Now add enough of the remaining unbleached flour, 1 cup at a time, to make a stiff but manageable dough. Turn out onto a lightly floured board (use only enough flour to keep the dough from sticking) and knead hard for 5 minutes. Shape the dough into a ball, place in a warm, greased bowl, and turn the dough in the bowl so that it is greased all over. Cover with a clean, dry cloth, set in a warm, draft-free spot, and allow to rise until doubled in bulk—about 1¼ hours. Punch the dough down, turn out onto a lightly floured board, and knead hard for 5 minutes.

Once again, shape the dough into a ball, place in a clean, warm, greased bowl, turn the dough in the bowl so that it is greased all over, cover with a cloth, and set in a warm, draft-free spot until doubled in bulk—about 1 hour. Again punch the dough down, turn out onto a lightly floured board, adding only enough flour to keep the dough from sticking. Knead hard for 5 minutes, then divide the dough in half. Knead each half hard for 2 to 3 minutes, then shape into a ball. Grease two 8-inch layer-cake pans well, and sprinkle 1 teaspoon of cornmeal over the bottom of each. Place the balls of dough in the two pans and dust the tops lightly with flour. Cover with a cloth, set in a warm, draft-free spot, and allow to rise until doubled in bulk—about 45 minutes.

Meanwhile, improvise the brick-and-steam oven as directed on page 223, setting the thermostat at very hot (500°F.) and preheating the oven a full 20 minutes. As soon as the loaves are risen, drizzle cold water directly onto the hot bricks, producing a head of steam. Arrange the loaves on the center rack at once so that they do not touch each other or the oven walls. Close the oven door securely and bake the bread 15 minutes, drizzling the bricks with cold water every 5 minutes. Reduce the oven temperature to hot (400°F.) and bake the loaves 15 minutes longer, again drizzling the bricks with cold water every 5 minutes. As soon as the loaves are richly browned, firm, and hollow-sounding when thumped, remove from the oven and transfer at once to wire racks to cool.

To mix the dough in a food processor: Unless you have a big, powerful machine, mix the dough in two batches lest you stall or burn out the processor motor. Begin by hand-mixing the sponge as the recipe directs, then let it rise until doubled in bulk. Scoop half of the sponge (all of it if you have a heavy-duty machine) into the work bowl of a food processor fitted with the metal chopping blade. Now add ½ of each of the remaining ingredients (all of them if using a big machine), and buzz nonstop about 60 seconds until the mixture forms a stiff dough that rides up on the central spindle. Empty the dough into a warm bowl, then processor-mix the remaining sponge and ingredients the same way, if mixing the bread in two batches. Add second ball of dough to the first and turn out onto a lightly floured board. Knead the two together hard to form a single large ball; continue kneading 5 to 10 times until smooth and elastic. Place the dough in a warm, greased bowl for the first rising and proceed as the recipe directs.

SHAPED BREAD
Pão de Forma

This bread is richer than the classic *Pão* because it contains butter, milk instead of water, and sugar. The dough is unusually stiff, meaning that it will hold almost any shape you give it. Bakers in the Alentejo Province favor a full-blown "bow tie" shape—easier to make than it sounds: Simply bracket a small ball of dough with two larger ones of roughly equal size.

Makes 2 large loaves

2	packages active dry yeast
4	tablespoons sugar
7½	cups sifted unbleached all-purpose flour (about)
2	cups scalded milk, cooled to lukewarm (105°F. to 115°F.)
4	tablespoons (½ stick) unsalted butter, at room temperature
2	teaspoons salt

First make a sponge: In a large, warm bowl combine the yeast, 2 tablespoons of the sugar, and 1 cup of the flour, pressing out any lumps. Add ¾ cup of the lukewarm milk and beat until smooth. Cover with a dry cloth and set in a warm, draft-free spot until spongy, light, and doubled in bulk—25 to 30 minutes. Meanwhile, combine the remaining 1¼ cups milk with the remaining sugar, the butter, and salt.

As soon as the sponge is properly bubbly, stir down, and blend in the milk mixture. Now add enough (about 6 cups) of the remaining flour, 1 cup at a time, to make a stiff but workable dough. Turn out onto a lightly floured board (use just enough of the remaining flour to keep the dough from sticking) and knead hard for 5 minutes or until the dough is smooth and elastic. Shape the dough into a ball, place in a warm, greased bowl, then turn the dough in the bowl so that it is greased all over; cover with a cloth and allow to rise in a warm, draft-free spot until doubled in bulk—about 1 hour. Punch the dough down, turn out onto a lightly floured board, and knead hard for 5 minutes. Now divide the dough in half and knead hard about 20 times. Divide each half in half and knead each of these quarters lightly 15 to 20 times.

To shape into "bow ties," pinch a little dough off each of the four pieces, then put together two pairs so that you have two small balls of equal size, and knead. Place each in the center of a lightly greased 8- or 9-inch layer-cake pan. Now shape the four quarters of dough into four balls of equal size and bracket each small ball with two larger ones. Sift a little flour on top, cover with a cloth, and set in a warm, draft-free spot until doubled in bulk—about 1 hour.

Meanwhile, improvise the brick-and-steam oven as directed on page 223, setting the thermostat at very hot (500°F.) and preheating the oven a full 20 minutes. As soon as the loaves are risen, drizzle cold water directly onto the hot bricks, producing a head of steam. Arrange the loaves on the center rack at once so that they do not touch each other or the oven walls. Close the oven door securely and bake the bread 15 minutes, drizzling the bricks with cold water every 5 minutes. Reduce the oven temperature to hot (400°F.) and bake the loaves 15 minutes longer, again drizzling the bricks with cold water every 5 minutes. As soon as the loaves are richly browned, firm, and hollow-sounding when thumped, remove from the oven and transfer at once to wire racks to cool.

To mix the dough in a food processor: Unless you have a big, powerful machine, mix the dough in two batches lest you stall or burn out the processor motor. Begin by hand-mixing the sponge as the recipe directs, then let it rise until doubled in bulk. Scoop half the sponge (all of it if you have a heavy-duty machine) into the work bowl of a food processor fitted with the metal chopping blade. Now add ½ of each of the remaining ingredients (all of them if using a big machine), and buzz nonstop about 60 seconds until the mixture forms a stiff dough that rides up on the central spindle. Empty the dough into a warm bowl, then processor-mix the remaining sponge and ingredients the same way, if mixing the bread in two batches. Add second ball of dough to the first and turn out onto a lightly floured board. Knead the two together hard to form a single large ball; continue kneading 5 to 10 times until smooth and elastic. Place the dough in a warm, greased bowl for the first rising and proceed as the recipe directs.

TABLE BREAD
Pão de Mesa

A spongy, slightly sweet bread that's an Easter favorite in the Azores. It bakes at a much lower temperature than the rugged everyday loaves.

Makes two tall 7-inch round loaves

2	packages active dry yeast
4	tablespoons sugar
5½	cups sifted unbleached all-purpose flour (about)
1½	cups scalded milk, cooled to lukewarm (105°F. to 115°F.)
2	large eggs
½	teaspoon salt
2	tablespoons unsalted butter, at room temperature

First make a sponge: In a large, warm bowl combine the yeast, 1 tablespoon of the sugar, and 2 cups of the flour, pressing out all lumps. Add the milk slowly, whisking all the while until smooth. Cover with a dry cloth and set in a warm, draft-free spot until spongy, light, and doubled in bulk—about 20 minutes.

As soon as the sponge is properly bubbly, stir down, then beat in the remaining sugar, the eggs, salt, and butter. Now mix in the remaining flour, 1 cup at a time, to make a soft but workable dough. Turn out onto a well-floured board and knead hard with well-floured hands for about 5 minutes or until the dough is smooth, elastic, and no longer sticky; shape into a ball, place in a warm, greased bowl, then turn the dough in the bowl so that it is greased all over. Cover with a cloth and allow to rise in a warm, draft-free spot until doubled in bulk—about 1 hour. Punch the dough down, turn out onto a lightly floured board, and knead lightly 8 to 10 times. Now divide the dough in half, knead each half lightly 15 to 20 times, and shape into a ball. Place the dough in two well-buttered 2½-quart charlotte molds or deep 7-inch casseroles. Cover with a cloth, set in a warm, draft-free spot, and allow to rise until doubled in bulk—about 45 minutes.

Meanwhile, preheat the oven to moderate (350°F.). As soon as the loaves are risen, arrange on the center oven rack so that the pans touch neither the oven walls nor each other. Bake about 40 minutes until nicely browned and hollow-sounding when thumped. Remove the bread from the oven, loosen around the edges, and turn out on wire racks to cool. Do not cut the bread until it has reached room temperature, and when you slice into it, use a very sharp serrated knife and a gentle sawing motion so that you don't destroy the light spongy texture. Serve with butter, if you like, although the bread is really rich enough not to need it.

To mix the dough in a food processor: Unless you have a big, powerful machine, mix the dough in two batches lest you stall or burn out the processor motor. Begin by hand-mixing the sponge as the recipe directs, then let it rise until doubled in bulk. Scoop half the sponge (all of it if you have a heavy-duty machine) into the work bowl of a food processor fitted with the metal chopping blade. Now add ½ of each of the remaining ingredients (all of them if using a big machine), and buzz nonstop about 60 seconds until the mixture forms a stiff dough that rides up on the central spindle. Empty the dough into a warm bowl, then processor-mix the remaining sponge and ingredients the same way if mixing the bread in two batches. Add second ball of dough to the first, and turn out onto a well-floured board. Knead the two together hard to form a single large ball; continue kneading 5 to 10 times until smooth and elastic. Place the dough in a warm, greased bowl for the first rising and proceed as the recipe directs.

SWEET BREAD
Pão-Doce

This sweet bread, or its fancily shaped and decorated descendants, is the traditional festival bread of both the Azores and mainland Portugal. It may be twisted up with almonds for Easter, studded with diced candied fruits for Twelfth Night, or simply baked as is. There are dozens of variations on the theme: Some of the breads contain no saffron, some are sweeter than others, some are more buttery or eggy. This recipe is my particular favorite.

Makes two 7-inch round loaves

¼	teaspoon saffron strands (measure loosely packed)
1	cup lukewarm water (105°F. to 115°F.)
2	packages active dry yeast
½	cup sugar
5¾	cups sifted all-purpose flour
5	tablespoons unsalted butter (at room temperature)
1	large egg (at room temperature)
4	large egg yolks (at room temperature)

First make a sponge: Crumble the saffron strands into the water and let stand 15 minutes. Meanwhile, combine the yeast, 1 tablespoon of the sugar, and 1 cup of the flour in a large warm bowl, pressing out all lumps. Pour in ⅔ cup of the saffron mixture, whisking all the while until smooth. Cover with a dry cloth and set in a warm, draft-free spot until spongy, light, and doubled in bulk—about 30 minutes.

As soon as the sponge has risen, stir it down, then beat in the remaining sugar, saffron mixture, the butter, and the egg. Now, one by one, beat in the egg yolks. Finally, add the remaining flour, a cup at a time—the dough will be too soft and sticky to knead at this point. Transfer it to a large, warm, well buttered bowl, butter your hands, then pat the top of the dough gently all over so that it is nicely buttered, too. Cover with a dry cloth, set in a warm, draft-free spot, and allow to rise until doubled in bulk—45 to 50 minutes.

Toward the end of the rising period, preheat the oven to hot (425°F.). When the dough has risen impressively, punch it down well and divide in half. Knead each piece of dough 35 to 40 times on a lightly floured pastry cloth, shape into a ball, and place in a well-buttered 7-inch charlotte mold or deep metal pan (use 1-pound coffee tins if necessary). Cover the loaves with a dry cloth, set in a warm, draft-free spot, and again let rise until doubled in bulk—about 20 minutes.

Bake the loaves on the middle oven rack, positioned so that they do not touch the oven walls or each other, about 25 minutes or until the loaves are puffed, richly browned, and sound hollow when thumped. Turn the loaves out onto wire racks to cool and do not cut before they have reached room temperature. *Note: Because these loaves are so light and spongy, use a sharp serrated knife and a gentle seesaw motion when slicing them.*

To mix the dough in a food processor: Hand-mix the sponge as directed, then let it rise until doubled in bulk. Scrape the sponge into the work bowl of a food processor fitted with the metal chopping blade. Add the remaining sugar, saffron mixture, the butter, egg, and egg yolks, and mix by snapping the motor on and off 8 to 10 times. Now mix in the remaining flour, 1 cup at a time, by snapping the motor on and off 8 to 10 times. Once all the flour is incorporated, machine-knead the dough by churning 30 to 40 seconds nonstop until the dough rolls into a ball and rides up on the central spindle. Turn the dough into a warm, greased bowl for the first rising, and proceed as the recipe directs.

BEER BREAD
Pão de Cerveja

This rough, moist bread owes its malty flavor to the stale beer used as the liquid ingredient and its tweedy texture to a mixture of whole wheat and unbleached flours. I first tasted *Pão de Cerveja* in the Algarve.

Makes two 7-inch round loaves

2	packages active dry yeast
5	cups sifted unbleached all-purpose flour (about)
1½	cups lukewarm stale beer (105°F. to 115°F.)
1½	cups unsifted whole wheat flour
2	teaspoons salt
½	cup scalded milk, cooled to lukewarm (105°F. to 115°F.)
¼	cup corn, peanut, or vegetable oil

First make a sponge: In a large, warm bowl combine the yeast and 1 cup of the unbleached flour, pressing out all lumps; beat in ¾ cup of the beer to make a smooth batter. Cover with a clean, dry cloth, set in a warm, draft-free spot, and allow to "work" until light and spongy and doubled in bulk—20 to 25 minutes.

Stir the sponge down, mix in the remaining beer, the whole wheat flour, salt, milk, and oil. Now add enough of the remaining unbleached flour, 1 cup at a time, to make a stiff but manageable dough. Turn out onto a lightly floured board (use only enough of the remaining flour to keep the dough from sticking) and knead hard for 5 minutes. Shape the dough into a ball, place in a warm, greased bowl, and turn the dough in the bowl so that it is greased all over. Cover with a clean, dry cloth, set in a warm, draft-free spot, and allow to rise until doubled in bulk—about 1¼ hours. Punch the dough down, turn out onto a lightly floured board, and knead hard for 5 minutes.

Once again, shape the dough into a ball, place in a clean, warm, greased bowl, turn the dough in the bowl so that it is greased all over, cover with a cloth, and set in a warm, draft-free spot until doubled in bulk—about 1 hour. Again punch the dough down, turn out onto a lightly floured board, using any remaining flour and adding more only if essential to keep the dough from sticking. Knead hard for 5 minutes, then divide the dough in half. Knead each half hard for 2 to 3 minutes, then shape each into a ball. Place in lightly greased 8- or 9-inch layer-cake pans and dust the tops of each loaf lightly with whole wheat flour. Cover with a cloth. Set in a warm, draft-free spot, and allow to rise until doubled in bulk—about 1 hour.

Meanwhile, improvise the brick-and-steam oven as directed on page 223, setting the thermostat at very hot (500°F.) and preheating the oven a full 20 minutes. As soon as the loaves are risen, drizzle cold water directly onto the hot bricks, producing a head of steam. Arrange the loaves on the center rack at once so that they do not touch each other or the oven walls. Close the oven door securely and bake the bread 15 minutes, drizzling the bricks with cold water every 5 minutes. Reduce the oven temperature to hot (400°F.) and bake the loaves 15 minutes longer, again drizzling the bricks with cold water every 5 minutes. As soon as the loaves are richly browned, firm, and hollow-sounding when thumped, remove from the oven and transfer at once to wire racks to cool.

To mix the dough in a food processor: Unless you have one of the extra-large, extra-powerful machines, mix the dough in two batches lest you stall or burn out the processor motor. Begin by hand-mixing the sponge as the recipe directs, then let it rise until doubled in bulk. Scoop half the sponge (all of it if you have a heavy-duty machine) into the work bowl of a food processor fitted with the metal chopping blade. Now add ½ of each of the remaining ingredients (all of them if using a big machine), and buzz nonstop about 60 seconds until the mixture forms a stiff dough that rides up on the central spindle. Empty the dough into a warm bowl, then processor-mix the remaining sponge and ingredients the same way, if mixing the bread in two batches. Add second ball of dough to the first, and turn out onto a lightly floured board. Knead the two together hard to form a single large ball; continue kneading 5 to 10 times until smooth and elastic. Place the dough in a warm, greased bowl for the first rising and proceed as the recipe directs.

BARLEY BREAD
Pão de Centeio

At country fairs and markets all over Portugal, you see round loaves of barley bread, often scored into quadrants and invariably fresh from the bakers' ovens. I puzzled for years over the bread's unusual "break"—that is, the way the top is crazed like that of a giant gingersnap. However, the mystery was solved the first time I made the bread. It contains such a high proportion of barley flour and such a low percentage of wheat flour that there is very little gluten or protein to stretch and form the framework of the bread. What happens as the yeast rises is that the fragile strands of dough rupture, causing an unusually dense texture and crispy crust with the network of cracks or "breaks." Next to *Pão,* this is probably Portugal's most popular country bread. *Note: Barley flour is available at specialty food shops and health-food stores.*

Makes three 7-inch round loaves

3   packages active dry yeast
3   cups sifted all-purpose flour
2   cups scalded milk, cooled to lukewarm (105°F. to 115°F.)
3   tablespoons lard (hog lard, not vegetable shortening), or unsalted butter
1   teaspoon salt
7   cups unsifted barley flour (about)

First make a sponge: In a large warm bowl, combine the yeast and 2⅓ cups of the all-purpose flour, pressing out all lumps. Now gradually add 1¼ cups of the milk, whisking all the while until smooth. Cover with a dry cloth and set in a warm, draft-free spot until spongy, light, and doubled in bulk—about 45 minutes.

    Stir the sponge down, then beat in the remaining all-purpose flour and milk, the lard, and salt. Now, 1 cup at a time, mix in enough of the barley flour to make a workable dough—it will be quite heavy and sticky, so you may have to knead in the last of the flour. Shape the dough into a large ball, place it in a large, warm, greased bowl, then turn the dough in the bowl so that it is greased all over. Cover with cloth and allow to rise in a warm, draft-free spot until doubled in bulk—about 1¼ hours. Punch the dough down and divide into three equal parts. Knead each on a pastry cloth topped with about ½ cup unsifted all-purpose flour. *Note: The dough will feel limp, almost lifeless, but that's because it contains too little gluten to give it the usual bounce of yeast breads.* Persist in kneading each piece of dough—hard—25 to 30 times; shape each into a ball and place in a well-buttered 7-inch charlotte mold or deep metal container. (You can use 1-pound coffee tins if need be.) Dust the top of each loaf lightly with a little sifted barley flour.

Again cover with a cloth and set in a warm, draft-free place to rise until doubled in bulk—about 45 minutes to 1 hour. Toward the end of the rising period, improvise the brick-and-steam oven as directed on page 223, setting the thermostat at very hot (500°F.) and preheating the oven a full 20 minutes. As soon as the loaves are risen, drizzle cold water directly onto the hot bricks, place the loaves on the center oven rack so that they touch neither the oven walls nor one another, and close the oven door securely. Bake for 15 minutes, drizzling the bricks with cold water every 5 minutes. Reduce the oven temperature to hot (400°F.) and bake the bread 20 minutes longer, drizzling the bricks with cold water several times. As soon as the loaves are richly browned, firm, and hollow-sounding when thumped, remove from the oven and transfer at once to wire racks to cool.

To mix the dough in a food processor: Don't attempt it unless you have a very large, very powerful machine. This dough is simply too heavy and sticky to be made by machine and you risk burning out your processor motor. If you have the big professional machine, here's the procedure: Hand-mix the sponge as the recipe directs, then let it rise until doubled in bulk. Scrape the sponge into the work bowl of the food processor fitted with the metal chopping blade. Add the remaining all-purpose flour and milk, the lard, and salt, and incorporate by snapping the motor on and off 5 to 6 times with each addition. Now add the barley flour, 1 cup at a time, by snapping the motor on and off 8 to 10 times. Once all the flour is incorporated, machine-knead by churning about 40 seconds nonstop until the dough rolls into a ball and rides up on the central spindle. *Note: Even with the heavy-duty processor, the motor may strain under the weight of the dough. If it does, uncover the work bowl and with a plastic spatula break the mass of dough into 3 or 4 pieces, then resume mixing as before.* Once the dough is properly kneaded, turn it into a large, warm, greased bowl for the first rising, and then proceed as the recipe directs.

DARK BREAD
Pão Preto

Few Portuguese breads are made with rye flour, so this loaf is unusual. It is altogether different from the caraway-flavored Jewish rye Americans are accustomed to. Despite the bread's name, it is not very dark—just a pleasant beige.

Makes one 7½-inch round loaf

2	packages active dry yeast
1	cup sifted unbleached all-purpose flour
1	cup scalded milk, cooled to lukewarm (105°F. to 115°F.)
¼	cup lukewarm water (105°F. to 115°F.)
1	teaspoon unsalted butter, at room temperature
½	teaspoon salt
½	cup unsifted gluten flour
3	cups unsifted rye flour (about)

First make a sponge: In a large, warm bowl combine the yeast and all-purpose flour, pressing out all lumps. Now add the milk gradually, whisking all the while until smooth. Cover with a dry cloth and set in a warm, draft-free spot until spongy, light, and doubled in bulk—about 30 minutes.

As soon as the sponge has risen, stir it down, then beat in the water, butter, salt, and gluten flour. Now add enough of the rye flour to make a stiff but manageable dough. Turn out onto a lightly floured board and knead hard for 5 minutes until the dough is smooth and elastic. Shape into a ball, place in a warm, greased bowl, then turn the dough in the bowl so that it is greased all over. Cover with a cloth and allow to rise in a warm, draft-free spot until doubled in bulk—about 1 hour. Punch the dough down, turn out onto a lightly floured board, and knead lightly about 20 times. Shape into a ball and place in a greased 8-inch layer-cake pan. Cover with a cloth, set in a warm, draft-free spot, and allow to rise until doubled in bulk—40 to 45 minutes.

Meanwhile, improvise the brick-and-steam oven as directed on page 223, setting the thermostat at very hot (500°F.) and preheating the oven a full 20 minutes. As soon as the loaf is risen, drizzle cold water directly onto the hot bricks, producing a head of steam. Place the loaf on the center rack at once, close the oven door securely, and bake 15 minutes, drizzling the bricks with cold water every 5 minutes. Reduce the oven temperature to hot (400°F.) and bake the bread 20 minutes longer, drizzling the bricks with cold water several times. As soon as the loaf is richly browned, firm, and hollow-sounding when thumped, remove from the oven and transfer at once to a wire rack to cool.

To mix the dough in a food processor: Hand-mix the sponge as the recipe directs, then let it rise until doubled in bulk. Scrape the sponge into the work bowl of a food processor fitted with the metal chopping blade. Add the water, butter, salt, and gluten flour, and mix by snapping the motor on and off 5 to 6 times. Now mix in the rye flour, 1 cup at a time, by snapping the motor on and off 8 to 10 times with each addition. Once all the flour is incorporated, machine-knead by churning 30 to 40 seconds nonstop until the dough rolls into a ball and rides up on the central spindle. Turn the dough out into a warm, greased bowl for the first rising, and proceed as the recipe directs.

YEAST-RAISED CORN BREAD
Broa

This sturdy bread from the North of Portugal, like most other country breads, is baked at intense heat in the presence of steam—which accounts for its thick brown crust. *Broa* is the perfect accompaniment to husky regional soups such as *Caldo Verde* and *Sopa de Pedra*. And, if the *Broa* you make is to have the proper dense and chewy texture, you must use the floury stone-ground cornmeal, not the mass-produced granular meal that's the supermarket staple. Health-food stores and specialty groceries now routinely stock stone-ground meals.

Makes two 7-inch round loaves

2	packages active dry yeast
2	cups sifted stone-ground cornmeal (preferably yellow)
1½	cups lukewarm water (105°F. to 115°F.)
1	cup scalded milk, cooled to lukewarm (105°F. to 115°F.)
2	tablespoons corn oil
1½	teaspoons salt
5½ to 6	cups sifted unbleached all-purpose flour

First make a sponge: In a large, warm bowl, combine the yeast and ⅔ cup of the corn meal, pressing out any lumps. Blend in ½ cup of the lukewarm water, beating until smooth. Set in a warm, draft-free spot, cover with a clean dry cloth, and allow to rise until light, spongy, and doubled in bulk—30 to 40 minutes. (You will notice a distinct smell of alcohol; this is as it should be and contributes to the bread's unique flavor.) Meanwhile, combine the remaining 1 cup lukewarm water, the milk, corn oil, and salt. As soon as the sponge is light and bubbly, stir it down, blend in the milk mixture and the remaining 1⅓ cups corn meal. Now add enough of the flour, 1 cup at a time, to make a soft but manageable dough—5 to 5½ cups should be about right. Turn the dough out onto a well-floured board (use some of the remaining flour) and knead hard for 5 minutes or until the dough is smooth and elastic. Shape the dough into a ball, place it in a warm, greased bowl, and turn the dough in the bowl so that it is greased all over. Cover with a clean dry cloth, set in a warm, draft-free spot, and allow to rise until doubled in bulk—about 1 hour.

Punch the dough down, turn out onto a well-floured board, and knead hard for 5 minutes. Again shape the dough into a ball, place in a clean, warm, greased bowl, turn the dough in the bowl so that it is greased all over, cover with a cloth, and set in a warm, draft-free spot until doubled in bulk—about 1 hour. Again punch the dough down, turn out onto a well-floured board, and knead hard for 5 minutes. Divide the dough in half, knead each half hard for 2 to 3 minutes, then shape into balls. Place each loaf in a lightly greased 8- or 9-inch layer-cake pan and sift a little cornmeal on top. Cover with a cloth, set in a warm, draft-free spot, and let rise until doubled in bulk—about 45 minutes.

Meanwhile, improvise the brick-and-steam oven as directed on page 223, setting the thermostat at very hot (500°F.) and preheating the oven a full 20 minutes. As soon as the loaves are risen, drizzle cold water directly onto the hot bricks, producing a head of steam. Arrange the loaves on the center rack at once so that they do not touch each other or the oven walls. Close the oven door securely and bake the bread 15 minutes, drizzling the bricks with cold water every 5 minutes. Reduce the oven temperature to hot (400°F.) and bake the loaves 15 minutes longer, again drizzling the bricks with cold water every 5 minutes. As soon as the loaves are richly browned, firm, and hollow-sounding when thumped, remove from the oven and transfer at once to wire racks to cool.

To mix the dough in a food processor: Unless you have a big, powerful machine, mix the dough in two batches lest you stall or burn out the processor motor. Begin by hand-mixing the sponge as the recipe directs, then let it rise until doubled in bulk. Scoop half the sponge (all of it if you have a heavy-duty machine) into the work bowl of the food processor fitted with the metal chopping blade. Now add ½ of each of the remaining ingredients (all of them if using a big machine), and buzz nonstop about 60 seconds until the mixture forms a stiff dough that rides up on the central spindle. Empty the dough into a warm bowl, then processor-mix the remaining sponge and ingredients the same way, if mixing the bread in two batches. Add second ball of dough to the first, and turn out onto a lightly floured board. Knead the two together hard to form a single large ball; continue kneading 5 to 10 times until smooth and elastic. Place the dough in a warm, greased bowl for the first rising, and proceed as the recipe directs.

YEAST-RAISED WHOLE WHEAT CORN BREAD
Broa de Barcelos

Portugal's liveliest country market takes place each Thursday in the historic river town of Barcelos, located some forty miles north of Porto. Here you will see stall after stall of the rough country breads for which Portugal is famous. One of the best is this dense, high-fiber, whole wheat corn bread. *Note: Few Portuguese bakers use sugar in their* broa *because they keep lively "starters" on hand. The sugar not only gets the yeast working faster, but also, I think, improves both texture and flavor.*

Makes two 7-inch round loaves

3	packages active dry yeast
3	tablespoons sugar
2	cups unsifted stone-ground yellow cornmeal
2	cups warm water (105°F. to 115°F.)
3	tablespoons bacon or meat drippings, or vegetable oil
2	teaspoons salt
1½	cups unsifted gluten flour (obtainable at health-food stores)
3	cups unsifted whole wheat flour
2	teaspoons granular cornmeal

First make a sponge: In a large, warm bowl, combine the yeast, 1 tablespoon of the sugar, 1½ cups of the stone-ground cornmeal, and ¾ cup of the water in a small bowl; beat hard to blend. Cover with a dry cloth, set in a warm, draft-free spot, and let rise until spongy and doubled in bulk—about 30 minutes.

Stir the sponge down, then mix in the remaining sugar and stone-ground cornmeal, and also the remaining 1¼ cups warm water, the drippings, salt, and gluten flour. Now add the whole wheat flour, 1 cup at a time, to make a fairly stiff but manageable dough. Turn the dough out onto a well-floured board and knead hard for 5 minutes or until the dough is smooth and elastic. Shape the dough into a ball, place in a warm, greased bowl, turn the dough in the bowl so that it is greased all over. Cover with a clean dry cloth, set in a warm, draft-free spot, and allow to rise until doubled in bulk—about 2½ hours. (This is a very heavy dough, so it takes longer than usual to rise.)

Punch the dough down, divide in half, and knead each half hard about 5 minutes on a lightly floured pastry cloth. Butter two 8-inch layer-cake pans well and sprinkle 1 teaspoon granular cornmeal over the bottom of each. Shape each piece of dough into a ball, dust the tops lightly with flour, and place in the pans. Cover with a cloth, set in a warm, draft-free spot, and let rise until doubled in bulk—about 1¼ hours.

Meanwhile, improvise the brick-and-steam oven as directed on page 223, setting the thermostat at very hot (500°F.) and preheating the oven a full 20 minutes. As soon as the loaves are risen, drizzle cold water directly onto the hot bricks, producing a head of steam. Arrange the loaves on the center rack at once so that they do not touch each other or the oven walls. Close the oven door securely and bake the bread 20 minutes, drizzling the bricks with cold water again after 10 minutes. Reduce the oven temperature to hot (400°F.) and bake the loaves 25 minutes longer, drizzling the bricks with cold water several times. As soon as the loaves are richly browned, firm, and hollow-sounding when thumped, remove from the oven and transfer at once to wire racks to cool.

To mix the dough in a food processor: Because this is such a heavy dough, I don't recommend mixing it in a food processor unless you have one of the big and powerful machines. If you do, first hand mix the sponge as directed, then let it rise until doubled in bulk. Scrape the sponge into the processor fitted with the metal chopping blade; add the remaining sugar, stone-ground cornmeal, and water, also the bacon drippings, salt, and gluten flour. Mix well using 6 to 8 on-offs of the motor. Add the whole wheat flour, 1 cup at a time, mixing each in with 6 to 8 on-offs of the motor. Now knead the dough by churning 30 seconds nonstop. Shape the dough into a ball, place in a large, greased bowl for the first rising, and proceed as the recipe directs.

HAM BREAD
Pão de Presunto

Although it is almost unknown in this country, *presunto* is one of Europe's choicest dry-cured hams. Like prosciutto, Bayonne, and Westphalian hams, it is eaten raw. Portugal's finest *presunto* comes from the northeastern province of Trás-os-Montes, especially from farms around the town of Chaves, where ham-curing is a cottage industry. Maria Eugénia Cerqueira da Mota, a food historian and gifted cook from Valpaços, explained to me: "When you want good hams in the autumn, you must feed the pigs every four hours in August, even at night. You must cook potatoes for them and also feed them corn and chestnuts and wheat."

"These are very special pigs," she continues. "Large white pigs with very big heads. The breed is Favios." Maria Eugénia cures hams for her family each fall and believes that hers are superior to those of Chaves. I would agree. Her technique is to rub the hams with a mixture of salt, sweet paprika, crushed garlic, and red wine, to let them cure for a month, then to smoke them for eight days over smoldering embers of oak. This bread recipe showcases the wonderful Portuguese *presunto*—which, alas, is unavailable here—but fortunately we do have fine prosciutto, which I have substituted.

Makes a 13 × 9 × 2-inch loaf

1	package active dry yeast
1	tablespoon sugar
5	cups sifted all-purpose flour (about)
1¼	cups scalded milk, cooled to lukewarm (105°F. to 115°F.)
½	teaspoon salt
2	medium eggs (at room temperature)
2½	tablespoons unsalted butter (at room temperature)
½	pound prosciutto, trimmed of fat and cut into fine julienne strips

GLAZE:

1	egg yolk mixed with 1 tablespoon cold water

First make a sponge: In a large warm bowl, combine the yeast, sugar, and 1 cup of the flour, pressing out all lumps. Pour in ½ cup of the milk, whisking all the while until smooth. Cover with a dry cloth and set in a warm, draft-free spot until spongy, light, and doubled in bulk—about 30 minutes.

Stir the sponge down and beat in the remaining milk, the salt, eggs, and butter. Now add enough of the remaining flour, 1 cup at a time, to make a soft but manageable dough. Turn out onto a lightly floured pastry cloth and knead hard 3 to 5 minutes; shape into a ball, place in a large, warm greased bowl, and turn the dough in the bowl so that it is greased all over. Cover with a dry cloth and set in a warm, draft-free spot to rise until doubled in bulk—50 to 60 minutes.

Punch the dough down and divide in half; knead one piece hard 2 to 3 minutes on a lightly floured pastry cloth, then roll into a rectangle approximately 14 inches long and 10 inches wide. Lay the rolling pin across the center of the dough, lap half the dough over the rolling pin, and ease it into a well-buttered 13 × 9 × 2-inch baking pan. Lightly press the dough over the bottom of the pan, pushing it into the corners and up the sides of the pan about ½ inch.

Sprinkle the ham strips evenly over the dough, leaving 1-inch margins all around; press the ham firmly into the dough. Now knead and roll the remaining dough the same way, but make the rectangle 13 inches long and 9 inches wide; ease into place on top of the ham. Press the dough into the ham; also tuck any loose ends in around the sides of the pan and pinch the top and bottom layers of dough together firmly all around. Cover with a dry cloth and set in a warm, draft-free place to rise until doubled in bulk—60 to 70 minutes.

Toward the end of the rising period, preheat the oven to moderately hot (375°F.). When the loaf has risen almost to the rim of the pan, brush it with the egg glaze and bake uncovered for 30 minutes until nicely browned and hollow-sounding when thumped. Remove the pan to a wire rack and cool the bread in it right-side up to room temperature. To serve, cut into large squares. *Note: This bread is hearty enough to serve as a main dish—you'll need only a green salad to accompany and fresh fruit for dessert.*

To mix the dough in a food processor: Hand-mix the sponge as directed, then let it rise until doubled in bulk. Scrape the sponge into the work bowl of the food processor fitted with the metal chopping blade. Add the remaining milk, the salt, eggs, and butter, and incorporate by snapping the motor on and off 8 to 10 times. Now mix in enough of the remaining flour, 1 cup at a time, to make a soft but workable dough, snapping the motor on and off 8 to 10 times after each addition. Once all the flour is incorporated, machine-knead the dough by churning about 30 seconds nonstop or until the dough rolls into a ball and rides up on the central spindle. Turn the dough out into a warm greased bowl to rise, and proceed as the recipe directs.

FRIED CORN BREAD
Milho Frito

The classic accompaniment to *Carne de Vinho e Alhos* (Pork with Wine and Garlic; page 138). Use the bread as the Portuguese do to sop up the savory juices. It is delicious, too, with any grilled pork or poultry.

Makes 4 to 6 servings

2½	cups water
1	tablespoon lard (hog lard, not vegetable shortening)
½	teaspoon salt
¼	teaspoon freshly ground black pepper
⅔	cup yellow cornmeal
3	tablespoons bacon drippings or lard (for frying the bread)

Bring the water, lard, salt, and pepper to a boil in a large heavy saucepan set over moderate heat. Whisking the mixture briskly, add the cornmeal in a slow but steady stream, then cook and stir 2 to 3 minutes until as thick as porridge. Slide a Flame-Tamer under the saucepan, turn the heat to its lowest point, and let the mixture cook slowly, uncovered, 25 to 30 minutes, stirring often, until it is very thick and no raw corn taste remains. Pour into a well greased 8 × 8 × 2-inch baking dish and cool to room temperature; cover and chill several hours or until firm enough to cut.

Cut into 12 domino-shaped pieces and drain well on paper toweling. Heat the bacon drippings in a medium-size heavy skillet over high heat 1 to 2 minutes until ripples appear on the skillet bottom. Brown the corn bread in 2 to 3 batches, allowing 3 to 4 minutes for the first side to brown, and 2 to 3 minutes for the flip side. Turn the bread only once as it fries, and give it a full 3 minutes before turning. Drain on paper toweling and serve.

KING'S CAKE
Bolo-Rei

Portuguese bakers begin making this sweet bread at the end of November and continue displaying fancily decorated loaves of it in their windows until the middle of January. It's the traditional Christmas bread of Portugal, shaped into rings to symbolize the crowns of the Magi. A fava bean or small trinket wrapped in paper is inserted into the unbaked bread—a penalty to whoever finds it. (He must buy the next year's *Bolo-Rei* and share it with all who partook of the loaf in which he found the fava.) Although popular throughout the *Festa do Natal* season, which in Portugal lasts through Twelfth Night (January 5) and Epiphany (January 6), the bread is also popular—particularly in the North of Portugal—at Eastertime (*Páscoa*).

Makes two 10-inch rings

2	packages active dry yeast
¾	cup sugar
8	cups sifted all-purpose flour (about)
½	cup lukewarm water (105°F. to 115°F.)
1	cup finely diced mixed candied fruits
⅓	cup golden seedless raisins (sultanas)
⅓	cup coarsely chopped piñons (pine nuts)
⅓	cup coarsely chopped blanched almonds or coarsely chopped walnuts
⅔	cup ruby Port
¼	pound plus 4 tablespoons unsalted butter
	Grated rind of 1 large orange
	Grated rind of 1 large lemon
4	large eggs
½	cup lukewarm milk (105°F. to 115°F.)

GLAZE:

1	large egg yolk lightly whisked with 2 tablespoons cold water

DECORATION:

20	thin slices candied citron (lay half a candied citron hollow-side down on the counter, then slice crosswise so that you have crescent-shaped pieces)

10 candied red cherries, halved
20 blanched whole almonds
40 piñons (pine nuts)
 2 tablespoons light corn syrup

First make a sponge: In a large warm bowl, combine the yeast, 1 tablespoon of the sugar, and 1 cup of the flour, pressing out all lumps. Pour in the warm water and whisk until smooth. Cover with a dry cloth and set in a warm, draft-free spot until spongy, light, and doubled in bulk—about 30 minutes.

Meanwhile, macerate the candied fruits, raisins, and nuts in the Port. Cream together the butter, orange and lemon rinds, and remaining sugar until light; beat in the eggs, one by one, then add the milk. Stir the sponge mixture down and add to the butter-egg-milk mixture, along with 1 cup of the flour, mixing until smooth. Add the macerated fruits and nuts and all their wine, then add enough of the remaining flour, cup by cup, mixing well after each addition, to make a very soft dough. *Note: The dough will be too soft and sticky to knead at this point; scoop into a well-buttered bowl and pat the surface well with buttered hands.* Cover with a dry cloth and set in a warm, draft-free spot to rise until doubled in bulk—about 1 hour.

Punch the dough down and divide in half; knead one piece hard 30 to 40 times on a well-floured pastry cloth, then shape into a chunky rope about 22 inches long; bend into a circle, knead the ends together well to seal, then ease the ring onto a greased baking sheet. Brush the top lightly with some of the glaze, taking care that it doesn't run down the sides onto the baking sheet. To decorate, lay 10 crescents of candied citron around the top of the ring, spacing evenly; arrange a row of candied cherries around the edge of the ring, in the spaces between the slices of citron; then place almonds and piñons in a decorative pattern in the space below the cherries. Knead, shape, glaze, and decorate the remaining dough the same way. Cover the loaves with dry cloths, then set in a warm, draft-free spot to rise until doubled in bulk—40 to 50 minutes.

Toward the end of the rising period, preheat the oven to hot (400°F.). Carefully glaze the tops of the loaves again with the egg mixture, taking care not to glaze the nuts or candied fruits or to let the mixture dribble down onto the baking sheets; it would act like glue and make the loaves very difficult to remove from the pans. Bake uncovered for 20 minutes; then lower oven temperature to moderate (350°F.) and bake 15 to 20 minutes longer until richly browned and hollow-sounding when thumped. Remove from the oven and ease the loaves onto racks to cool. While the breads are still hot, brush each piece of candied fruit well with the light corn syrup. When cool, cut into wedges, and serve as a holiday breakfast bread. *Note: These sweet breads, snugly wrapped in aluminum foil or plastic freezer wrap, freeze well and will retain their just-baked flavor for several months.*

To mix the dough in a food processor: Hand-mix the sponge as directed, then let it rise until doubled in bulk. Meanwhile, macerate the fruits and nuts. Then remove the zest from the orange and lemon with a swivel-bladed vegetable peeler and drop into the work bowl of a food processor fitted with the metal chopping blade; add the remaining sugar and churn 60 seconds nonstop; scrape down the sides of the work bowl and snap motor on and off 8 to 10 times—this will finish grating the orange and lemon rinds. Add the butter and buzz 15 seconds nonstop. With the motor running, drop the eggs, one by one, down the feed tube. Stop the motor, add 1 cup of the flour, and mix in with 8 to 10 on-offs of the motor. Add the milk, the stirred-down sponge, and 3 cups of the flour, and mix in by snapping the motor on and off 8 to 10 times. Now add the macerated fruits and nuts and all their wine. With a long-handled plastic spatula (do not buzz the machine), partially and *carefully* mix in the fruits and nuts, keeping your distance from the chopping blade. Now add the last of the flour and mix in by snapping the motor on and off quickly 8 to 10 times. Turn out the dough at once into a warm, buttered bowl for the first rising, and proceed as the recipe directs.

Sweets

Doces

BACON FROM HEAVEN I
Toucinho do Céu I

There must be a hundred different versions of this rich egg-and-almond sweet, which some say originated in a convent near Guimarães. Not so, says Maria Eugénia de Castro Cerqueira da Mota, a pharmacist and culinary historian who lives in the little town of Valpaços in the Trás-os-Montes Province. She insists that the dessert was created in the neighboring town of Murça, that it originally contained fat bacon, which accounts in part for the recipe's unusual name (the flavor explains the rest). Many recipes for *Toucinho do Céu* contain *abóbora,* a small orange pumpkin with flesh much like that of butternut squash. Others glisten with candied *chila,* an unusual gourd with flesh that "strings" rather like spaghetti squash. This recipe, although not the Murça original, is nonetheless celestial. Be forewarned: Cut the pieces small!

Makes 16 servings

FOR PREPARING THE PAN:

2 teaspoons unsalted butter, at room temperature
1 tablespoon sugar

TOUCINHO DO CÉU:

1¾	cups sugar
½	cup water
½	cup thawed frozen puréed winter squash, drained very dry
2	cups whole blanched almonds
¾	teaspoon ground cinnamon
3½	ounces marzipan (half a 7-ounce package), cut in small pieces
10	jumbo egg yolks
2	jumbo eggs
3	tablespoons finely minced crystallized ginger, or drained preserved ginger

TOPPING:

1	tablespoon sugar
1	tablespoon finely minced blanched almonds (optional)

To prepare the pan: Butter well the bottom and sides of a 9- or 9½-inch springform pan. Add sugar and tilt the pan from side to side to coat the bottom and sides; tap out excess sugar; set pan aside.

For the Toucinho do Céu: Combine the sugar and water in a large heavy saucepan over moderate heat and bring to a boil, stirring constantly. Reduce heat slightly and boil gently, without stirring, 5 minutes. Blend in the squash and boil gently 5 minutes, stirring occasionally. Meanwhile, buzz the almonds and cinnamon 60 seconds in a food processor fitted with the metal chopping blade; scrape down workbowl sides and buzz 60 seconds longer. With the processor motor running, drop the pieces of marzipan down the feed tube and buzz 60 seconds longer until fine and feathery. Blend almond mixture into saucepan, turn heat down low, and cook uncovered 25 minutes, stirring now and then. *Note: If you do not have a food processor, grind the almonds in a blender, a little bit at a time, until they are very fine. Or put them through a grinder fitted with the fine blade. Once almonds are ground, beat hard with the cinnamon and marzipan until uniformly smooth; add to saucepan and cook as directed.*

Meanwhile, preheat the oven to slow (300°F.). Beat the egg yolks and eggs until frothy; blend in 1 cup of the hot almond mixture, stir back into pan, set over low heat, and cook, stirring constantly, 5 minutes until slightly thickened. Stir in the ginger and pour all into prepared springform pan. Top with a sprinkling of sugar and, if you like, the minced blanched almonds. Bake uncovered on the middle oven shelf 40 to 45 minutes until the torte pulls from the sides of the pan and a toothpick inserted near the center comes out clean. Place the pan right-side up on a wire rack, loosen the torte around the edges with a spatula, then release and remove the

springform sides. Cool the torte at least 2 hours before cutting; it will soften somewhat, taking on a firm, jellylike consistency. Cut into slim wedges and serve. Top, if
you like, with dollops of whipped cream, although the Portuguese would never
dream of such a thing.

BACON FROM HEAVEN II
Toucinho do Céu II

This recipe is even richer than the preceding one and about as close to the old
"convent" sweet as you can get. Portuguese cooks would decorate the top of it with
confectioners' sugar sifted through a fancy paper cutout; you can achieve the same
effect using a lacy paper doily. *Note: It's essential that you grease and flour the pan in
which you bake this egg sweet very lavishly.*

Makes 16 servings

FOR PREPARING THE PAN:

2	tablespoons unsalted butter, at room temperature
¼	cup unsifted all-purpose flour

TOUCINHO DO CÉU:

2⅓	cups sugar
1¼	cups water
1	cup blanched almonds, ground very fine
¾	cup *Doce de Chila* (Candied Chila Gourd, page 286), drained well
20	large egg yolks
2	large eggs
1½	teaspoons ground cinnamon

TOPPING:

2	tablespoons confectioners' (10X) sugar

To prepare the pan: Butter well the bottom and sides of a 9- or 9½-inch springform
pan. Add the flour and tilt the pan from side to side to coat the bottom and sides;

tap out about half of the excess flour, then shake the pan slowly from side to side to distribute the remaining flour in a thin even layer over the bottom of the pan; set pan aside.

For the Toucinho do Céu: Combine the sugar and water in a large heavy saucepan over moderate heat and bring to a boil, stirring constantly. When all the sugar is dissolved, insert a candy thermometer and cook, without stirring, until the mixture reaches the soft-ball stage (236°F.). Remove the candy thermometer, blend in the almonds and *Doce de Chila,* reduce heat to low, and cook, stirring often, about 20 minutes until very thick.

Meanwhile, beat the egg yolks, eggs, and cinnamon until light. Blend in hot almond mixture, little by little, then return all to the saucepan and cook over lowest heat, stirring almost constantly, 25 to 30 minutes until the mixture is about as thick as a thick cream sauce. Meanwhile, preheat the oven to very slow (275°F.).

Pour the almond mixture into the prepared springform pan and bake uncovered for about 2 hours or until a toothpick inserted in the center comes out clean. Cool the *Toucinho do Céu* right-side up in the pan on a wire rack 1 hour; carefully loosen it around the edges, then loosen and remove the springform sides. Now cool the dessert completely—about another hour. Place a dessert plate on top of the *Toucinho do Céu,* invert, then with a large thin spatula carefully separate the bottom of the springform pan from the dessert and lift off.

To decorate the *Toucinho do Céu,* lay a large lacy round doily on top of it, sift the 10X sugar evenly over all, and lift off doily. When serving this dessert, cut the pieces very small—it is unconscionably rich.

RICE PUDDING
Arroz Doce

Portuguese rice pudding is quite different from our own. It's cooked entirely on top of the stove and the technique for making it is similar to that used for *risotto;* that is, liquid (milk) is added slowly—and in stages—so that the rice absorbs it gradually and completely. The only rice that will cook down to the proper smoothness is short-grain rice, so make sure that's what you use. The classic seasonings for Portuguese rice pudding are lemon and cinnamon—no vanilla. Usually the lemon zest is steeped in the initial cooking water and removed before the rice is added. The cinnamon not only goes into the pudding but is also used to decorate the top of it—

frequently in a simple grid or harlequin pattern but sometimes in a more fanciful design of hearts. If your hand isn't steady enough to add the cinnamon in fine, ruler-straight lines, make a cone of typing paper and snip a tiny hole at the point; spoon cinnamon into the cone; then, by tapping the side of it gently, force the cinnamon out in a thin stream.

Makes 6 to 8 servings

4½	**cups water**
½	**teaspoon salt**
	Zest of 1 large lemon, cut in long thin strips
2	**cups short-grain rice**
4½	**to 5 cups scalding hot milk (use part cream, if you like)**
¾	**cup sugar**
1	**tablespoon unsalted butter**
4	**large egg yolks, lightly beaten**
1½	**teaspoons ground cinnamon (about)**

In a large heavy saucepan set over moderate heat, bring the water, salt, and lemon zest to a simmer; reduce heat so that water barely trembles, cover, and steep the lemon zest 10 minutes; remove and discard the zest. Bring the water to a rolling boil, then stir in the rice. Adjust the heat so that the water bubbles gently, and cook the rice uncovered 10 to 15 minutes until all water is absorbed. Now add about 1 cup of the hot milk, stir gently, adjust the heat so that the milk just ripples, ocver, and cook, stirring occasionally, until all the milk is absorbed—about 10 minutes. Continue to add the milk in stages, allowing the rice to absorb each addition completely before pouring in more. Keep the heat very low and the pan covered; stir the rice now and then, but not too often or it will become gummy. The idea is to let the rice swell and soften so that the final pudding will be supremely creamy.

When you add the final ½ to 1 cup of milk, also mix in the sugar, butter, egg yolks, and ½ teaspoon of the cinnamon. Reduce heat to its lowest point, cover, and cook, stirring occasionally, about 15 to 20 minutes or until the mixture is very creamy and no raw egg flavor remains. Spoon the pudding into a well-buttered shallow 3-quart casserole, decorate the top with the remaining cinnamon, and chill 1 to 2 hours before serving.

CARAMELIZED FLAN FROM PINHÃO
Pudim Flan de Pinhão

Pinhão, a little whitewashed village some eighty miles up the Douro River from Porto, is the hub of the Port wine grape-growing district. This gossamer flan spiked with Port is one I enjoyed while staying at a *quinta* there some years ago.

Makes 8 to 10 servings

CARAMELIZED SUGAR SYRUP:

½   cup sugar
½   cup boiling water

FLAN:

2   cups half-and-half cream
2   cups heavy cream
1   cup sugar
4   strips orange zest, each about 2 inches long and ½-inch wide
2   tablespoons caramelized sugar syrup (above)
12   jumbo egg yolks
¼   cup tawny Port

For the caramelized sugar syrup: Place the sugar in a medium-size heavy skillet (not iron), set over moderately low heat, and allow to melt and caramelize to a rich golden brown (this will take about 40 minutes). Do not stir the sugar as it melts but do shake the skillet from time to time. Add the boiling water, teaspoon by teaspoon at first, stirring briskly to dissolve the caramelized sugar. Simmer uncovered 8 to 10 minutes until the consistency of maple syrup. Reserve 2 tablespoons of the caramelized sugar syrup for the flan; pour the balance into a chilled, well-buttered, shallow fluted 2-quart mold. Set the mold in the freezer while you prepare the flan.

For the flan: Preheat the oven to moderately slow (325°F.). Combine the half-and-half, heavy cream, and sugar in a large heavy saucepan; drop in the orange zest and bring to a simmer over moderately low heat, stirring now and then; blend in the 2 tablespoons of reserved caramelized syrup. Beat the egg yolks until frothy; blend 1 cup of the hot cream mixture into the yolks, stir back into pan, and heat, stirring constantly, 1 minute. Remove from the heat and mix in the Port. Strain all through a fine sieve, then pour into the prepared mold. Set the mold in a shallow baking pan and pour in enough hot water to come halfway up the mold. Bake uncovered 1½ hours or until a toothpick inserted near the center of the flan comes out clean. Remove from the oven and the water bath; cool 1 hour, then refrigerate 4 to 5 hours until firm. To invert the flan, dip the mold quickly in hot water, then turn out on a dessert plate with a turned-up rim; the caramel syrup will come cascading down over the flan. Cut into slim wedges and serve.

TEA PUDDING
Pudim de Chá

Because tea is the principal flavoring of this rich custard, you should use a particularly fine and fragrant one. Portuguese farm women would make the tea pudding without cream, but in the fancier houses, milk or cream are often added. This may seem like too many eggs for just three cups of liquid, but the tannin in the tea seems to reduce the thickening power of the eggs. And the pudding is still too fragile to unmold easily, so it's best to bake it in individual small decorative ramekins that can be brought to the table.

Makes 8 servings

- 2   cups very strong and fragrant tea
- 1   cup heavy cream, half-and-half, milk, or water
- 1   cup sugar
- 4   large whole eggs
- 8   large egg yolks

Preheat the oven to moderate (350°F.). Combine the tea and cream; beat together the sugar, eggs, and egg yolks lightly just to blend; stir in the tea mixture, then strain all through a fine sieve. Pour into 8 well-buttered 4- to 5-ounce ramekins, set in a large shallow baking pan containing about 1 inch of hot water, then bake uncovered about 45 minutes or until a toothpick inserted halfway between the edge and the center of a pudding comes out clean. Remove the puddings from the oven and from the hot-water bath, cool ½ hour, then cover each ramekin with plastic food wrap and chill several hours before serving. Top, if you like, with whipped cream, but this is not the Portuguese way.

ORANGE TORTE
Torta de Laranja

A remarkable dessert. It contains no flour and it's a bit tricky to make because you must work at lightning speed once the torte comes from the oven. Make sure that the wax paper you use to line the bottom of the pan is well buttered *and* floured. Do not use baking parchment to line the pan because the torte mixture would slither over it as it bakes and be extremely uneven, making the torte difficult to roll.

Makes 6 to 8 servings

- 1½   cups sugar
- 3   jumbo eggs
- Juice of 1 navel orange
- 1   tablespoon finely grated orange rind
- ⅛   teaspoon ground cinnamon

Preheat the oven to hot (425°F.). In an electric mixer set at high speed, beat ¾ cup of the sugar with the eggs 5 minutes until the color and consistency of mayonnaise. Meanwhile, line the bottom of a 15½ × 10½ × 1-inch jelly-roll pan with wax paper. Butter the wax paper generously and also the pan sides; sprinkle 2 tablespoons of flour over the wax paper, then tip the pan from side to side and back and forth to coat both the wax paper and the pan sides with flour. Rap the pan lightly against the counter, then tip out the excess flour; set the pan aside.

As soon as the sugar-egg mixture is fluffy-light, stir in the orange juice, rind, and cinnamon. Pour batter into the prepared pan and bake uncovered on the middle oven rack 12 to 15 minutes until the surface is richly browned. *Note: As it bakes, the batter will billow into alarming "hills and valleys," but this is perfectly normal.* While the torte bakes, spread a clean dishtowel across the counter so that one of the short sides faces you. Now sprinkle the remaining ¾ cup sugar over the towel to cover an area slightly larger than that of the jelly-roll pan.

The instant the torte is done, remove from the oven and loosen around the edges with a thin-bladed knife or small spatula. Quickly invert the pan on top of the sugared towel and, wasting no time, gently pull off the wax paper. (Never mind if a few holes appear in the torte; they won't show once the torte is finished.) Now, with a sharp knife dipped in hot water, quickly trim off any crisp edges around the torte. To roll the torte, lift the front end of the towel up, letting the torte roll up on itself, jelly-roll style. Leave the torte wrapped up in the towel for 3 to 4 hours (the torte will make its own jellylike filling), then carefully unwrap. To serve, slice the torte about ⅜-inch thick and slightly on the bias. Allow 2 to 3 slices per serving.

LEMON TORTE
Torta de Limão

Another of Portugal's flourless, rich-as-sin egg sweets. This lemon torte is served all over Portugal, but no one makes it better than the pastry chef at the Pousada do Castelo, the government inn built inside the medieval castle that crowns the storybook walled town of Óbidos north of Lisbon.

Makes 6 to 8 servings

1¾	cups sugar
5	jumbo eggs
¼	cup lemon juice
1	tablespoon finely grated lemon rind

Preheat the oven to hot (425°F.). In an electric mixer set at high speed, beat 1 cup of the sugar with the eggs 5 minutes until the color and consistency of mayonnaise. Meanwhile, line the bottom of a 15½ × 10½ × 1-inch jelly-roll pan with wax paper. Butter the wax paper generously and also the pan sides; sprinkle 2 tablespoons of flour over the wax paper then tip the pan from side to side and back and forth to coat both the wax paper and the pan sides with flour. Rap the pan lightly against the counter, then tip out the excess flour; set the pan aside.

As soon as the sugar-egg mixture is fluffy-light, fold in the lemon juice and rind. Pour batter into the prepared pan and bake uncovered on the middle oven rack 12 to 15 minutes until the surface is richly browned. *Note: As it bakes, the batter will billow into alarming "hills and valleys," but this is perfectly normal.* While the torte bakes, spread a clean dishtowel across the counter so that one of the short sides faces you. Now sprinkle the remaining ¾ cup sugar over the towel to cover an area slightly larger than that of the jelly-roll pan.

The instant the torte is done, remove from the oven and loosen around the edges with a thin-bladed knife or small spatula. Quickly invert the pan on top of the sugared towel and, wasting no time, gently pull off the wax paper. (Never mind if a few holes appear in the torte; they won't show once the torte is finished.) Now, with a sharp knife dipped in hot water, quickly trim off any crisp edges around the torte. To roll the torte, lift the front end of the towel up, letting the torte roll up on itself, jelly-roll style. Leave the torte wrapped up in the sugared towel for 3 to 4 hours (the torte will make its own custardy filling), then carefully unwrap. To serve, slice the torte about ⅜ inch thick and slightly on the bias. Allow 2 to 3 slices per serving.

DELICIOUS ORANGE PUDDING
Delícias de Laranja

For a Portuguese egg sweet, this one is surprisingly airy. It's the specialty of Reid's, that grand old resort hotel on the green Atlantic island of Madeira. Start it the day before you plan to serve it. *Note: Because this recipe contains raw egg whites, use only eggs from a known source—safe and salmonella-free.*

Makes 6 servings

> 2 envelopes plain gelatin
> Juice of 2 medium oranges
> Grated rind of 2 medium oranges
> 1 cup sugar
> 1 quart milk, scalded
> 12 large eggs, separated
> 6 tablespoons confectioners' (10X) sugar

Soften the gelatin in the orange juice 5 minutes. Add the rind, sugar, and softened gelatin mixture to the pan of hot milk; stir until dissolved. Beat the egg yolks lightly, mix in a little of the hot milk, then stir yolk mixture into pan. Set over low heat and cook, stirring constantly, 15 to 20 minutes until slightly thickened—about like a thin custard sauce. Do not boil or the mixture may curdle; remove from the heat.

  Beat the egg whites to soft peaks, gradually adding the confectioners' sugar. Gently but thoroughly fold the beaten whites into the orange mixture. Pour into a large bowl and chill for 24 hours. Serve in stemmed goblets, sprigged, if you like, with lemon verbena, lemon geranium, or mint.

SOUP OF GOLD
Sopa Dourada

In many parts of Portugal this beloved egg sweet is made with *Pão de Ló* (Portuguese Sponge Cake, page 272), but I prefer this version from the palatial, antique-filled Pousada da Rainha Santa Isabel in Estremoz, which uses crisp cubes of toast. *Sopa Dourada* is so rich it doesn't need the added sweetness of cake! *Note: This dessert will be more flavorful if you make it the day before you plan to serve it.*

Makes 4 to 6 servings

3	slices stale firm-textured white bread, cut into ¼-inch cubes
4	tablespoons unsalted butter
2	tablespoons vegetable oil
1¼	cups sugar
1	cup water
5	large egg yolks
1	large egg
⅛	teaspoon ground cinnamon
⅛	teaspoon ground nutmeg
⅛	teaspoon salt
2	tablespoons almond paste (it must be soft and malleable)
	Light sprinklings of ground cinnamon

Sauté half the bread cubes in 1 tablespoon each butter and oil in a large heavy skillet over moderate heat. When crisply golden, drain on paper toweling. Wipe the skillet clean with paper toweling and brown the remaining bread cubes the same way in 1 tablespoon each butter and oil; drain on toweling as before and reserve.

Combine the sugar and water in a small heavy saucepan; insert a candy thermometer and bring to 230°F. without stirring. Meanwhile, beat together the egg yolks, egg, ⅛ teaspoon cinnamon, nutmeg, and salt in a double-boiler top until frothy; set aside. Cream the remaining 2 tablespoons of butter with the almond paste until smooth; reserve. When the syrup reaches the proper temperature, drizzle slowly into the egg mixture, beating hard with a whisk or a hand electric mixer set at medium speed. Place over simmering water and beat 10 minutes, until the consistency of hollandaise. Remove from the heat. Whisk a little of the hot sauce into the creamed almond paste, stir the almond paste back into the sauce, and beat until smooth. Add the bread cubes, stir lightly, and cool to room temperature.

Spoon into 4 to 6 small crystal goblets, cover, and refrigerate at least 24 hours. About 30 minutes before serving, remove the goblets from the refrigerator, sprinkle each portion lightly with cinnamon, and let stand at room temperature.

MOLOTOV PUDDING I
Pudim Molotov I

On my first trip to Portugal thirty years ago I tasted for the first time this quivery poached meringue topped with a fragrant apricot sauce. I've enjoyed *Pudim Molotov* on every subsequent trip and in dozens of permutations: meringue made with burnt sugar syrup (as here), snowy meringue topped with *Ovos Moles* (sweet soft eggs) of pouring consistency, with thin custard, but only in the Algarve with that golden apricot sauce. *Pudim Molotov* is new as Portuguese sweets go, possibly less than fifty years old. And yet no one in Portugal's food fraternity with whom I spoke—chefs, cooking school teachers, hoteliers, restauratuers, cookbook authors, culinary historians—could tell me the origin of the dessert or of its name. Perhaps some frugal cook simply whipped up the meringue to rid his refrigerator of excess egg whites (given that the usual egg sweets so dear to the Portuguese are made with such a quantity of yolks). Was his name Molotov (seems unlikely), or did he cook for someone named Molotov?

Makes 6 to 8 servings

- 1 **cup plus 2 tablespoons sugar**
- ⅔ **cup boiling water**
- 1 **tablespoon lemon juice**
- 10 **large egg whites**

Place ½ cup of the sugar in a small heavy skillet and set over moderately low heat to caramelize; this will take about 40 minutes. Do not stir the sugar as it melts but do shake the skillet from time to time. When the sugar has completely liquefied and turned a rich amber-brown, pour in the boiling water and lemon juice. The mixture will sputter furiously and the burnt sugar will harden, but let it simmer uncovered over low heat about 30 minutes, stirring from time to time, until it is liquid again and about the consistency of pancake syrup.

Meanwhile, preheat the oven to moderate (350°F.). Also butter well a 10-inch tube pan, then add 2 tablespoons sugar and tilt the pan from side to side until the bottom, sides, and central tube are all well coated with sugar; tap out the excess sugar. Beat the egg whites until frothy; add the remaining ½ cup sugar gradually, beating all the while. Measure out ½ cup of the burnt sugar syrup and drizzle into the egg whites, beating slowly. Continue beating just until the whites mount in the bowl and billow—they will not peak even softly. Reserve the remaining burnt sugar syrup to use as a sauce.

Pour the meringue (it *will* pour provided you haven't overbeaten the whites) into the prepared tube pan. Rap the pan sharply a couple of times against the counter to burst any large air bubbles in the meringue, then set in a large shallow baking pan, and pour about 1 inch of hot water into the baking pan. Set on the middle oven rack and bake the meringue uncovered for 45 minutes or until just set. Remove from the oven and from the water bath, carefully loosen the meringue around the edges and central tube with a spatula dipped in hot water, then turn out onto a large colorful dessert plate.

Return the reserved burnt sugar syrup to moderate heat. If it has solidified, add about ⅓ cup additional boiling water and heat, stirring now and then, until the syrup liquefies; continue boiling uncovered until the consistency of pancake syrup— this will take about 10 minutes. Drizzle the burnt sugar syrup artfully over the top of the *Pudim Molotov*. Cool the pudding to room temperature, then cut into wedges and serve.

MOLOTOV PUDDING II
Pudim Molotov II

An easier recipe than *Pudim Molotov I* because there is no burnt sugar syrup to be made. In Portugal, this poached meringue would be served with *Ovos Moles* (sweet soft eggs) or Apricot Sauce (pages 282 and 284). I also like it with sliced fresh strawberries or peaches.

Makes 6 to 8 servings

10	large egg whites
¼	teaspoon salt
1	cup sugar
1	teaspoon lemon juice
1	teaspoon vanilla (optional)

Preheat the oven to moderate (350°F.). Also butter well a 10-inch tube pan, add a little sugar (about 2 tablespoons), and tilt the pan first to one side, then the other until the pan bottom, sides, and central tube are all well coated with sugar; tap out excess sugar. In an electric mixer set at moderate speed, beat the egg whites together with the salt until frothy; add the 1 cup sugar gradually, beating all the while, just until soft and billowing. (When the bowl is tilted, the beaten whites should just flow—not run—from the bowl.) Pour the meringue into the prepared pan, rap sharply once or twice against the counter to burst large air bubbles in the meringue, then place in a large shallow baking pan, and pour about 1 inch of hot water into the baking pan. Set on the middle oven rack and bake the meringue uncovered for 45 minutes or until just set. Remove from the oven and from the water bath, carefully loosen the meringue around the edges and central tube with a spatula dipped in hot water, then turn out onto a large colorful dessert plate. Cool to room temperature before cutting into wedges and serving.

CHEESE TARTS FROM SINTRA
Queijadas de Sintra

These bite-size sweets are sold by street vendors in Sintra, a lushly landscaped castle town some fifteen miles west of Lisbon. (Lord Byron wrote some of "Childe Harold's Pilgrimage" here, and Sintra has since been known as "Byron's Eden.") The tarts are sold in sets of six, stacked in pairs, and rolled up in white paper. They are made with *queijo fresco,* a smooth white sheep's milk cheese unavailable here, but I've hit upon a recipe using fresh mozzarella (plus a little butter to give the filling the requisite richness) that comes close to the Sintra original. The tarts' pastry is neither short nor tender—its purpose is merely to provide a little shell for the filling—so it must be rolled as thin as paper. *Note: If you should visit Sintra, find your way to Sapa, a venerable family-run pastelaria where queijadas are made fresh every day the old-fashioned way—by hand. They are Sintra's—and Portugal's—best and, I'm sorry to say, positively addicting.*

Makes about 3½ dozen tarts

PASTRY:

> 2 cups sifted all-purpose flour
> ¼ teaspoon salt
> 2 tablespoons lard (hog lard, not vegetable shortening)
> ½ to ⅔ cup ice water

CHEESE FILLING:

¾	pound fresh mozzarella, cut into ½-inch cubes (at room temperature)
4	tablespoons unsalted butter, cut into pats
1¾	cups sugar
1	teaspoon ground cinnamon
4	large egg yolks
½	cup unsifted all-purpose flour

For the pastry: Combine the flour and salt in a large bowl; then, with a pastry blender, cut in the lard until the texture of fine meal. Forking briskly, drizzle just enough ice water over the mixture to make it hold together. Shape into a ball, wrap in wax paper, and refrigerate several hours.

Meanwhile, prepare the filling: In a food processor fitted with the metal chopping blade (or in a blender or electric mixer set at highest speed), buzz the mozzarella, butter, sugar, and cinnamon about 60 seconds nonstop until smooth and creamy; scrape down the work bowl sides with a rubber spatula and beat 60 seconds longer. *Note: It will take longer for the electric mixer to reduce the mixture to creaminess—perhaps 3 to 4 minutes of steady beating.* Add the egg yolks, one at a time, beating well after each addition; add the flour and snap the motor on once or twice to blend in. Transfer the mixture to a small bowl, cover, and chill several hours.

When ready to bake the *queijadas,* preheat the oven to hot (400°F.). Divide the pastry in half and roll, first one half, then the other, as thin as paper on a lightly floured pastry cloth with a lightly floured, stockinette-covered rolling pin. Cut into rounds with a 3½-inch cutter. Also reroll and cut the scraps. Fit the pastry into plain or fluted tart tins measuring 2½ inches across the top. Set the tins on baking sheets, then half-fill each tart shell with the cheese mixture.

Bake uncovered for 18 to 20 minutes, just until the filling is puffy and a rich amber-brown. Remove the tarts from the oven, cool until easy to handle; then, using a small, pointed knife, gently pry the tarts from the tins. Serve at room temperature.

ALMOND TART À LA RITZ HOTEL
Torta de Amêndoa Feito à Moda do Hotel Ritz Lisboa

This diet-busting almond tart has been served at Lisbon's Ritz as long as I can remember. Today, it's one of the regional (Algarve) specialties featured on the daily menu at the hotel's Varanda Restaurant overlooking Eduardo VII Park. In the old days the tart was made with a short pastry, which I'm convinced contained almond paste or marzipan. Today, the Ritz pastry chef is more likely to use puff pastry, which gives the tart a Gallic character. By all means use puff pastry if you like (remember, you need enough for top and bottom crusts). What I use here is my interpretation of the more Portuguese almond pastry; it's also quicker and easier than puff pastry.

Makes a 9-inch pie

PASTRY:

    3⅓   cups sifted all-purpose flour
    2   tablespoons sugar
    ½   teaspoon salt
    ¼   pound (1 stick) plus 2 tablespoons cold unsalted butter, cut into slim pats
    2   ounces marzipan or almond paste, cut into small cubes
    2   large egg yolks, lightly beaten
    ½   to ⅔ cup ice water

FILLING:

    ½   pound *less* 2 tablespoons (1¾ sticks) unsalted butter
    2   cups very finely ground blanched almonds
    1   cup sugar
    4   large eggs
    2   tablespoons all-purpose flour
    1   tablespoon anise liqueur

For the pastry: Sift the flour, sugar, and salt into a large, broad-bottomed bowl. Dot the surface with butter and marzipan. Using a pastry blender or two knives, cut the butter and marzipan into the dry ingredients until the texture of coarse meal. Add the egg yolks and toss quickly; then, forking the mixture constantly, drizzle in just enough ice water to make the pastry hang together. Divide the pastry in half; wrap half in plastic food wrap and refrigerate; roll out the remaining half on a well-floured pastry cloth with a well-floured stockinette-covered rolling pin into a circle about 12 inches across and ¼-inch thick. Lay the rolling pin across the center of the pastry, then *carefully*—for this pastry is extra short, extra tender—lop half of it over the rolling pin and ease into a 9-inch pie pan. Trim the pastry so that it overhangs the pan rim about 1 inch all around, and set aside.

Now prepare the filling: Cream together the butter, ground almonds, and sugar until light; then beat the eggs in, one by one. Mix in the flour and anise liqueur. Set filling aside for the moment. Preheat the oven to very hot (475°F.). Remove remaining pastry from the refrigerator and roll into a 9-inch circle just as you did the first half. Pour the filling into the pie shell. Now lay the rolling pin across the center of the pastry circle, lop half of it over the rolling pin, and ease into place on top of the filling. Trim the pastry overhang so that it is about 1 inch larger all around than the pie pan. With well-floured fingers, roll the top and bottom crusts together up onto the rim of the pie pan, sealing the filling in, and crimp all around in a zigzag pattern. With a metal skewer, prick the top crust in a decorative all-over pattern. (These steam vents are necessary to keep the top crust from cracking under the pressure of the rising filling.) I like to work out a design of big and little hearts (*very Portuguese!*), but let your own creativity dictate; just be sure you prick the top crust well.

Place the tart on the middle oven shelf, reduce the temperature at once to moderately hot (375°F.), and bake 45 to 50 minutes, just until the tart is puffed and lightly browned. Remove the tart from the oven, set on a wire rack, and cool to room temperature before cutting.

DREAMS
Sonhos

Once you've sampled one of these airy puffs straight from the deep-fat fryer, you'll understand why the Portuguese call them "dreams." They're really nothing more than sweetened *choux* paste, fried until golden, then served either with lavish dustings of cinnamon-sugar or topped by *Molho de Caramelo* (Caramel Sauce, page 285) or *Molho de Morango* (Strawberry Sauce, page 285).

Makes about 2½ dozen

¼   **pound (1 stick) unsalted butter**
2   **tablespoons sugar**
¼   **teaspoon salt**
1   **cup water**
1   **cup sifted all-purpose flour**
4   **large eggs**
     Vegetable oil or shortening for deep-fat frying (about 2 quarts oil or 2 pounds shortening)
½   **cup sugar blended with 1 teaspoon ground cinnamon (optional cinnamon-sugar)**

In a small heavy saucepan set over high heat, bring the butter, sugar, salt, and water to a boil. Now pull the pan almost off the burner, dump in all the flour, and beat hard with a wooden spoon until the mixture comes together in a ball. Set the pan on a damp cloth on the counter and add the eggs, one at a time, beating well after each addition. *Note: The mixture will seem to curdle each time you add an egg, but continue beating and it will smooth out nicely. Always beat each egg in thoroughly before adding the next one.*

Pour the oil into a large deep-fat fryer, insert a deep-fat thermometer, set over high heat, and heat until the thermometer registers 375°F. Drop the *sonhos* into the hot fat by rounded tablespoonfuls and fry, 3 to 4 at a time, just until puffed and golden-brown on all sides—2 to 3 minutes. Keep the temperature of the fat as nearly as possible at 375°F. by raising and lowering the burner heat as needed. Drain the fried *sonhos* on several thicknesses of paper toweling, and if you like, sprinkle with cinnamon-sugar while hot. If you prefer, omit the cinnamon-sugar and top the *sonhos* instead with *Molho de Caramelo* or *Molho de Morango*. *Note: When topping the* sonhos *with sauce, serve them on individual plates, allowing three per serving.*

FIG TORTE
Morgado de Figo

The Portuguese aren't noted for chocolate desserts, yet this Algarve sweet is loaded with cocoa. Like most *morgados,* it's compounded of finely ground dried figs and almonds and is no doubt one of the sweets introduced by the Moors, who occupied the Algarve for more than five hundred years. Few *morgados* are made with chocolate and certainly the Moorish original would have been devoid of it, for this New World delicacy wasn't introduced to Europe until the sixteenth century, some three hundred years after the Moors had been driven from the Algarve. This particular recipe comes from Mário Palma, Maître d'Hôtel at the *Escola de Hotelaria e Turismo do Algarve* (Algarve Hotel and Tourism School) in the cubistic white port city of Faro.

Makes a 9-inch torte

1¼   cups sugar
⅔   cup water
½   pound dried figs, ground very fine
½   pound blanched almonds, ground very fine
1½   cups cocoa powder (not a mix)
    Grated rind of 1 lemon
10   large egg yolks, lightly beaten
1   cup *Doce de Chila* (Candied Chila Gourd, page 286), or, if you prefer, orange marmalade

Preheat the oven to slow (300°F.). In a medium-size heavy saucepan set over low heat, combine the sugar and water, stirring until all the sugar dissolves. Insert a candy thermometer, raise the heat to moderate, and cook without stirring until the syrup reaches 215°F. Meanwhile, combine the ground figs and almonds, cocoa, and lemon rind. As soon as the syrup reaches the proper temperature, blend it into the fig mixture; then beat in the egg yolks. Spread half the mixture in a well-buttered 9-inch springform pan. *Note: Because the mixture is so thick, I find it easiest to pat it over the bottom of the pan with buttered hands.* Spread the *Doce de Chila* evenly on top, leaving a ½-inch margin all around. Now pat the remaining fig mixture firmly on top. Bake uncovered about 45 minutes, just until the surface of the *morgado* no longer feels moist. Remove from the oven and cool right-side up in the pan on a wire rack for 10 minutes; loosen around the edges with a small spatula, then release the springform sides and remove. Let the *morgado* cool to room temperature before serving. Cut the pieces small—the *morgado* is devastingly rich; in fact, it tastes very much like those unbaked chocolate fudge cakes so popular in trendy American restaurants today.

FILLED ALMOND COOKIES
Morgados

These little ground-almond pillows filled with both *Ovos Moles* (sweet soft eggs) and *Doce de Chila* (candied squash) are another sweetmeat introduced by the Moors. It was a Moorish king who planted almond groves all over the Algarve (so that, the legend goes, their February flurries of blossoms might remind his homesick Scandinavian wife of the snows of home). This recipe given to me by Mário Palma of the Algarve Hotel School also contained *Fios de Ovos* (thread eggs), but they are difficult to make without the proper equipment. Given America's growing cholesterol-consciousness, I have not only omitted them here but also from the book itself; the Portuguese use these rich candied strands of poached egg yolk primarily as decoration, and they are not something many Americans like. As a friend of mine once observed, "They've got your basic sugar flavor but not much else." Besides, these *morgados* are plenty rich without the added calories and cholesterol of the *Fios de Ovos*.

Makes about 1½ dozen

> 1⅓   cups sugar
> ⅔   cup water
> ½   pound blanched almonds, ground very fine
> 3   large egg yolks, lightly beaten
> ¼   cup *Ovos Moles* (page 282 or 283)
> ¼   cup *Doce de Chila* (page 286)

Combine the sugar and water in a medium-size heavy saucepan, set over low heat, and stir until the sugar is completely dissolved. Insert a candy thermometer, raise the heat to moderately low, and heat without stirring until the syrup reaches 215°F. Dump in the ground almonds, stirring briskly, then cook and stir about 30 minutes until very thick. Add the egg yolks, turn the heat to low, and cook, stirring often, 15 to 20 minutes until very thick. Remove from the heat and cool until thick enough to shape. (Don't chill, or the mixture may become too crumbly to work.)

Preheat the oven to moderate (350°F.). Pinch off a small chunk of the almond mixture and shape into a deep little cup about 1½ inches across the top; spoon in first a little dab of the *Ovos Moles,* then one of the *Doce de Chila.* Shape a second little cup just like the first, then invert it on top, forming a small globe. With moistened hands, pinch the two halves together, then roll in your palms into a smooth ball. Repeat until you have used up all the almond mixture.

Place the balls about 2 inches apart on a greased and floured baking sheet and bake uncovered for 15 minutes—the balls will flatten into little pillows as they bake. Transfer while warm to wire racks to cool. Store airtight.

SIGHS
Suspiros

I love the name the Portuguese have given to these crisp meringue cookies; to eat one is surely to sigh with happiness. I have visions of Portuguese cooks baking these by the hundreds simply to use up all the egg whites left after making so many yolk-rich confections. The variation added below is a favorite in the Algarve Province; you can buy these "yolk-filled" meringues at any good pastry shop there. *Note: Do not attempt to make* suspiros *in rainy or humid weather, because the meringues will absorb atmospheric moisture and lose their shattery crispness.*

Makes about 5 dozen

2½	cups sugar
1	cup water
6	large egg whites
1	tablespoon lemon juice
¼	teaspoon salt

Combine the sugar and water in a medium-size heavy saucepan and set over moderately low heat, stirring occasionally, until the sugar dissolves completely. Insert a candy thermometer, then cook without stirring until the syrup reaches the soft-ball stage (236°F.). As the temperature nears the appropriate mark, preheat the oven to slow (300°F.). Also beat the egg whites together with the lemon juice and salt until silvery—it's best to do this with an electric mixer. As soon as the syrup reaches 236°F., drizzle it slowly into the egg whites, beating all the while at highest mixer speed. Continue beating for 2 to 3 minutes after all the syrup has been incorporated—the mixture should be very stiff and stand up in peaks.

Drop the meringue by the rounded tablespoonful onto baking sheets lined with aluminum foil (dull side up) and bake uncovered 30 minutes. Turn the oven off and let the meringues dry out in the oven for 1 hour. Peel from the foil and store airtight.

VARIATION:

Suspiros com Ovos Moles (Meringues with Sweet Soft Egg Filling): For this you'll need about 1 cup of *Ovos Moles* (page 282 or 283). Make the *suspiros* as directed, then sandwich pairs together with about 1 rounded teaspoon of *Ovos Moles*. Store airtight. Makes about 2½ dozen.

PINEAPPLE IN PORT WITH FRESH CHOPPED MINT
Ananás em Porto com Hortelã Picada

The mellowest pineapples on earth are those grown in the Azores because they ripen in greenhouses under waftings of smoke. Most of the pineapple served in mainland Portugal comes from the Azores, the mid-Atlantic archipelago discovered and claimed for Portugal by Prince Henry-the-Navigator's captains early in the fifteenth century. This particular recipe couldn't be easier or more refreshing. It also proves that not all Portuguese desserts are desperately rich.

Makes 6 servings

> 1   **large ripe pineapple (3¾ to 4 pounds)**
> 3   **tablespoons fine ruby Port**
> ¼   **cup freshly minced mint**

Slice the top and bottom off the pineapple, stand it on end, and slicing straight down, remove all the prickly peel. Cut the pineapple lengthwise into 8 wedges, slice off the hard core at the point of each wedge, then slice the wedges about ¼-inch thick, making small fan-shaped pieces. Place the pineapple fans in a large non-metallic bowl, add the Port, and toss to mix. Cover and chill 3 to 4 hours. Add the mint, toss again, and chill 30 minutes longer. To serve, spoon into stemmed goblets, and if you like, sprig with fresh mint.

STRAWBERRIES IN PORT
Morangos em Porto

Makes 4 to 6 servings

3　pints ripe strawberries, washed, hulled, and halved. (If berries are very large, slice about ¼ inch thick.)
3　tablespoons sugar
¼　cup ruby Port or, if you have a bottle open, fine vintage Port
4　to 6 mint sprigs

Place the strawberries in a large bowl (preferably nonmetallic), add the sugar and Port and toss lightly. Cover and macerate in the refrigerator 2 to 3 hours. To serve, spoon berries into stemmed goblets and sprig with mint.

SPONGE CAKE
Pão-de-Ló

Every Portuguese town, it seems, has its own recipe for *Pão-de-Ló*. Alfeizerão, for example, near the "movie-set" fishing village of Nazaré, is famous for a *Pão-de-Ló* that is only half baked and eaten like pudding. Most of them, however, are fairly classic sponge cakes with higher or lower proportions of eggs and sugar. They are a bakery staple and you see them in *pastelarias* (pastry shops) everywhere, with their baking parchment serving as wrappers. Portuguese women use *Pão-de-Ló* as the foundation of a huge repertoire of sweets. Portuguese children are content just to eat chunks of the cake out of hand.

Makes one 10-inch tube cake

- 4 large eggs
- 8 large egg yolks
- 1¼ cups sugar
- 1½ cups sifted all-purpose flour

Preheat the oven to moderate (350°F.). Cut six 7-inch squares of baking parchment, then line a well-buttered 10-inch tube pan this way: Place a parchment square on the diagonal in the bottom of the pan so that one of its points touches the central tube; now flatten the square against the bottom of the pan and up the side, pleating it as needed for a smooth fit. Next lay a second square of parchment in the pan the same way, so that it slightly overlaps the first square, and smooth it against the pan bottom and side, pleating it as necessary for a snug fit. Continue lining the pan with the parchment squares, each one overlapping the previous one, until you've completely covered the bottom and sides of the pan; you'll need all six squares. The points of the squares will stand several inches above the rim of the pan all around; this lends a decorative touch and is characteristic of *Pão-de-Ló*.

Beat the eggs and egg yolks in an electric mixer at high speed 1 minute; now add the sugar in a slow but steady stream, beating all the while, and when all the sugar is incorporated, beat at highest mixer speed for 15 minutes. Reduce the mixer speed to low and add the flour, 1 heaping tablespoon at a time, beating all the while. Stop the machine about midway through the addition of the flour and scrape down the sides of the mixer bowl thoroughly. Resume adding the flour at low mixer speed and when all of it is incorporated, spoon the batter at once into the prepared pan. Bake uncovered for 40 minutes or until the cake is lightly browned and spongy to the touch. Remove the cake from the oven and from its pan, then cool it right-side up in its parchment liner on a cake rack. Let the cake come to room temperature before serving or using in recipes.

SPONGE PUDDING-CAKE
Pão-de-Ló de Alfeizerão

I can't help but believe that this beloved dessert was born of a mistake because it looks like such a disaster—sunken in the center, oozing liquid, barely brown. It is in truth a half-baked cake, but to the Portuguese it is ambrosia. Usually baked one day and served the next, this soft *Pão-de-Ló* is cut into wedges and served utterly plain— no snifters of confectioners' or cinnamon sugar are put out, as they frequently are with so many of Portugal's other egg sweets. The dessert is a snap to make; indeed, the most demanding thing about it is lining the baking pan with parchment.

Makes one 10-inch tube cake

4   large eggs
8   large egg yolks
¾   cup sugar
¾   cup sifted all-purpose flour

Preheat the oven to very hot (450°F.). Cut 2 circles of baking parchment with holes in the centers to line the bottom of a 10-inch tube pan. Also cut two long strips to line the sides of the pan. Finally, cut a third circle with a hole in it, this circle about 2 inches larger all around than the top of the pan; this will serve as a cover. Butter the pan bottom, sides, and central tube well, then lay one of the parchment circles in the bottom of the pan. Now smooth the strips of parchment against the sides of the pan, pleating here and there as needed for a smooth fit. Lay the second parchment circle in the bottom of the pan, covering the bottom edge of the side strips; set the pan aside.

In an electric mixer set at high speed, beat the eggs and egg yolks until frothy; add the sugar in a slow but steady stream, beating all the while. Now beat the mixture 10 minutes at highest mixer speed. Reduce mixer speed to low and add the flour, heaping tablespoon by heaping tablespoon. About halfway through the addi- tion of the flour, stop the machine and scrape down the sides of the mixer bowl thoroughly.

The minute all the flour has been added, stop the machine, then mix the batter 8 to 10 times in a gentle over-and-over folding motion with a rubber spatula. Pour the batter into the prepared pan, cover with the third parchment circle, bending the edges down around the sides of the pan. Bake for 12 minutes exactly.

Remove the cake from the oven, and without removing the parchment cover, invert at once onto a large round plate; gently peel the baking parchment from the bottom and sides of the cake. Invert quickly again onto a second large round plate and carefully peel off the parchment cover. Let stand at room temperature at least 1 to 2 hours before serving.

HONEY CAKES
Bolos de Mel

To the Portuguese, molasses is "honey" (*mel da cana,* or "cane honey," as opposed to *mel da abelha,* which is "bee honey"). These dark spicy loaves made with molasses are a specialty of Madeira, where sugarcane has been an important crop since Prince Henry-the-Navigator directed his colonists to plant cuttings of Sicilian cane there early in the fifteenth century. At harvest time today, everywhere about the island you see trucks of cane lumbering along the mountain roads, and children racing to snatch up whatever stalks fly off. To most Madeira youngsters, sucking a chunk of sugar cane is better than munching a candy bar.

Makes 2 (9 × 5 × 3-inch) loaves

⅔	cup moderately finely chopped mixed candied fruits
⅔	cup moderately finely chopped walnuts
⅔	cup moderately finely chopped blanched almonds
4½	cups sifted all-purpose flour
2	teaspoons baking soda
½	teaspoon ground cloves
½	teaspoon ground cinnamon
½	teaspoon ground anise
½	pound (2 sticks) unsalted butter, at room temperature
½	cup vegetable shortening
1	cup sugar
3	large eggs
2	packages active dry yeast softened in ½ cup lukewarm water (105°F. to 115° F.)
1¼	cups molasses (preferably light, unsulfured molasses)

Dredge the fruits and nuts in ½ cup of the sifted flour and set aside. Sift the remaining flour with the baking soda, cloves, cinnamon, and anise onto a piece of wax paper and set aside also. Cream together the butter, shortening, and sugar until fluffy-light; beat in the eggs, one at a time. Mix in the softened yeast. Add the sifted dry ingredients alternately with the molasses, beginning and ending with the dry. Fold in the fruits and nuts and all their dredging flour.

Transfer the batter to a large well-greased bowl, cover with a clean dry cloth, and allow to rise in a warm, draft-free spot for 2 hours. *Note: The batter will rise only slightly, but it will become spongy and light.* Stir the batter down, divide between two well-greased and floured 9 × 5 × 3-inch loaf pans; cover with a cloth and allow to rise 1½ hours.

Toward the end of the second rising, preheat the oven to moderately hot (375°F.). When the loaves are properly risen, bake for 50 to 60 minutes or until they begin to pull from the sides of the pans and feel springy to the touch. Cool the cakes right-side up in their pans on wire racks 10 minutes; loosen around the edges with a spatula, turn the cakes out, and cool to room temperature before cutting. *Note: In Madeira, a popular way to decorate these cakes is to sift bands of confectioners' sugar diagonally across the tops. The cakes will keep well in the freezer for about 6 months if you've wrapped them snugly in foil or plastic food wrap.*

PUTRID CAKE
Bolo Podre

Usually clever about naming their desserts, the Portuguese missed the mark on this one! This moist and spicy honey cake is from the olive-rich Alentejo Province. The cake *is* made with oil—vegetable or peanut oil. I wonder if olive oil was used long ago, when it might have become rank or rancid. That might explain why the cake is inelegantly called "putrid," but in consulting my Portuguese dictionary, I see that *podre* also means "depraved" or "corrupt." Certainly the cake is of a richness decadent enough to appeal to depraved souls, and it's guaranteed to corrupt or sabotage any diet. One of its principal ingredients is *erva-doce,* a sweet herb that grows on the plains of the Alentejo and tastes very much like licorice. I've substituted freshly ground anise seeds, which also taste like licorice. *Note: The cake is so sweet and rich that it will crack on top as it bakes and it will brown deeply. This is the way every good* Bolo Podre *should look.*

Makes a 10-inch tube cake

2½	cups sifted all-purpose flour
1	teaspoon ground cinnamon
1	teaspoon finely ground anise seeds
6	large eggs, separated
⅔	cup sugar
	Finely grated rind of 1 orange
1¼	cups peanut or vegetable oil
1¼	cups honey
¼	cup brandy (the Portuguese would use *aguardente,* the local fire-water)
	Pinch of salt

Preheat the oven to moderately hot (375°F.). Sift together the flour, cinnamon, and anise onto a piece of wax paper and set aside. In an electric mixer set at highest speed, beat the egg yolks, sugar, and orange rind 5 minutes until the color and consistency of mayonnaise. Reduce the mixer speed to moderate, drizzle in the oil, then the honey, then the brandy. Reduce mixer speed to low, add the sifted dry ingredients in 3 to 4 batches, beating only enough after each addition to incorporate. Beat the egg whites and salt to soft peaks and fold gently but thoroughly into the batter.

Pour into a well-buttered 10-inch tube pan, rap the pan sharply on the counter two or three times to burst large air bubbles, then bake uncovered 50 to 55 minutes until the cake begins to pull from the sides of the pan and is springy to the touch. Remove the cake from the oven, cool it right-side up in its pan on a wire rack 10 minutes, then loosen around the edges and around the central tube with a small spatula. Turn the cake out, then invert at once so that it is right-side up. Cool completely before cutting. There's no need to frost this cake; it's rich enough as is.

ALMOND CAKE FROM THE POUSADA DA OLIVEIRA
Bolo de Amêndoa da Pousada da Oliveira

One evening at the delightful Pousada da Oliveira in historic Guimarães, the dining room waiter, having heard me order this glorious cake for the third night in a row, whispered the news that "the cake is made entirely of mashed potatoes. It contains no wheat flour at all." Well, not quite. It does have mashed potatoes, but it also has flour, and the two combine to give it a dense texture similar to poundcake. The *pousada's* skilled pastry chef tops the finished cake with the thinnest glaze of almond praline, a difficult feat. I've taken the coward's way out by calling for crushed almond praline. (And if you don't want to bother making that, you can simply top the cake with chopped toasted almonds.)

Makes one 2-layer, 10-inch cake

12	large eggs, separated
2	cups sugar
1¼	cups cold unseasoned mashed potatoes (measure firmly packed)
⅔	cup very finely ground blanched almonds
2¼	cups sifted cake flour

FILLING:

⅔	cup cold *Ovos Moles* (page 282 or 283)

TOPPING:

¼	cup cold *Ovos Moles*
½	cup finely chopped *Praline de Amêndoa* (page 287), or coarsely chopped toasted blanched almonds

Preheat the oven to moderately slow (325°F.). Butter a 10-inch tube pan well, then dust it with flour, and set aside. In an electric mixer set at high speed, beat together the egg yolks and 1¾ cups of the sugar for 5 minutes. Slowly beat in the mashed potatoes, then the almonds. Sift a little of the cake flour over the batter, then fold it in gently but thoroughly; fold in the remaining flour the same way, using 4 to 5 separate additions. Beat the egg whites together with the remaining ¼ cup of sugar to soft peaks. Mix about one fourth of the beaten whites into the cake batter to lighten it (it's a very heavy mixture), then spoon the remaining beaten whites on top and fold in gently until no streaks of white show.

Pour the batter into the prepared pan and bake uncovered for 1 hour or until the cake begins to pull from the sides of the pan, feels springy to the touch, and is lightly browned. Cool the cake right-side up in its pan on a wire rack for 15 minutes, then loosen around the edges and around the central tube, invert on the rack, and remove the pan. Cool several hours before proceeding.

With a sharp serrated knife, halve the cake horizontally. Place the bottom layer cut-side up on a large colorful cake plate, then spread thickly with the ⅔ cup *Ovos Moles*. Set the top layer into place (no matter if some of the filling should run down the sides of the cake). Now spread the top of the cake thickly with the ¼ cup *Ovos Moles* and pat the *Praline de Amêndoa*, or chopped almonds, evenly over all. Let the cake stand for about an hour before cutting. Cut the pieces small—the cake is very rich.

DUKE OF BRAGANÇA CAKE
Bolo Duque de Bragança

This excruciatingly rich almond cake is believed to have been created by the pastry chef at the palace at Vila Viçosa in the Alentejo Province to honor one of the dukes of Bragança. There's no flour to give it body, only finely ground almonds, mashed potatoes, and eggs. The cake's texture is very much like that of the chess pies so popular in the American South.

Makes one 9-inch cake

2¼	cups sugar
¼	pound (1 stick) unsalted butter
10	large egg yolks
1	cup cold unseasoned mashed potatoes (measure firmly packed)
½	pound unblanched almonds, ground very fine
5	large egg whites
¼	teaspoon salt

Preheat the oven to moderately slow (325°F.). Beat together 2 cups of the sugar and the butter until light (the mixture will be crumbly because of the high proportion of sugar); then beat in the yolks one by one. Mix in the mashed potatoes, then the almonds. Now beat together the egg whites and salt until frothy; beat in the remaining sugar, a tablespoonful at a time, and continue beating to soft peaks; fold gently but thoroughly into the batter. Pour into a well-buttered 9-inch springform pan and bake 1 hour and 50 minutes until the cake pulls from the sides of the pan. The cake's surface will seem crisp, but will yield to the slightest pressure. Let the cake cool right-side up in the pan on a wire rack 15 minutes, then loosen around the edges with a spatula; remove the springform sides, then carefully separate the cake from the pan bottom. Turn the cake over onto a dessert plate and cool thoroughly before cutting into slim wedges. *Note: The cake will fall slightly as it cools, but this is as it should be.*

MADEIRA CAKE
Bolo da Madeira

This unusual yeast-raised fruitcake is drizzled with Madeira wine before it's served. The Portuguese also like to sip a fine sweet Madeira—a Malmsey, perhaps, or a Boal—with the cake. This may seem like overkill, but somehow the cake and wine complement one another perfectly.

Makes one 10-inch tube cake

4½	cups sifted all-purpose flour
½	cup finely diced candied citron
½	cup finely diced candied lemon peel
½	cup coarsely chopped candied red cherries
1	tablespoon baking powder
1	pound (4 sticks) unsalted butter, at room temperature
1½	cups sugar
¼	cup dark corn syrup
¼	cup molasses
8	large eggs
2	packages active dry yeast softened in ¼ cup lukewarm water (105°F. to 115° F.)
	Juice of 1 large lemon
1	tablespoon finely grated lemon rind
⅓	cup sweet Madeira (Malmsey or Boal)

Preheat the oven to moderately hot (375°F.). Place 1 cup of the flour in a small bowl, add the candied fruits, and toss well to dredge; set aside. Sift the remaining flour with the baking powder onto a piece of wax paper and set aside also. Cream together the butter and sugar until fluffy-light; beat in the corn syrup and molasses. Add the eggs, one at a time. Mix in the yeast mixture, the lemon juice, and rind. Add the flour gradually, beating lightly after each addition. Fold in the fruits and their dredging flour. Pour the batter into a well-greased and floured 10-inch tube pan and bake for about 1¼ hours or until the cake begins to pull from the sides of the pan and is springy to the touch. Cool the cake right-side up in its pan on a wire rack 10 minutes, loosen, invert on the rack, and remove the pan. Cool to room temperature, then drizzle evenly with the Madeira. Let stand at least 1 hour before cutting.

REID'S HOTEL MADEIRA CAKE
Bolo da Madeira Feito à Reid's Hotel

This fruit cake, much lighter than the family-style Madeira Cake that precedes, is often found aboard the pastry cart that is trundled out every afternoon to the tea terrace at Reid's Hotel in Funchal, Madeira. Reid's pastry chef tops it with butter cream frosting, but I think the cake is quite rich enough without it. The English who frequent Reid's like the cake with tea, but the Portuguese prefer it with Madeira.

Makes one 10-inch tube cake

4½ cups sifted all-purpose flour
1 cup chopped mixed candied fruits
1 tablespoon baking powder
1 pound (4 sticks) unsalted butter, at room temperature
2 cups sugar
8 large eggs
2 packages active dry yeast softened in ¼ cup lukewarm water (105°F. to 115°F.)
   Juice of 1 large lemon
1 tablespoon finely grated lemon rind
½ cup sweet Madeira (Malmsey or Boal)

Preheat the oven to moderately hot (375°F.). Place ½ cup of the flour in a small bowl, add the candied fruits, and toss well to dredge; set aside. Sift together the remaining flour and the baking powder onto a piece of wax paper and set aside also. Cream together the butter and sugar until fluffy-light, then beat in the eggs, one at a time. Mix in the yeast mixture, the lemon juice, and rind. Add the flour gradually, beating lightly after each addition. Fold in the fruits and their dredging flour. Pour into a well-greased and floured 10-inch tube pan and bake for about 1¼ hours or until the cake begins to pull from the sides of the pan and is springy to the touch. Cool the cake right-side up in its pan on a wire rack 10 minutes, loosen, invert on the rack, and remove the pan. Cool to room temperature, then drizzle evenly with the Madeira. Let stand at least 1 hour before serving.

GINGER CAKE
Bolo de Gengibre

Another of those celestial cakes from the pastry cart at Reid's Hotel in Madeira. It's really a spice cake because it contains cinnamon and ginger and, in lesser amounts, cloves and nutmeg. It also contains Madeira wine. In texture, this cake is quite dense, much like our poundcake.

Makes one 10-inch tube cake

4	cups sifted all-purpose flour
1	teaspoon baking soda
1	teaspoon baking powder
1	teaspoon ground cinnamon
1	teaspoon ground ginger
½	teaspoon ground cloves
½	teaspoon freshly grated nutmeg
¼	pound (1 stick) plus 3 tablespoons unsalted butter, at room temperature
⅔	cup vegetable shortening
1⅔	cups sugar
⅓	cup light molasses or dark corn syrup
5	large eggs, separated
⅓	cup sweet Madeira (Malmsey or Boal)
1	cup milk

Preheat the oven to moderately slow (325°F.). Sift together the flour, baking soda, baking powder, and spices onto a piece of wax paper and set aside. Cream together the butter, shortening, and sugar until fluffy-light. Add the molasses, and cream well; beat in the egg yolks, one at a time. Combine the Madeira and the milk. Add the sifted dry ingredients to the creamed mixture alternately with the combined liquids, beginning and ending with the dry ingredients. Beat the egg whites to soft peaks and fold in gently but thoroughly.

Pour the batter into a well-greased and floured 10-inch tube pan and bake about 1 hour and 15 minutes or until the cake begins to pull from the sides of the pan and feels springy to the touch. Cool the cake right-side up in its pan on a wire rack 10 minutes; loosen with a spatula, then turn the cake out on the rack, remove the pan, and cool to room temperature before cutting. Serve plain, or frost if you like with your favorite butter cream to which you have added about 1 tablespoon of Madeira wine and 2 to 3 tablespoons of chopped preserved ginger.

SWEET SOFT EGGS
Ovos Moles

Most Portuguese cooks would feel less deprived if you took their kitchen whisks away than if you denied them their *Ovos Moles*. These golden sweet eggs, which have the consistency of lemon-pie filling, are used in virtually everything. You'll find them spread between layers of pastry, smoothed across the tops of cakes, squirted inside little marzipan candies, and stirred into dozens of lavish egg sweets. In the northern town of Aveiro, where they are said to have originated, you can buy *Ovos Moles* in little wooden barrels in the pastry shops. The nuns who created *Ovos Moles* used only egg yolks, sugar, and water. Latter-day cooks, with an eye on both their budgets and bulges, prefer to substitute rice flour for at least some of the egg yolks. *Note: This recipe and the one that follows for* Ovos Moles *made the Aveiro way may be used interchangeably in recipes.*

Makes about 1¾ cups

- 1½   cups sugar
- 1¾   cups water
- 7   tablespoons rice flour
- 8   large egg yolks

Place the sugar and 1 cup of the water in a heavy medium-size saucepan, insert a candy thermometer, set over moderately low heat, and cook until the syrup's temperature reaches the hard-ball stage (246°F.). Meanwhile, combine the remaining ¾ cup water with the rice flour and set aside. When the syrup has reached 246°F., beat the egg yolks until frothy, then drizzle the syrup into the yolks, beating hard all the while; then stir in the rice-flour solution. Return all to the original pan, set over low heat, and cook, stirring almost constantly, for about 30 minutes or until the mixture becomes quite thick; when you move a spoon across the bottom of the pan, the crease should show and so should the pan bottom—for a second or so. Spoon the mixture into a 1-pint preserving jar, cap, and store in the refrigerator to use as needed. The *Ovos Moles* will keep fresh for a week to 10 days.

VARIATION:

Molho de Ovos Moles (Sweet Egg Sauce): Prepare exactly as directed for *Ovos Moles,* but take the completed mixture from the stove when it is about the consistency of a medium white sauce, not too thick. Serve warm over cakes, puddings, or other desserts. Or chill and serve cold. Stored tightly covered in the refrigerator, the sauce will keep well for a week to 10 days.

SWEET SOFT EGGS IN THE MANNER OF AVEIRO
Ovos Moles Feito à Maneira de Aveiro

Because they are made with rice cooking water instead of rice flour, these soft, sweet eggs made the old-fashioned Aveiro way are supremely silky. The rice must be sacrificed to obtain the properly starchy cooking water, but only ⅓ cup of it is needed.

Makes about 1¼ cups

- ⅓ cup short-grain rice
- 3 cups boiling water
- 1 cup sugar
- 8 large egg yolks, lightly beaten

Cook the rice in the boiling water in a covered heavy saucepan set over low heat 40 minutes; drain and reserve the cooking water. (If you can find a use for the well-cooked rice, so much the better.) Place 1 cup of the rice cooking water in a small heavy saucepan and mix in the sugar. Set over low heat and cook, stirring occasionally, 2 to 3 minutes until the sugar is completely dissolved. Insert a candy thermometer, raise the heat to moderate, and boil without stirring until the temperature reaches 225°F. Very slowly drizzle the hot syrup into the beaten egg yolks, whisking all the while. Pour the mixture into the saucepan, set over low heat, and cook, stirring constantly, until it is the consistency of a thick white sauce and no raw egg flavor remains—25 to 30 minutes. *Note: Do not allow the mixture to boil or it will curdle.* Strain through a fine sieve (do not force any of the solids through), then cover tight and store in the refrigerator to use as recipes direct.

APRICOT SAUCE
Molho de Alperce

This is the golden sauce I was served with *Pudim Molotov* (page 260) on my first trip to the Algarve thirty years ago at a little inn by the sea. The inn has long since vanished, but not my memories of this ambrosial sauce. Praise be, variations of the sauce are still served in the Algarve.

Makes 3 cups

½	pound dried apricots
3½	cups cold water
1	cinnamon stick, broken in several places
	Zest of 1 large lemon
2	tablespoons lemon juice
2	tablespoons sugar
1	tablespoon unsalted butter

Place the apricots in a heavy saucepan, add the water, cinnamon, and lemon zest, cover, and let stand at room temperature 3 hours. Set over moderate heat, bring to a simmer, then reduce heat so that the mixture bubbles gently; simmer, covered, 35 to 40 minutes until the apricots are very soft. Discard the cinnamon stick and lemon zest, then purée the apricots with their cooking water by buzzing 30 seconds non-stop in an electric blender or food processor fitted with the metal chopping blade; scrape down the blender cup or work bowl sides, then buzz 30 seconds longer. If you have neither blender nor food processor, force the mixture through a food mill or fine sieve.

Return the purée to the saucepan, add the lemon juice, sugar, and butter, set over low heat, and simmer uncovered, stirring occasionally, 10 minutes. Cool to room temperature, then ladle over *Pudim Molotov II* (page 261) or slices of *Pão de Ló* (page 273).

CARAMEL SAUCE
Molho de Caramelo

The Portuguese do like their sweets twice-gilded, so this sauce is a popular topping for *Pudim Molotov II* (page 261), as well as for assorted egg-yolk desserts and flans. I like it ladled over tart sliced oranges or wedges of fresh pineapple.

Makes about ¾ cup

½ cup sugar
¾ cup boiling water
1 tablespoon lemon juice
1 tablespoon unsalted butter

Melt the sugar in a small heavy skillet over moderately low heat—this will take about 40 minutes. Do not stir the sugar as it melts, but do shake the skillet from time to time. When the sugar has completely liquefied and turned a rich amber-brown, pour in the boiling water and lemon juice. The mixture will sputter violently and the melted sugar will harden; let it simmer uncovered over low heat about 20 minutes, stirring from time to time, until it is liquid again. Add the butter and simmer uncovered, stirring occasionally, until the consistency of thin maple syrup— about 5 minutes. Cool to room temperature before serving.

STRAWBERRY SAUCE
Molho de Morango

This is a favorite sauce to ladle over *Sonhos*, or "Dreams," crisply fried puffs of sweet pastry, and it is very good, too, over *Pudim Molotov II* (see pages 266 and 261).

Makes about 1⅓ cups

1 cup strawberry jelly or jam (You may substitute raspberry or red currant jelly, if you like, although strawberry is the Portuguese favorite.)
⅓ cup water
1 tablespoon lemon juice

In a small heavy saucepan set over moderate heat, heat the jelly, water, and lemon juice 4 to 5 minutes until the jelly melts; sieve the mixture, then cool to room temperature. Serve as a dessert topping.

CANDIED CHILA GOURD
Doce de Chila

A staple in the kitchen of every good Portuguese cook is candied *chila,* a gourd that "strings" much like our spaghetti squash. *Doce de chila* is integral to many of Portugal's devastating egg sweets, including the Algarve's *morgado,* several versions of *Toucinho do Céu,* and too many tarts and puddings to name. *Chila* is not available here, but I have worked out a way of candying the threads of spaghetti squash, which both look and taste like *chila* and can be substituted for it with excellent results. I won't pretend that pulling the filaments from raw spaghetti squash is a snap; it's tedious work, so enlist as much help as you can. Once the threading's done, however, the rest is easy.

Makes 2 to 2½ cups

- 2 medium spaghetti squash (about 2½ pounds each)
- 6 cups boiling water plus 1 tablespoon salt
- 4 cups sugar (about)
- 2 cinnamon sticks, broken in half

Break open the spaghetti squash, then break into 1½- to 2-inch chunks. *Note: Maria De Lourdes Modesto, Portugal's Julia Child, says it's best not to use any metal implements when handling* chila *because it affects the flavor. So I've followed her advice in working with spaghetti squash. It's easier than you think to break open a spaghetti squash; simply crack it sharply on the corner of the kitchen counter, then press down with all your might and the squash will break into pieces.* Discard all seeds, also all soft yellow threads in the center of the squash. What you want are the tougher, cream-colored strands. Immerse the chunks of squash at once in a very large kettle of cold water, remove the pieces one by one, and pull out all the threads, rubbing them lightly between your fingers to separate into thin filaments. Place in a large bowl, cover with cold water, and refrigerate overnight.

Next day, drain the squash, blanch 30 seconds in the boiling salted water, and drain well again. Weigh the squash, dump into a very large heavy kettle, and add an equal weight of sugar. Set over moderate heat, and cook, stirring often with a long-handled fork, 5 minutes. Drain, reserving both the squash and their liquid. (Even though you have drained the squash, considerable water will have clung to the spaghetti-like strands—enough, in fact, to dissolve the sugar and form a syrup.) Return the liquid to the kettle, add the cinnamon sticks, insert a candy thermometer, raise heat to moderate, and boil uncovered until the temperature reaches 240°F. Quickly dump the squash back in, turn the heat off, and with a long-handled fork, briskly mix the squash into the syrup so that every strand glistens. Cool 10 minutes, drain off the excess syrup, then spoon the candied squash and cinnamon sticks lightly into a wide-mouthed preserving jar. Cover tight and store in a cool, dark place. Use as individual recipes specify. *Note: You'll have to fork the squash into individual strands before you add it to any recipe. If the strands of squash should crystallize, add 2 to 3 tablespoons of water to the jar and gently turn upside-down and back several times to moisten the squash throughout.*

ALMOND PRALINE
Praline de Amêndoa

Portuguese chefs go all-out when it comes to decorating their cakes, puddings, and pastries. A favorite topping is chopped almond brittle or praline. It's easy to make and, if stored in a tightly covered container in the freezer, will keep well for several weeks. *Note: Do not attempt to make this praline in rainy or humid weather because it will not harden properly.*

Makes about 1½ cups

1	cup sugar
¼	cup water
3	tablespoons light corn syrup
1	tablespoon lemon juice
1	tablespoon unsalted butter
¾	cup lightly toasted blanched almonds

Place the sugar, water, corn syrup, and lemon juice in a small heavy saucepan; insert a candy thermometer, set over moderate heat, and heat slowly, without stirring, until the thermometer registers 310°F. This will take some time—30 to 40 minutes—and the syrup at this point will be deep-amber in color. Remove the syrup from the heat, drop in the butter, and remove the candy thermometer. Quickly stir in the almonds, then pour all onto a well-buttered heavy baking sheet or marble slab. Cool to room temperature, break into chunks; then, with a very sharp knife, chop as coarse or fine as you like.

LEMON TEA
Chá de Limão

An aromatic digestive popular throughout Portugal. I like to sip it just before going to bed and am convinced that it lulls me to sleep.

Makes 4 servings

3   cups cold water
    Zest of 3 large lemons
1   tablespoon sugar or honey (optional)

Bring the water and lemon zest to a simmer in a small heavy saucepan set over moderately low heat, turn the heat to its lowest point, cover, and let the mixture steep 20 minutes. Do not allow the mixture to boil at any time or the "tea" may become bitter. Sweeten, if you like, with sugar or honey; then strain, and serve steaming hot.

Acknowledgments

I am indebted to the following individuals, firms, and organizations who, over the years, have made my many trips to Portugal both productive and enjoyable by introducing me to the country's superb foods and wines, its splendid *pousadas* (government inns), its warm and caring people and, not least, to Portugal itself, which for me will always be a second home:

Fernando Moreira Paes Nicolau de Almeida, A. A. Ferreira, Sucrs., Porto; José Eduardo Simões de Almeida, Director, Pousada de São Filipe, Setúbal; Luis Simões de Almeida, Director, Hotel Albatroz, Cascais; Nuno Mendes de Almeida, formerly Director, Portuguese National Tourist Office, New York, and presently Director, Madrid; Jean-Claude Annen, Assistant Director, Reid's Hotel, Funchal, Madeira; Fernando Lopes Autunes, formerly Maître d'Hôtel, Pousada dos Lóios, Évora; Richard Blandy, Madeira Wine Company, Funchal, Madeira; Anthony Bradford, formerly Manager, Quinta do Lago, Almansil; Alvaro Braga-Lopes, formerly Director, Pousada do Castelo de Palmela, Palmela, presently Director, Pousada de Santa Marinha da Costa, Guimarães; João G. Borges, President, Madeira Tourist Board, Funchal, Madeira; Engenheiro João de Brito e Cunha, formerly Director, The Port Wine Institute, Porto; A. A. Cálem & Filho, Lda., Porto; Joaquim José Cristo Calixto, Chef de Cuisine, Pousada dos Lóios, Évora; José Carrasco, Director, Planning, Services, Markets and Products, Portuguese National Tourist Office, Lisbon; Mary Carroll, Director, Public Relations, Inter-Continental Hotels, New York; Maria Guadalupe Costa Carvalho, Director, Public Relations, Hotel Ritz Lisboa, Lisbon; Esteban Medel do Carmo, Assistant Director, Escola de Hotelaria e Turismo do Algarve, Faro; Clotilde dos Santos Correia, formerly Chef, Pousada de São Filipe, Setúbal; Dinorah Costa, Managing Director, Pousada da Oliveira, Guimarães; Maria Filomena de Abreu Coutinho, Casa de Cortegaça, Subportela, Viana do Castelo; Maria da Graça, Funchal, Madeira; Luis Manuel da Silva, Assistant Manager, Pousada do Castelo, Óbidos; Vitor Francisco Fonte da Silva, Chef de Cuisine, Pousada do Castelo de Palmela, Palmela; Mário Felix, Director, Public Relations, TAP–Air Portugal, Lisbon; António Gil Alves Machado Guedes, Quinta da Aveleda, Penafiel; Luis Guedes, Managing Director, Aveleda, Porto.

Grateful thanks are also due the invariably charming, always efficient Georges C.A. Hangartner, formerly Director General, Reid's Hotel, Funchal, Madeira; to Ana Maria Horta, ENATUR, Lisbon; Jorge Felner da Costa, Director, Portuguese National Tourist Office, New York; Domingos Manuel Sardo Lameiras, Concierge, Pousada da Rainha Santa Isabel, Estremoz; Carlos Lameiro, formerly Director, Portuguese National Tourist Office, New York; João Alegria Lima, Director, Algarve Regional Tourist Office, Faro; José Luis Fernandes Lima, Chef de Cuisine, Pousada de Dom Dinis, Vila Nova de Cerveira; Maria do Céu Gonçalves da Rocha Sá Lima, Ponte do Lima Tourist Board, Ponte do Lima; Semão Marcus, Tagide Restaurant, Lisbon; José A. Meireles, Promotional Manager, Costa Verde Tourist Board, Porto; Gloria Melo, Public Relations Manager, USA, TAP–Air Portugal, Newark; and Encarnação (Enca) Mello, Portuguese National Tourist Office, New York.

Many, many thanks, too, to friend, colleague, and gourmand Walter Menke, formerly TWA–Trans World Airlines, New York; to unfailingly gracious and giving Maria de Lourdes Modesto, Portuguese cookbook author without peer and culinary star of RTP-TV, Lisbon, and to her incredibly trusting and hospitable friend (and now mine) Maria Eugénia de Castro Cerqueira da Mota of Valpaços, Trás-os-Montes, who welcomed two total strangers into her home and prepared one of the most memorable Portuguese meals I have ever eaten; to gracious host Francisco Javier de Olazabal, A. A. Ferreira, Sucrs., Porto; Isabel Oliveira, Algarve Regional Tourist Office, Faro; Isabel Pacheco, Algarve Regional Tourist Office, Praia do Carvoeiro; José Manuel Paiva, Assistant Manager, Hotel Porto Santo, Porto Santo Island, Madeira; Mário Palma, Maître d'Hôtel, Escola de Hotelaria e Turismo do Algarve, Faro; Manuel Mendes Perreira, Chef de Cuisine, Pousada da Oliveira, Guimarães; José Manuel Reis, Resident Manager, Vilalara, Armação de Pêra; Manuel Paulino Revéz, Assistant Director, Escola de Hotelaria e Turismo do Algarve, Faro; José Santos, Manager, Palace Hotel, Bussaco; Rosinha Santos, supremely talented executive cook for A. A. Feirreira, Sucrs., Porto.

And thanks to that extraordinary host and hotelier Jacques Chevasson, General Manager, Hotel Ritz Lisboa, Lisbon; Vasco Seabra, Manager, Pousada de Dom Dinis, Vila Nova de Cerveira; Carlos Silva, Sous-Chef, Pousada da Oliveira, Guimarães; Jose-Maria Soengas, Director General, Hotel Meridien, Porto and Lisbon; Solar do Vinho do Porto, Lisbon; Manuel Sousa, Portuguese Trade Commission, New York; José Manuel Carvalho Alves Teixeira, Chef de Cuisine, Pousada de São Teotónio, Valença do Minho; Maria de Graça de Castro Guimarães Teixeira, Valpaços; João Trindade, O Castelo Restaurant, Praia do Carvoeiro; João Bello van Zeller, General Manager,

Pousada de Barrão Forrester, Alijó; Fernando Xavier, A. A. Ferreira, Sucrs., Porto; and Helmut Ziebell, gifted Chef de Cuisine, Hotel Ritz Lisboa, Lisbon, who knows Portuguese country cooking as well as he does the classical French cuisine.

A very special thank you goes to Pasquale Iocca, Portuguese Trade Commission, New York, for unraveling the mysteries of Portuguese wines and keeping me up-to-date on the very newest labels; and to that ever-willing, ever-able miracle worker António Madeira of Heyward Associates, Lisbon, for thirty years of assists, favors, and too many kindnesses and courtesies to count.

Finally, my deepest gratitude to colleague and dear friend Evelyn Heyward of Heyward Associates, New York, who introduced me to Portugal thirty years ago, who has been there even more times than I, and who loves the country, the people, the food, and the wine with a passion to equal my own.

Bibliography

Allen, H. Warner. *The Wines of Portugal*. New York: McGraw-Hill, 1963.

Andersen, Hans Christian. *A Visit to Portugal, 1886,* trans. with Introduction, Notes and Appendices by Grace Thornton. Indianapolis: Bobbs-Merrill, 1972.

Atkinson, W. C. *A History of Spain and Portugal*. London: Penguin Books, 1960.

Baedeker's Portugal. Englewood Cliffs, N.J.: Prentice-Hall, 1983.

Bello, António M. de Oliveira. *Culinária Portuguesa*. Lisbon: Edição do Autor, 1936.

Bradford, Ernle. *Southward the Caravels*. London: Hutchinson, 1961.

Bridge, Ann, and Susan Lowndes. *The Selective Traveller in Portugal,* rev. ed. New York: McGraw-Hill, 1967.

Croft-Cooke, Rupert. *Madeira*. London: Putnam, 1961.

da Costa, Francisco Carreiro. *Açores*. Lisbon: Olisipo Editorial de Publicações Turísticas, 1969.

da Maia, Carlos Bento. *Tratado Completo de Cozinha e de Copa,* orig. ed. Lisbon: Livraria Editora Guimarães, 1904. Facsimile ed. Lisbon: Publicações Dom Quixote, 1984.

Davidson, Alan. *North Atlantic Seafood*. New York: Viking, 1979.

Dervenn, Claude. *The Azores*. London: Harrap, 1956.

———. *Madeira*. Paris: Horizons de France, 1957.

de Sampaio, Albino Forjaz. *Volu'pia a Nona Arte a Gastronomia*. Porto: 1940.

Edita Lausanne, creator and producer, *The Great Book of Wine*. New York: World, 1970.

Feibleman, Peter S., and the editors of Time-Life Books. *The Cooking of Spain and Portugal*. New York: Time-Life Books, 1969.

Gonçalves, Francisco Esteves. *Portugal, A Wine Country*. Lisbon: Editora Portuguesa de Livros Tecnicos e Cientificos, 1984.

Grigson, Jane. *Jane Grigson's Book of European Cookery*. New York: Atheneum, 1983.

Isalita. *Doces e Cozinhados*, 23rd ed. Lisbon: Livraria Sá da Costa, 1969.

Johnson, Hugh. *The World Atlas of Wine*, rev. ed. New York: Simon and Schuster, 1978.

Kaplan, Marion. *The Portuguese, The Land and Its People*. New York: Viking, 1991.

Landström, Björn. *The Quest for India,* trans. M. Phillips and H. W. Stubbs. Garden City, N.Y.: Doubleday, 1964.

Lichine, Alexis. *Alexis Lichine's Encyclopedia of Wines & Spirits.* New York: Knopf, 1967.

Lowndes, Susan. *Travellers' Guide to Portugal.* London: Thornton Cox Travellers Guides, Geographia, 1982.

Marjay, F. P. *Portugal and the Sea.* Lisbon: Livraria Bertrand, 1957.

Miréne (Maria Iréne Andrade Braga). *Tesouro das Cozinheiras,* Porto: Porto Editora.

Modesto, Maria de Lourdes. *Cozinha Tradicional Portuguesa.* Lisbon: Verbo, 1982.

——. *Receitas Escolhidas,* 2nd ed. Lisbon: Verbo, 1982.

Portugal, Madeira, Michelin, 1st ed. Norwich, England: Jarrold, 1969.

Portugal, Madeira, Azores. Paris: Librairie Hachette, 1956.

Renault-Roulier, G. *Portugal.* New York: Hastings House, 1957.

Root, Waverly. *Food.* New York: Simon and Schuster, 1980.

Roteiro Gastronómico, Portugal, 6th ed. Lisbon: Publicações Turísticas Corte-Real, 1981.

Sarvis, Shirley. *A Taste of Portugal.* New York: Scribner's, 1967.

Schmaeling, Tony. *The Cooking of Spain & Portugal.* Secaucus, N.J.: Chartwell, 1983.

Seligo, H. *Portugal,* trans. G.A. Colville. Garden City, N.Y.: Doubleday, 1959.

Soares, E. *O Infante D. Henrique.* Lisbon: Livraria S. Carlos, 1960.

Tesouros da Cozinha Tradicional Portuguesa, Selecções do *Reader's Digest,* Lisbon, 1984.

Thomas, Gertrude Z. *Richer than Spices.* New York: Knopf, 1965.

Tucker, Alan, editor. *The Berlitz Travellers Guide, Portugal.* New York: Berlitz, 1993.

Valente, Maria Odette Cortes. *Cozinha Regional Portuguesa.* Coimbra: 1973.

Villier, F. *Portugal,* trans. J. and C. Pace. New York: Viking, 1963.

Vizi, Iréne. *Cozinha no Lar.* Lisbon: Livraria Bertrand.

Ward, Artemas. *The Encyclopedia of Food.* New York: Artemas Ward, 1923.

Warner, O. H. *Portugal.* Geneva: Les Editions Nagel, 1956.

Wohl, Hellmut and Alice. *Portugal.* New York: Scala Books, 1983.

Wright, David, and Patrick Swift. *Algarve.* London: Barrie and Jenkins, 1965.

Younger, William. *Gods, Men and Wine,* The Wine and Food Society. Cleveland: World, 1966.

Index